FLY WITH THE STARS

British South American Airways
The Rise and Controversial Fall of a Long-Haul Trailblazer

Susan Ottaway and Ian Ottaway

SUTTON PUBLISHING

First published in the United Kingdom in 2007 by
Sutton Publishing, an imprint of NPI Media Group Limited
Cirencester Road · Chalford · Stroud · Gloucestershire · GL6 8PE

British Library Cataloguing in Publication Data
A catalogue record for this book is available from the British Library.

Hardback ISBN 978-0-7509-4448-9

Typeset in Photina MT.
Typesetting and origination by
NPI Media Group Limited.
Printed and bound in England.

Contents

Acknowledgements		v
Map of BSAA Routes		viii
Introduction		ix
1	From the Sea to the Air	1
2	Pathfinder, Pioneer and Leader	8
3	An Airline is Born	20
4	The Government Decides	32
5	The People Behind the Airline	48
6	Ministry Interference	62
7	A Bad Year For Safety	84
8	A Very Suspicious Death	95
9	STENDEC	109
10	The Tudor Fiasco	125
11	A Tiger Goes Missing	143
12	Lord Nathan Deals a Crushing Blow	160
13	A Magnificent Achievement in Berlin	183
14	The Disappearance of *Star Ariel*	192
15	'I think I'll have a spot of lunch!'	212
	Epilogue: An Unpopular Merger	224
	Appendix I. Aircraft Performance Comparison	226
	Appendix II. Accidents to Aircraft of BSAA	227
	Appendix III. Accidents to BOAC and BEA aircraft	228
	Appendix IV. Proving Flight on 1 January 1946	229
	Appendix V. Aircraft Operated by British South American Airways	230
	Bibliography	237
	Index	238

For Dad

Acknowledgements

When we first decided to write a book about BSAA we were not certain if we would be able to find enough people to tell us their memories of the airline; it had, after all, been merged with BOAC nearly sixty years before. We decided to place advertisements in newspapers in the first instance to test the response and it was overwhelming. We have been privileged to meet and talk to many of the people who made BSAA the unique company that it was, acquiring some valuable friendships along the way.

We would like to thank the following for their kindness in writing, telephoning or meeting us and for their help and encouragement in our project: Barry Abraham, Cliff Alabaster, Peter Amos, Fred Appleby, Michael Aries, Albert Axten, Harry Bartholomew, Rosemary and Eric Beales, Richard Beith, Peter Berry, Maggie Bird, Jim Blackburn, Peter Campbell, David Capus, Nick Carter, Alan Cole, Dorothy Connal, Dave Cotterell, May Cox, Mary Cunningham, Ann Davidson, Robert Davidson, Fred Davis, Jim Davis, John Davis, Derek Davison, Ken Ellis, Gerry Farnsworth, Sandy Foster, Chris Gardner, Steve Gardner, Mark Gibbons, Tim Gibson, Peter Gill, Richard Glover, Rod Goff, David Goldsmith, Eileen Gunnell, David Hammocks, Eileen Hallett, Shona Handford, Pat Harmer, Malo Harvey, John Haslett, John Havers, Ted Hayden, Sylvia Haynes, Darrell Hillier, Bob Hobbs, Raymond Hoddinott, Mike Hudson, Derek Hughey, Archie Jackson, Roger Jackson, Paul Jarvis, Lionel Jeans, George Jenks, Peter Jenny, Neil Jeppeson, Richard Kebabjian, John Kendrick, Lincoln Lee, David Lindbergh, Donald Macintosh, Simon Maidment, Mr L. Marks, Michael Marsden, Amy Minns, Mike Mitchell, Mr A. Morley, Tony Morris, Geoffrey Negus, Helen Noble, Brian Pickering, Martin Powell, Frank Price, Jack Randell, Barry Raymond, Edna Riddell, Brian Riddle, Ernie Rodley, Nils Rosengaard, Douglas Rough, Bob Sale, Ken Sanford, Chris Semmens, Chris Seymour, John Silver, John Smurthwaite, Geoff South, Nick Stroud, Frank Taylor, Julian Temple, Carol Thompson, Brian Turpin, Wilf Vevers, Ed Walters, Harry Webster, John

West, Mick West, Cynthia White, Joan Wilby, Mel Wilby, John Wilkinson, Brian Williams, Geoff Womersley.

Thanks are due also to the staff at the National Archive in Kew, the RAF Museum, the British Airways Museum and the Avro Heritage Centre.

This book would have been particularly difficult to produce without the special help of a number of people. Audrey Ford of the Hampshire Library Service has been her usual helpful self, handling requests for urgent information with great speed and enthusiasm. Derek A. King (British Transport Aircraft Histories) put in a great deal of effort to provide accurate information for the fleet list. Peter Duffey scanned and emailed many gems of unique information. Roy Day, John Brennan, Dick Beddoes, Paddy Cormican, Aubrey Dare, Jack Eade, Richard Enser, Ron Forrester and Fred Whitworth gave up many hours of their time to relate interesting anecdotes, and lent many items from their personal collections. Richard Riding has offered valuable advice and lent unique photos from his late father's collection. Keith Hayward's enthusiasm and expert help has been invaluable. Tony Doyle has contributed an immense amount of priceless research material, giving up a lot of his own time for our benefit and providing constant encouragement. Annette Hedges not only helped with snippets of information, but also introduced us to her friends Priscilla and Wyn Fieldson who have welcomed us into their home, given us a great deal of help and support and have become dear friends. Our thanks to them all.

* * *

Special thanks to my brother and co-author, Ian, for his patience, humour and expertise; to my sister-in-law Carolin for her work on the appendices; to my nephews – James, for his interest and support, and William for all the research he did on our behalf; to Mum for her love and her memories of those long-ago days and to my partner Nick who read the book for us and, knowing how important it was to me, has constantly supported and encouraged me in all my efforts.

Susan Ottaway

Special thanks to my wife and two wonderful sons. My youngest son William has continually offered his time and help with this project. He has unearthed many useful pieces of information which would otherwise have escaped me, and was responsible for discovering the stunning cover photograph of *Star*

Watch. He has helped with research, with compiling the Aircraft Performance table, and he even gave up valuable Playstation time one afternoon to design a sample front cover (which can be seen on the www.flywiththestars.co.uk website)! My eldest son James has been a constant source of encouragement and has never once complained about the lack of attention from me while I've been engrossed in research and writing. We'll try and see Arsenal play more often from now on James! Finally, my lovely wife Carolin has put up with me droning on for the past six years about 'Star' this and 'Avro' that, including valiantly trying to understand, and more impressively to appear interested in the intricacies of the Avro Tudor fuel system. She spent a great many hours compiling the Fleet List, for which I'm extremely grateful. She has put up with a house full of notes, files, photos and aviation books. Most importantly, over the past few years she's seen me spend a great deal of time researching BSAA and very little time on work around the house, without a word of complaint. I couldn't ask for more.

Ian Ottaway

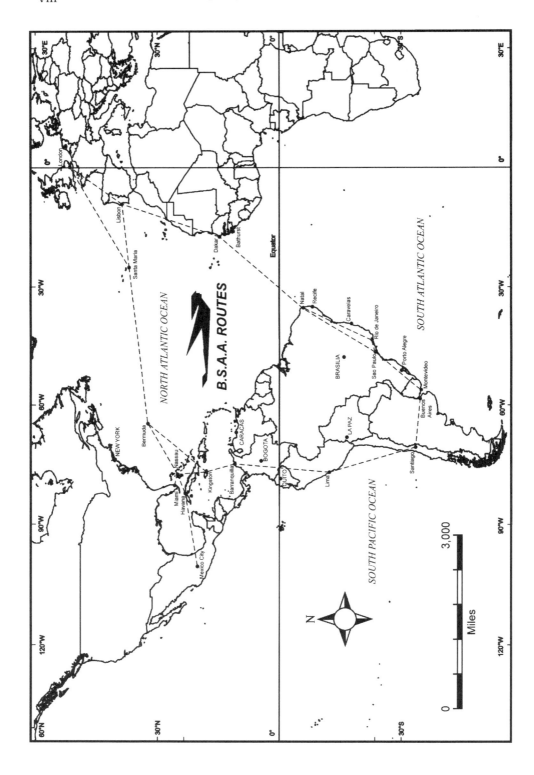

Introduction

The mention of British South American Airways (BSAA) to people with an interest in aviation will often elicit comments alluding to a dubious safety record. Many people will immediately refer to the unexplained losses of the Avro Tudors *Star Tiger* and *Star Ariel*, or to stories of poor maintenance and over-ambitious scheduling. Unfortunately, these beliefs are perpetuated and often exacerbated by authors for whom the sensational is more appealing than plain facts, and who often do not take the trouble to research the full story to give a more balanced view.

There can be no denying the fact that the airline suffered many more accidents and mishaps than would be considered acceptable now. Indeed it could be argued that even one accident is unacceptable. To look at the statistics in isolation, however, would be to do the airline an injustice.

The interpretation of aircraft accident statistics is a notoriously inexact science, as the very same facts can be used in subtly different ways to support completely opposing arguments. Many accounts of the short history of BSAA refer to the eleven accidents the airline suffered. To the uninformed, this gives the impression of eleven accidents on the scale of the July 2000 Air France Concorde disaster or any one of a number of more recent airliner accidents involving large loss of life. This is not the case. The BSAA 'accidents' range from the tragic loss of twenty-five passengers and the crew in the Tudor *Star Tiger* to the collapse of a Lancaster undercarriage on landing at Heathrow after a night training exercise with no injuries to the four crew members on board. Indeed, the total number of passenger fatalities during BSAA's history is seventy-three. Of this figure, fifty-eight passengers were in just three of the eleven accidents and of those, thirty-eight passenger fatalities were due to the disappearance of the two Tudors; accidents for which the cause, in all probability, will never be explained. While the loss of seventy-three passengers is a tragedy, that figure is not excessive compared with those of other airlines of the late 1940s, especially when one considers the demanding routes BSAA was operating.

These were pioneering days for global air travel, with many routes unproven by other airlines before being initiated by BSAA. The accident record would be shocking for an airline in the twenty-first century, but technology was very different in the 1940s. Not only were the aircraft and their engines relatively primitive compared with today's ultra-reliable airliners, but so were navigation aids, radio communications and the understanding of meteorology. Many will have read that the most likely explanation for the loss of the Avro Lancastrian *Star Dust* in the Andes is that it encountered headwinds of up to 150mph in a phenomenon known as the jetstream. This is something of which there was little detailed knowledge in 1947, although it will be seen later that Air Vice-Marshal Don Bennett, Chief Executive of BSAA, was aware of the existence of these dangerous, high altitude, high speed winds and had been pressing for government assistance to learn more about them.

Instead of comparing the BSAA safety record with that of a present day airline, a much fairer comparison would be with some of the other major airlines of the 1940s. During the same period that BSAA was operating, Air France, in nine accidents with fatalities, killed over 110 passengers while KLM's toll was 126 passengers in five accidents. BOAC suffered thirty-two accidents, killing seventy people, and BEA thirteen accidents with the loss of fifty-two lives. In the case of BEA, thirty-five of these fatalities were in accidents on flights within the UK. Most of them were on routes which were far less challenging than those which BSAA was operating.

There have been suggestions that one of the failings of BSAA was to employ crews straight from RAF Bomber Command (often from the elite Pathfinder Force, commanded by Don Bennett during the war years) and that this resulted in pilots who were willing to take risks inappropriate to civilian operations. In his 1964 autobiography *Out on a Wing*, Sir Miles Thomas, Chairman of BOAC in 1949 at the time of the merger with BSAA, says:

> Many people have the idea than an airline captain and his officers are gay cavaliers of the air, dashing, brave and bold. In point of fact they are very serious-minded gentlemen indeed. Crews were mostly recruited from RAF Bomber Command or Transport Command. Fighter pilots usually did not make good airline captains. What you want in an airline is not impetuosity but dogged dependability.
>
> When BOAC absorbed British South American Airways we received several first-class ex-bomber pilots. Many of them had been Pathfinders and

were 'the tops' in airmanship. But even with them there was no policy of 'bash on regardless', or 'charge and cheer'. It was cool, calculated courage that was inculcated.

The rather ill-informed accounts one sees from time to time regarding poor maintenance standards on BSAA aircraft are simply untrue. BSAA engineering was of a high standard. If an engineer required a special tool or item of equipment to do a job, its purchase was approved. The company's maintenance facilities at Langley near Slough were typical of any major airline of the period. After the demise of the airline, a great many of the BSAA engineering and maintenance staff moved on to long careers working for BOAC and then British Airways. These airlines were generally recognised as having a very high standard of maintenance, so there was clearly no problem with the competence of the staff.

When searching for causes of the BSAA accidents, it is easy to point the finger at the crews for taking too many unnecessary risks, at the maintenance staff for cutting corners, or at the management for over-ambitious scheduling and routing. However, there is something which BSAA seemed to suffer in abundance, and that is sheer bad luck. In looking at the details of the accidents there are many examples where an unlucky chain of events combined to cause a disaster. No airline, however well prepared, can safeguard against bad luck.

* * *

Fly with the Stars shows another side to this much maligned company; a side that, itself, is not without controversy. As well as the bad luck it suffered, BSAA had enemies who, for reasons known only to themselves, did not want the company to succeed and did their best to ensure that it failed. Despite these attempts the airline forged ahead, establishing a British aviation presence in South America. When it was on the point of entering a new era in air transport, the government, in a state of blind panic or, perhaps, deliberate intent, removed its franchise and handed over its routes and its pioneering work to BOAC, with little concern for the people who had made it all possible and who were the heart of BSAA. Time has buried their story; *Fly with the Stars* seeks to resurrect it.

Chapter 1

From the Sea to the Air

British South American Airways had its genesis in the late nineteenth century with five shipping lines. Drawn by the opportunities offered by the far distant continent, English, Scottish and Irish emigrants from farming, industrial and business communities journeyed 5,000 miles to South America in the early nineteenth century to seek their fortunes, settling in Argentina, Bolivia, Chile, Paraguay, Peru and Uruguay.

They introduced the Presbyterian Church and founded banks, trading companies, farms, cattle ranches and sheep stations. South America was a land rich in mineral resources, especially precious metals, which attracted settlers from British mining communities; the largest number were Cornwall's tin-miners.

The Welsh arrived, too, but wanted something different. They longed for a land where they could establish a Welsh-speaking society with a Welsh culture and lifestyle. They chose the remote region of Patagonia at the southern tip of South America and the first settlers arrived in 1865 after a two-month voyage from Liverpool on board the ship *Mimosa*. Their descendants still live in the area, celebrating the arrival in their new homeland every year on 28 July, The Landing Day.

Through the necessity for importing equipment and the constant passenger traffic to the continent, shipping companies grew up serving the routes from Britain to South America. Of these companies, five were to be the founding fathers of the airline that would become British South American Airways. They were the Pacific Steam Navigation Company, Royal Mail Steam Packet Company, Lamport and Holt Line, Booth Steamship Company and Blue Star Line.

The last of the five companies was formed by a Liverpool family named Vestey, who owned a butchery business. They were one of the first companies in the United Kingdom to use refrigerators, which made it possible for them to import meat from South America. They bought their own cattle ranches in South America, opened a meat processing works, the Anglo Frigorifico, in

Buenos Aires, and built the first cold store in London in 1895. They were so successful that the family started the Blue Star Line in 1911 to transport meat from Argentina to the United Kingdom. By the start of the First World War the company had twelve refrigerated ships which were used during the war to supply beef to the Army. For these patriotic services the founder, William Vestey, was created a baronet.

The Blue Star Line prospered and in the early 1920s launched a ship named *Albion Star*, which was the first in a long line of ships named 'Star'. At the start of the Second World War it had thirty-eight ships, many of which were requisitioned, along with their crews, by the British government to bring food to Britain. By the end of the war thirty-nine of these ships and 646 personnel had been lost to enemy attacks.

The Blue Star Line operated after the war as part of the Vestey Group until the latter decided to sell all its interests in shipping and it was bought in 1998 by P&O Nedlloyd.

* * *

Following an attack on Imperial Airways in the House of Commons by two Tory MPs, John Moore-Brabazon, later Lord Brabazon of Tara, and Robert Perkins, who declared the airline to be 'the laughing stock of the world', a committee was set up in November 1937 under the chairmanship of Lord Cadman to look into the state of British civil aviation. Its report, published on 8 February 1938, made several recommendations. It suggested that British Airways, formed in 1936 with the merger of United Airways, Hillman's Airways and Spartan Airlines, should expand its services in Europe; Imperial Airways should concentrate on increasing its flights to the British Empire; and, most radically of all, the two airlines should merge.

The report was especially critical of Imperial Airways which it accused of having 'poor staff relations, inefficient operations and obsolete equipment'. Disgusted by this slur, George Woods-Humphrey, managing director of Imperial Airways, resigned.

On 12 June 1939 the British Overseas Airways Corporation Ltd Bill was introduced in the House of Commons by Sir Kingsley Wood, Secretary of State for Air, to allow the merger to take place. On 24 November British Overseas Airways Corporation (BOAC) came into being with Sir John Reith as its chairman.

Cadman had also noted that there was no British airline flying to South America and proposed that this omission should be rectified as soon as possible.

* * *

The war had made the prospects of many shipping companies seem bleak. So many of their ships had been requisitioned and sunk that it was unlikely that they would ever be able to operate as they once had and, if they were to remain profitable, they had to find ways to diversify. Realising that air transport would offer strong competition, the directors of the five shipping companies decided to explore the possibilities of starting their own airline to cover the routes they knew well, between Britain and South America.

In 1943 John W. Booth, of the Booth Steamship Company, and chairman of the General Council of British Shipping, had approached American-educated New Zealander, Lowell Yerex, founder in 1931 of Honduran airline Transportes Aeros Centro Americanos (TACA), to see if he was interested in operating an air service between South America and Great Britain; an approach made largely at the behest of the Air Ministry.

Yerex was a pilot of some note in Central America and by the end of the 1930s his airline was flourishing. But he wanted to expand it to include other countries such as Costa Rica and Panama, which is when his troubles started.

Pan American Airways (PAA) was the predominant airline in the area and it did not intend to give this up to anyone, especially a foreigner like Yerex, who was regarded as being 'British'. It had powerful backing, being regarded as the American government's 'preferred' airline. PAA began a campaign to discredit TACA including its president, Juan Trippe, making false claims about the safety of the smaller company. He even criticised it for not being American as if that, somehow, made it less reliable. The underhand efforts to ruin TACA came to a head when it was discovered that PAA had paid another small company in the area to undercut its fares in an attempt to poach passengers and force TACA out of business.

The US government was appalled but its hands were tied. It was doing its own dirty deals in the area using PAA as a front to build bases which it knew would never have been allowed by the governments concerned, had they known of its involvement.

Around this time Yerex made the acquaintance of British Consul General John Leche. Leche took such an interest in the aviator and his airline that he began bombarding the Foreign Office with reports about his friend, declaring him to be an ardent supporter of Britain and begging the government to help him in his struggle to keep his airline going. The reactions were mixed. Some thought that it was a lost cause while others wondered if there was a possibility of cooperating with Yerex in the West Indies. There was a suggestion that TACA could be useful to BOAC when it established its routes to South America after the war. However BOAC and the Air Ministry were concerned that, by supporting Yerex and operating in South America, the British airline would offend PAA, which it did not want to do. By the end of the war BOAC seems to have completely forgotten its desire not to upset the American carrier and was actively campaigning to be the government's chosen company to operate those same routes.

Leche continued championing Yerex and urged the government to act quickly before it was too late, but by 1940 American Export Airlines made a bid to buy TACA and, with no comparable offer from the British, Yerex accepted. Leche was distraught, sending more messages of complaint back to Britain accusing everyone concerned of being too slow to recognise what would have been a great opportunity. Ultimately the deal did not go ahead, encouraging Leche to send more communications to London. British officials were tiring of his obsession with Yerex. They felt that he lacked a sense of proportion and that his ideas and suggestions were not always logical. Some thought that his adulation was entirely inappropriate as there was a feeling that Yerex, although an able pilot and administrator, was self-seeking and untrustworthy. It is an interesting insight into the workings of British bureaucracy in those days that, in spite of Leche's almost manic activities, involving himself in something that was most definitely not part of his remit, his peculiar behaviour was quickly forgotten and he was later appointed British Ambassador to Chile, receiving the customary knighthood too.

* * *

At a cocktail party towards the end of 1940, Lady Young, wife of Trinidad and Tobago's governor, Sir Hubert Young, is said to have asked Yerex if he would start an airline for the West Indies. Never one to refuse a challenge he got to work immediately and on 27 November 1940, British West Indian

Airways (BWIA) took to the air for the first time, flying from Trinidad to Tobago and back in a Lockheed Lodestar. The airline was soon operating daily from Trinidad to Barbados and ten times a week to Tobago using an airfield in east Trinidad that eventually became the nation's main airport, Piarco International.

Although BWIA expanded its services throughout the Caribbean it was not long before Yerex wanted to enlarge it further. He used BWIA and TACA aircraft to operate charter flights between Trinidad and Miami and before long he had applied for the rights to operate scheduled services. The British government was alarmed as it rightly suspected that the American government would think that it was behind the request and would demand rights to operate to British colonies in return. It tried to calm the situation but by then Yerex had more plans and envisaged an airline that would link both North and South America via the West Indies. In line with his plans for expansion, Yerex started another airline, Aerovias Brasil. Although on paper it was Brazilian, the Americans regarded it as British and thought that it had been set up to pave the way for BOAC to operate into South America. Once again Yerex's actions caused friction between Britain and the USA and encouraged John Leche to renew his attempts to seek support for his friend. He must have been delighted by John Booth's approach to Yerex, but when this, too, came to nothing he seemed to harden his attitude to Booth's fledgling company. His blind devotion did not even waver when Yerex sold 28 per cent of BWIA shares to the Americans. The British government dithered about what it should do and things came to a head when the new governor of Trinidad and Tobago, Sir Bede Clifford, pressed the board of BWIA to issue new stock to the shareholders making both the Americans' and Yerex's interests minority holdings, thus taking control of the company away from him.

By April 1944 Yerex resigned. BWIA was left in limbo and the British government had to decide what to do with it.

* * *

Although the shipping companies were unable to do very much during the war, by 1944 there was hope that the tide was turning for the Allies, and so on 25 January 1944 British Latin American Air Lines Ltd (BLAA) was formed. Its first office was borrowed from the Royal Mail Lines and its chairman was John Booth; the directors were C.C. Barber, S.W. Black, W.H. Davies, L. Dewey and F.H. Lowe. Before the war was over the airline had established itself at 14 Leadenhall Street, London EC3.

The directors of BOAC were not happy about BLAA. BOAC had operated, albeit on a limited scale, throughout the war and, despite their initial reticence about upsetting PAA, they felt that they had more right to develop these new routes than a new, as yet unproven, company.

In 1938, before the merger with Imperial Airways, British Airways, although flying almost exclusively to Europe, had drawn up tentative plans to begin a service to South America. It had made some survey flights to Lisbon and to Bathurst (now Banjul) in The Gambia on the west coast of Africa, but because British Airways used short-range Lockheed 14s and the Spanish authorities refused it landing rights in any of the West African Spanish-held territories, it was forced to abandon its plans. Without Spanish cooperation, the routes were just too long for the range of its fleet.

* * *

In May 1944 land to the west of London in an area known as Heath Row was acquired by the government with a compulsory purchase order and on 6 June 1944 work began to build the runways for what would become the new London airport. Work on the site progressed slowly. As late as autumn 1945, runways suitable for civilian use were still being built and there were no terminal buildings and very few maintenance facilities. This was due partly to the war, but even after it was over there was a lack of urgency in the development of the site. A journalist, writing in *The Aeroplane* on 5 October, commented:

We have a tendency in this country to put off doing things until the last possible moment and to regard those who agitate for advance and preventive action as well-intentioned nuisances . . .

Though the gentlemen in whose hands is placed the ultimate responsibility for the direction of the general policy of our civil aviation have, therefore, some cause to expect the indulgence of both British and foreign opinion for London's lack of adequate airport facilities, we are bound to point out that this self-same lack of airport policy and facilities was a cardinal feature of pre-war London. This fact was underlined in the 1938 Cadman report, which, once again, we commend to the attention of all new Civil Aviation Ministers and officials charged with office, since that report was consigned to the archives soon after it first saw the light of day.

So although plans were afoot for Heathrow to become London's main airport, just over five months after BLAA became a registered company, none of the airlines that would operate from there knew how long it would take for them to be able to move in and, in the case of BLAA, whether or not it would be allowed to use the airport at all.

A government White Paper published in March 1945 recognised some of the proposals outlined in the Cadman report. It set out policy for three main British airlines with clearly defined routes. The first was to operate on what was called the Commonwealth air routes, serving nations such as Kenya, Uganda, South Africa, India, Ceylon, Australia, New Zealand and Canada, as well as the USA, the Far East and China. The second would serve the capitals and major cities of Europe and internal British destinations and the third would operate to South America. It also recommended that the company formed by the shipping lines should be assigned the routes to South America. BOAC, however, still planned to take them and would fight hard to get them.

When the war in Europe ended on 8 May 1945 the directors of British Latin American Air Lines began work in earnest to develop the airline. Having decided against asking Lowell Yerex to be a part of the new company, one of their first tasks was to appoint a general manager. The man that they chose for this role was Donald Bennett, a 34-year-old Australian. He took up his position on 1 June 1945.

Chapter 2

Pathfinder, Pioneer and Leader

BLAA's newly appointed general manager, Don Bennett, had achieved great things already in the world of aviation. An accomplished pilot and air navigator even before the Second World War had begun, he went on to become the youngest ever air vice-marshal in the Royal Air Force, and group commander of Bomber Command's elite Pathfinder Force in 1942. As an airman and leader of men, Bennett was second to none. The fortunes of BLAA and its successor BSAA are inextricably linked with him.

Donald Clifford Tyndall Bennett was born on 14 September 1910 in Toowoomba, Queensland, the youngest of George and Celia Bennett's four sons. Don's father ran a business in Toowoomba and owned a cattle station that covered 180 square miles at Kanimbla on the Condamine river. His mother, Celia Juliana Lucas, was English. Her father, T.P. Lucas, was a doctor with an interest in cancer research, but the BMA treated his findings with scepticism. Lucas became so disillusioned with the British medical establishment that, when his wife died, he took his daughter to live in Australia.

The sad irony was that a century later medical researchers found Lucas's original research was likely to have important implications for cancer treatment. In his autobiography, *Pathfinder*, Don Bennett tells how his grandfather taught him that 'the only crime an Englishman cannot forgive is to be right'.

The Bennett boys all grew into ambitious and successful young men. They learnt to ride horses and to drive cars at an early age – Don was about 10 or 11 when he learnt to drive – and they swam, canoed and went shooting. He admits that while his brothers were all 'brainy types' he was 'officially the disgrace of the family'. In any other family this would not have been so, but Don's brothers were exceptional: the eldest, Clyde Kinsey, 10 years his senior, became a barrister; the second eldest, Aubrey George, trained as a doctor and became an eye specialist; and Arnold Lucas, who was two years older than Don, achieved great success as a QC in Queensland.

The boys were sent to a private preparatory school, but when the family moved to Brisbane they attended Brisbane Grammar, a state maintained school. Don would only work hard in the subjects that interested him like maths, physics and chemistry, preferring instead to cram for exams at the last minute. He planned to become a doctor like Aubrey, but when he brought home a bad school report his father decided there was no point in financing his son's education any longer. George Bennett told the young man that he would have to work in his office in Brisbane. Horrified, Don asked if he might work on the cattle station instead.

With his father's blessing Don became a jackaroo, mending boundary fences, branding the cattle, moving them around the station and helping to kill them to provide the family with meat. His father was pleased that he had taken an interest in the cattle station and hoped that eventually he would become the manager, but it was not to be. For the three months that he worked at Kanimbla, Don thought about what he really wanted to do with his life. He realised that managing a cattle station was not a serious option because, although he believed it would be a happy life, it had no prospects. He also knew that he no longer wanted to become a doctor and so eventually he decided to try for a career in aviation.

In July 1930, 19-year-old Don Bennett reported to Royal Australian Air Force (RAAF) headquarters in Melbourne. In common with many other countries, Australia was experiencing difficult times and was not able to finance the training of the fifteen RAAF recruits it had chosen that year. However, there was a chance for them to be accepted if they would agree to transfer to the Royal Air Force (RAF) in the United Kingdom at the end of their training. Although he had no real desire to leave his homeland, Don decided that it would be better to do so than to lose his chance of a career in aviation and agreed to go to England. At the end of his year-long training course he came second in the ground school exam and first in the flying, and then left Point Cook as a pilot officer to return home for leave prior to sailing for England. In his book *Pathfinder* he says how proud he was to have become a qualified pilot, but also that 'the only comfort in having little knowledge is to have little knowledge of how little knowledge one has!'

When his leave ended Pilot Officer Bennett, along with the other successful cadets, boarded the P&O liner *Narkunda* to begin a new life in England. On arrival, he went first to RAF Uxbridge in Middlesex and then to the Flying Training School at Seeland near Liverpool. Following some flying tests he was sent to RAF North Weald in Essex where he joined 29 Squadron and flew the Armstrong Whitworth Siskin, a biplane fighter with an open cockpit which he described as being '. . . one of the worst aeroplanes ever produced'. It was, however, in a Siskin that he learnt many of the things which were to be invaluable to him later on, such as the 'new-fangled' device of radio telephony and the art of night flying.

He put himself forward for any new course that he could and by doing so learnt to parachute and, more importantly for him, to navigate. It was to become a lifelong interest and an invaluable skill in the war to come and beyond.

Having been accepted on a flying boat course, Bennett, by then a flying officer, was posted to RAF Calshot on Southampton Water for six months – three months' theory and three months' flying. The flying was done in twin-engined Supermarine Southampton biplane flying boats, described by Bennett as '. . . the most beautiful examples of wooden construction I have ever seen in aircraft, and they were certainly a delight to fly'.

At the end of the course he was posted again, this time to 210 Squadron at Pembroke Dock in South Wales from where he later returned to Calshot as an instructor in the navigation school.

At the beginning of 1934 an air race from England to Melbourne was announced to mark the centenary of the Australian city – the MacRobertson Trophy Air Race. Bennett decided that in order to take part he would need to obtain his First Class Navigator's Licence. He studied every evening and sometimes well into the night and obtained the licence, only the seventh person in the world to do so at that time. Finding a suitable aeroplane proved more difficult and he eventually had to accept an offer to navigate for another Australian pilot, Jimmy Woods. The venture was under-financed and their second-hand Lockheed Vega monoplane needed some maintenance before they were able to set off. Having no radio on board, they relied entirely on Bennett's ability to navigate and progressed well until coming into land at Aleppo in Syria. They touched down with a heavy thump and Bennett was thrown from the back to the front of the little aircraft, damaging his spine in three places and his knee. He was unable to move his head or his shoulders and was removed to a convent where he was nursed by the nuns. Jimmy Woods, although bleeding, was soon fit again, but the air race was over for the two Australians and Bennett returned to England by ship.

It was, perhaps, fortuitous that he returned earlier than planned as he met a beautiful blonde from Switzerland named Ly who was in England to learn

English. A year later, ten days after Bennett left the RAF, they were married and set off on a lengthy honeymoon, first to Switzerland to meet the bride's family and then to Brisbane to meet the groom's.

During the time that he had been in the RAF, Bennett had not only gained his First Class Navigator's Licence, he had also obtained his B Pilot's Licence, his Ground Engineer's Licence in categories A, C and X, his Wireless Operator's Licence and his Instructor's Certificate. His intention was to look for a position in civil aviation and he had made some preliminary enquiries before leaving the RAF. The trip to Australia was not just a honeymoon and a chance for his wife Ly to meet her new family. Bennett had been offered a position with New England Airways flying between Sydney and Brisbane. He had also taken the precaution of contacting Imperial Airways to enquire if they needed a well-qualified pilot.

During the honeymoon cruise Bennett wrote the first chapter of his book about air navigation. After contacting New England Airways in Australia and discovering that the pay and conditions were not as favourable as those offered by Imperial Airways, the Bennetts decided to return to England and the book, *The Complete Air Navigator*, was finished on the return voyage. It became the navigators' 'bible' and continued to be used and reprinted many times over the following years.

In January 1936 Bennett joined Imperial Airways and settled into the life of a civilian pilot. He began by flying the HP 42 biplane, but after a posting to Egypt transferred to flying boats and operated between Alexandria and the southern Italian port of Brindisi. On one five-day layover in the Adriatic port he wrote another book, *The Air Mariner*, about the handling of flying boats.

In 1938 Imperial Airways decided that its Atlantic flights, transporting cargo and mail, would be operated using the Mayo composite. This was a Short flying boat carrying another smaller flying boat in a piggy-back position, designed by the airline's technical manager Major Robert Mayo. The bigger aircraft, *Maia*, would take-off with the smaller, *Mercury*, attached and the two would not separate until they were in level flight, thus assisting the small aircraft on its way across the ocean. When he heard of this pioneering procedure, Bennett at once applied to pilot the smaller *Mercury* and was accepted.

Following the first highly successful return trip to Botwood in Newfoundland, Bennett met Sir Kingsley Wood who had just been appointed British Secretary of State for Air. He used this meeting as a chance to broach the subject of an attempt he wanted to make on the world long-distance seaplane record and asked Wood if he would be able to obtain official approval. Wood was interested and approval was given for Bennett to make the attempt using a modified version of *Mercury* with the floats doubling as extra fuel tanks. The flight was to be between Dundee and Cape Town, South Africa.

On 6 October 1938 *Mercury*, atop *Maia*, took off from Dundee and separated from the mother ship. In doing so part of an engine cowling became dislodged causing drag, and Bennett realised this would make it almost impossible to reach Cape Town non-stop. Because of the heavy fuel load, he could not return to Dundee for nearly 12 hours and, fearful that if he did, the authorities would cancel the record attempt, he decided to continue for as far as he could and then make a decision about where to land.

After a flight lasting 42 hours 30 minutes Bennett, his wireless operator Ian Harvey, and *Mercury* had covered 6,000 miles and had broken the existing record. Disappointed that he had not been able to reach his original destination, he made an intermediate landing up-country on the Orange River where he refuelled before continuing south-west to Cape Town. Although he received a rapturous reception from the South African crowds, when he returned to England his feat was ignored by Imperial Airways, Short Brothers who manufactured the aircraft, Napiers, manufacturers of the engine, and the British government. It was the first of many occasions where his great achievements were, inexplicably, treated with petty displays of jealousy and spite rather than the acclaim that they deserved.

After the record flight *Mercury* went back to the role for which it had been developed and carried Christmas mail from England to Egypt on the first non-stop commercial flights of this route – another record for Bennett, since he was the pilot.

Early in 1939 Imperial Airways began trials with Sir Alan Cobham's company, Flight Refuelling Ltd, to refuel a flying boat in mid-air during a transatlantic flight. They used an adapted Short S30 Empire flying boat and let out a fuel line from the tail which was then picked up by the receiving aircraft and attached to its fuel tanks. Fuel was then pumped to the flying boat enabling it to greatly extend its range. The trials went very well, so well in fact that the airline took on two more pilots to complete the tests, Irishman Jack Kelly-Rogers from Aer Lingus and South African Gordon Store.

* * *

When, in late 1939, the British Overseas Airways Corporation Act came into being, Bennett's reaction was typically outspoken. He found it hard to understand how a Conservative government could nationalise an airline – BOAC – that had been formed by a merger of Imperial Airways, which he believed to be the major airline in the world, and the much less efficient British Airways. Neither did it seem logical that the men who had pioneered Imperial Airways and its routes should receive no recognition for their achievements, but should be discarded in favour of others far less competent. He made his feelings known by declaring that 'it is as deplorable as it is typical that the country of their birth gave them no honour'. In expressing his sincerely held beliefs he was guaranteeing that the wrath of the establishment would, one day, fall upon him and that he would have to endure endless battles with bureaucratic nobodies in his attempts to make his company the best it could be.

* * *

In June 1940, on the day Italy entered the war, Bennett flew to Rome to fetch as many BOAC staff as he could and take them back to England.

Soon afterwards the Polish General Sikorski escaped to England and asked Prime Minister Winston Churchill for help in evacuating his staff and members of the Polish government in exile from France. Bennett was given this task and brought the Poles safely to England despite being shot at by a Royal Navy cruiser.

He also took the Duke of Kent to Lisbon for an international exhibition. While waiting for the Duke to return he found himself staying in a hotel room on the same floor as the German crew of a Lufthansa aircraft. Having seen what the Germans were doing in France and to shipping in the English Channel, he declared himself to be 'hardly on friendly terms!'

For the return flight he gave his destination as West Africa and took off in that general direction before turning about and heading out over the Bay of Biscay and then towards Poole where he landed in the early morning of 2 July 1940. It was the last flight he ever made for BOAC.

Not long after this, Bennett was called to the Ministry of Aircraft Production and told that he had been chosen to operate the Atlantic Ferry Organisation, flying American-built aircraft across the North Atlantic to save them being transported by ship. He was delighted to have been picked for this role and set about it with great enthusiasm. With two other ex-Imperial Airways pilots,

Ian Ross and Humphrey Page, Bennett sailed from Liverpool for Canada in an unescorted ship packed with evacuees.

On arrival they travelled on to California where they were the guests of the American aircraft manufacturer Lockheed. Bennett got to work straight away and took the controls of the Lockheed Hudson on a test flight. The Hudson was the first US aircraft type to be ferried to the UK. The Lockheed engineers thought that the British party would just accept their figures without question and were taken aback when Bennett insisted on working out his own. They realised the value of this later when Bennett proved that they were incorrect by as much as 8 per cent and that more fuel would be required to get the Hudson safely across the ocean.

The British authorities in Washington had been told to find American pilots to supplement those arriving from the UK as the RAF had none to spare; there were some Canadians and BOAC sent twelve, one of whom was Gordon Store, who had worked on the in-flight refuelling trials across the Atlantic.

Within a few weeks they were ready to send a formation of seven Hudsons to Britain. Aircraft and crews gathered in Gander, Newfoundland, at the beginning of November. The aircraft needed to be de-iced and they eventually left Canada on 10 November. A formation such as this had never flown across the Atlantic in wartime and there had never been a flight so late in the season but, despite the weather conditions, six of the seven aircraft landed at Aldergrove airport in Belfast the following day, the seventh landing at a nearby airfield. Having spent the night in Belfast they flew onwards to Blackpool airport where the ferry crews parted company. The American and Canadian pilots went to Liverpool to board a ship back to Canada, while Bennett went to London to report to Lord Beaverbrook, the Minister for Aircraft Production. Bennett convinced Beaverbrook that while this trip had been successful, it was unlikely that, as the winter progressed, they would be able to keep to formation flying. Arrangements were made to have navigators who had been newly trained in Canada to return to Britain on delivery flights, assisting the pilots in finding their way. The system worked well and the delivery flights continued throughout the winter of 1940 and into the New Year. Soon it was working like clockwork with new aircraft being delivered to Britain and the pilots being flown back to Canada by BOAC to complete the next deliveries. By July 1941 the Atlantic Ferry Organisation came under the control of the RAF with Air Chief Marshal Sir Frederick Bowhill in command. Bennett was told by Sir Frederick that he was to go back to England where he would return to the

RAF with the rank of group captain. Bennett found it rather ironic that the man who was taking over the organisation that he had set up and developed into the streamlined operation it now was, had the rank of air chief marshal while he, himself, was being offered the rank of group captain.

Bennett's wife Ly, and the couple's two children, daughter Noreen and son Torix, had been in Canada with him. He returned to Britain on a Hudson delivery flight while the family went by BOAC flying boat, Noreen and Torix becoming the first children to fly across the Atlantic.

During the entire time that Bennett had been in charge of the Atlantic Ferry only one aircraft had been lost. The excellence of Bennett's organisation, compared with that which followed, was emphasised when three Liberators crashed with no survivors and six Hudsons disappeared without trace during the first six weeks of the new administration.

* * *

Promised that he would be made a group captain, Bennett came up against civil service bureaucracy when he was told that he could not possibly be a group captain when he was merely an airline pilot and was grudgingly offered the rank of squadron leader. He was exasperated by this state of affairs and harsh words were spoken, the result of which was that he was sent to the new navigation school at Eastbourne, as an acting wing commander. It was at least something in which he had an interest and he stayed long enough to ensure that the courses were running. Then he went to see Group Captain Dawes, the Personnel Officer at Bomber Command, who immediately gave him command of 77 Squadron at RAF Leeming in Yorkshire.

He took over at the beginning of December 1941 just as the Americans came into the war. He found that his crews were inexperienced, with very little technical knowledge, but were enthusiastic, brave and usually fatalistic about their slim chances of surviving a tour of thirty operations. Their navigational skills were poor and even if they did successfully reach their designated targets, they had trouble in accurately bombing them. He set about improving their navigation skills and insisted that an aiming-point photograph be taken on each raid. By the time Bennett left in April 1942 to command 10 Squadron, also at RAF Leeming, 77 Squadron's bombing results had greatly improved.

Soon after arriving at 10 Squadron Bennett made a trip to Norway in a Handley Page Halifax to bomb the German battleship *Tirpitz* in Aasfjord near Trondheim. The ship was well defended and anti-aircraft fire hit his aircraft, setting one of the wings on fire. Realising that he would not be able to bring the crippled aircraft back home, he turned it in the general direction of neutral Sweden and told the crew to prepare to bale out. He then discovered to his horror that he had left his own parachute at the back of the aircraft. His life was saved by the flight engineer, Flight Sergeant Colgan, who found the parachute and came back to the cockpit to give it to him. Colgan helped the tail gunner out before finally jumping himself. Bennett baled out at around 200ft, hitting the ground a split second after his parachute opened.

Soon he met up with the wireless operator, Sergeant Forbes, and together they headed for Sweden. They walked for nearly two days in freezing conditions before coming across a small house where they stopped to ask for food. It was provided, as well as guides to get them across the border into Sweden where a Swedish army officer, Captain Skoogh, arrested them and sent them to an internment camp. Bennett managed to persuade the captain to send a telegram to his wife with just one word – love – which he knew Ly would understand meant he was safe. Having received the telegram and informed the station commander at Leeming that her husband was alive, she was amused, several days later, to receive notification from the Air Ministry that 'from an unreliable source it had been learnt that Wing Commander Bennett was alive and in Sweden'.

Bennett was determined not to remain in captivity. After a few days' rest nursing a frostbitten foot and regaining some of the weight he had lost during his walk from Norway, he got permission to travel to Stockholm where he contacted the British Air Attaché with the help of a friendly Swede. Finding that the British officials were courteous but otherwise unhelpful, Bennett enlisted the help of his new friend, Ake Sundell, who arranged for him to meet the Swedish Under Secretary of State in the Foreign Office, Count Bernadotte. He also met the Swedish Naval Attaché who told him that information which would have prevented the disastrous attack on the *Tirpitz* had been sent to the British Admiralty two months before. On his return to Britain he enquired why this information had not been passed to the RAF and was told that 'it was not considered worthwhile to pass it on to the Royal Air Force, but was purely used for Naval purposes'.

Bernadotte was able to arrange for Bennett to be returned to Britain. He was flown to RAF Leuchars in Scotland by a Norwegian pilot in a Lockheed 14 from where he went straight home, annoying the British authorities who thought he should first have gone to London to be debriefed. He had been gone just one month.

Resuming command of 10 Squàdron, Bennett was surprised to learn that the unit was being sent to the Middle East to bomb the Italian fleet. He thought this a worthless exercise since he did not believe that the Italian Navy had any clout whatsoever, and that 10 Squadron's deployment was a complete waste of resources. When he reached Hurn, near Bournemouth, on the first leg of his journey to the Middle East, he was suddenly told to hand over command to one of the flight commanders and to report to the Commander-in-Chief at Headquarters, Bomber Command.

The C-in-C had been informed by Winston Churchill that he was to set up a Pathfinder Force to lead bombers to their targets and mark those targets, ensuring greater bombing accuracy and therefore better results. It was something that Bennett had long favoured, but the C-in-C, Sir Arthur Harris, thought it a bad idea and had vetoed its formation. With the direct order coming from Churchill he had no choice but to implement it and insisted that the force be commanded by Don Bennett, whom he had known at RAF Pembroke Dock and whose progress he had monitored in the intervening years. Bennett was immediately promoted to group captain, taking up his new position on 5 July 1942. He was told that he could set up his headquarters at an aerodrome of his own choosing and chose RAF Wyton in Huntingdonshire.

Although Harris was not in favour of the Pathfinder Force he was always supportive of Bennett himself, and said of him in his book *Bomber Offensive*:

His courage, both moral and physical, is outstanding, and as a technician he is unrivalled. He will forgive me if I say that his consciousness of his own intellectual powers sometimes made him impatient with slower or differently constituted minds, so that some people found him difficult to work with. He could not suffer fools gladly, and by his own high standards there were many fools. . . . we were lucky to get a man of such attainments to lead and form the Pathfinders.

In many ways the two men were similar. Neither tolerated fools gladly and both were exasperated when coming into contact with bureaucratic pen-pushers. Although they had the greatest respect for each other, that did not stop them clashing over things about which they felt strongly and neither was afraid to say what he really believed despite the effects that this openness may have had.

Having been given the go-ahead to set up the Pathfinders, Bennett devoted himself to making it the best, most efficient force he could. He felt that the selection and training of the crews was most important, but initially there was no time to do any training as they were sent on their first mission to Flensburg on the German/Danish border on 18–19 August. The raid was not a success, due to inaccurate weather reports, but techniques soon improved.

Bennett was concerned not only with conventional navigation methods but also with the new navigation aids that were becoming available, first GEE and then Oboe, which allowed his crews to fix positions much more accurately than before. Later he became the first pilot to land an aeroplane in bad weather using FIDO (Fog Investigation Dispersal Operation). The system, developed by scientists at the Ministry of Petroleum Warfare, used petrol burners along each side of a runway, the intense heat from which dispersed the fog and showed inbound pilots where the runway was located, enabling them to land safely.

By January 1943 the Pathfinder Force was doing so well that Harris decided it should be upgraded. It became No. 8 Group with Don Bennett as its Air Officer Commanding. He was given the rank of air commodore, but when Harris tried to promote him to air vice-marshal in line with other group commanders, the Air Ministry refused because, they said, he was too young. They were treated to the full force of Harris's temper and at the age of 32 Bennett became the youngest ever air vice-marshal of the RAF.

What had started as a small outfit grew, under Bennett's guidance, into one of the most important groups in the RAF, improving the accuracy and efficacy of Bomber Command's operations. It was an accomplishment of which Bennett was proud and when he wrote his autobiography he called it *Pathfinder*.

Don Bennett's achievements throughout the Second World War had been great but he received scant recognition for them. Following the *Tirpitz* incident he had been awarded the DSO for gallantry and was given the CBE in 1943 and the CB in 1944. At the end of the conflict all RAF group commanders received knighthoods – except Don Bennett.

Towards the end of the war Bennett had been encouraged by Conservative MP Harold Balfour, then Parliamentary Under-Secretary of State for Air, to write a booklet setting out his ideas for ensuring world peace by the use of an international police force. As a serving officer, he had obtained permission for its publication from the Air Ministry and the day before the booklet was due to be published was surprised to be summoned to the office of Chief of the Air Staff, Air Chief Marshal Sir Charles Portal, and told, in no uncertain terms, that he was not to publish. When Bennett pointed out that he had already obtained permission, Portal replied: 'This will jeopardise you in my eyes – I am giving you an order not to publish.' Bennett, never one to be intimidated, went ahead anyway, but the whole incident left a sour taste and he felt he could no longer remain in the RAF.

Sir Archibald Sinclair, Secretary of State for Air, had a friend, Harcourt 'Crinks' Johnstone, who had been a prominent Liberal minister in the wartime coalition government and was MP for Middlesbrough West. When Johnstone died suddenly in March 1945 Sinclair asked Bennett if he would stand as unopposed Liberal candidate for the constituency. Bennett had already been asked to become general manager of British Latin American Air Lines when the war was over, but following the argument with Portal about the booklet, he decided to stand.

Bennett's time as an MP was short. Less than two months after his election the war ended and in July 1945 a general election was held in which he lost his seat. This was probably a blessing as, by then, he had taken up his post as general manager of BLAA and would need all his time and effort for setting up the new airline.

Chapter 3

An Airline is Born

On 9 February 1945 a report was sent from the British Air Attaché in Buenos Aires to the Air Ministry in Whitehall. The attaché had been approached by Señor Dodero of the Dodero Shipping Line which handled the interests of the British shipping companies behind British Latin American Air Lines. Dodero appeared to be disturbed at a press report which stated that BOAC would resent the competition of the British shipping companies and their airline to South America and he wanted to know if the British government intended to support BOAC to the exclusion of any other company. The air attaché was anxious to reassure Dodero, who was an important figure in Buenos Aires, and told him that although he had no official information he felt sure that the government did not intend to grant BOAC a monopoly. It was important to keep Dodero on side as he had made a proposal in which Britain would participate in the setting up of internal Argentinian airlines, providing feeder services from outlying towns and cities to the gateway of Buenos Aires. This would obviously benefit whichever carrier the government chose to fly from Britain to South America and, since PAA also had an interest in the venture which would further increase its dominance in the area, the British government could not afford to upset Dodero.

When in March 1945 the government's White Paper on civil aviation was published it came as no surprise that the routes to the Commonwealth countries, America, the Far East and Australia were allocated to BOAC, being the only company actually flying at that time. European and internal routes were to be undertaken by a new company comprising railway companies, short sea shipping lines, travel agencies and BOAC. This company would be called British European Airways. For the South American routes, the following was reported to the British ambassadors of several South American countries, in a telegram from the Foreign Office dated 14 March 1945:

South American Services will be assigned to a new company in which majority participants will be those British shipping lines operating to South

America who have associated together for this purpose in British Latin American Airways Ltd. It is proposed that BOAC should participate in capital and management of this new corporation but its shares in the capital will be smaller than that allotted to it in the corporation responsible for European and internal services.

Fourteen months after British Latin American Air Lines had been set up, it had received government permission to operate the routes from Britain to South America, albeit with some participation of the state airline, BOAC. It is ironic that BEA, with much more participation by BOAC envisaged, was allowed to operate independently for another twenty-nine years before it and BOAC joined forces to become British Airways. BLAA was not so lucky.

After the publication of the White Paper, Lord Swinton, Minister for Civil Aviation, asked the Foreign Office if it would set up a meeting with officials from the Brazilian, Argentinian and Uruguayan embassies to discuss arrangements for the new air services. This suggestion was taken up with great speed and the meeting was held on 19 March. The reaction of the South Americans to the plans was favourable. The Uruguayan counsellor, Señor de Arteaga, had already studied the White Paper and the various debates in Parliament and was drawing up a report for his government. He welcomed the proposal to enter into negotiations for an agreement. The Brazilian Chargé d'Affaires, Senhor Sousa Leao, also hoped his government would be able to begin negotiations for an agreement as soon as possible and hinted that Brazil might also welcome British interest in their internal airlines.

The situation with Argentina was rather more complicated. When the Japanese bombed Pearl Harbor in December 1941, most of the South and Central American countries had supported the Allies. Argentina, however, had remained neutral and only broke off diplomatic relations with the Axis powers in 1944. She was not invited to take part in the Chicago Convention later that year, which set up the International Civil Aviation Organisation (ICAO) and attempted to standardise facilities and traffic rights between nations, and was excluded from the Inter-American Conference on Problems of War and Peace, which opened in Mexico City on 21 February 1945. Argentina was told that she would not be allowed to join the United Nations unless she entered the war and accordingly did so on the side of the Allies on 27 March 1945. Since the meeting with the embassy officials only took place on 19 March, she was still not regarded as having toed the line and John Cheetham of the Foreign Office reported:

> Owing to the delicacy of the political situation we were unable to tell Señor Siri (Argentina) in so many words that we hoped to conclude an agreement as soon as possible with the Argentine government, but we left him in no doubt that as soon as normal relations were restored we should not hesitate to approach them. We also reassured Señor Siri that we were still greatly interested in the possibilities of the Dodero scheme, and had recently sought and obtained an assurance from the Argentine government that they would not clinch a deal with Panamerican [sic] Airways for participation in local airlines without first giving British interests an opportunity to associate themselves with the transaction.

Cheetham also said that he had met the Peruvian Chargé d'Affaires, Señor Berckemeyer, at a party and had discovered that Peru hoped to be included in the routes of the new airline. In view of this interest he wondered if he should contact the Chilean Embassy to canvass opinion as to the inclusion of Santiago for the final stop on the route between Rio de Janeiro, Montevideo and Buenos Aires.

Of the three countries, the one that had the closest relationship with Britain was Uruguay. At the same time she had the most to lose by not being included in the routes of BLAA. Even before the meeting, the Uruguayan authorities had been making representations to the British Embassy in Montevideo to ensure that their capital city would be included in whatever plans the British government had regarding postwar aviation. An article in a Uruguayan evening newspaper, El Diario, had stated that of nine international airlines present at the Chicago Convention in November 1944 who had expressed an intention of serving South American cities, only three were planning to land in Montevideo. The writer of the article, who was later discovered to have been the Uruguayan Director General of Civil Aviation, was concerned that their excellent modern facilities were likely to be bypassed in favour of Buenos Aires and Rio de Janeiro. He felt that this would be a tragedy for the country, especially since it now had a modern, new airport at Carrasco with one of the best runways in the world.

The British Ambassador to Montevideo, Gordon Vereker, also felt that the Uruguayan concerns were important and sent a confidential memo by diplomatic courier to the Foreign Secretary, Anthony Eden. He told Eden:

I venture, therefore, to express the hope that, if and when British air lines to South America are established, every effort will be made to include Montevideo in their itinerary, not only on account of the psychological value of such a provision from the point of view of propaganda but also . . . because of the benevolent attitude of the Uruguayan government towards British interests in postwar aviation. Moreover, I understand that it is unlikely that, for the next two years at least, the Argentine Republic will have an aerodrome in the vicinity of Buenos Aires capable of accommodating the large transatlantic liners which will presumably be employed on the route from Europe to South America.

BLAA director S.W. Black produced a list of the eleven basic requirements of the airline:

- The right of passage over foreign territory.
- The right to land for traffic purposes. Authority to cater for external traffic to and from destinations other than the UK.
- Landing rights at airports with facilities adequate for large passenger aircraft.
- Availability of radio and meteorological services.
- Basis and amount of airport dues.
- Customs facilities for traffic and for fuel and supplies.
- Conditions for carriage of mail.
- Technical personnel – recruitment locally and admission of all necessary technicians of British nationality.
- Cooperation with governmental authorities, and with national airlines for interchange of traffic, technical advice etc.
- Formal authority to establish offices and agencies and generally to engage in business within territory.
- The adoption of British radar apparatus at national airports.

Discussions between representatives of government offices and BLAA began on 12 April 1945 at a meeting chaired by the Director General of Civil Aviation, Sir William Hildred, and attended by members of the Ministry of Civil Aviation (MCA), the Air Ministry and, for BLAA, director S.W. Black and chairman John Booth. Brigadier General A.C. Critchley and Group Captain Wilson represented BOAC.

London at that time did not have an airport capable of handling aircraft as
large as Tudor IIs, so it was initially planned by the MCA that BLAA should
use Hurn near Bournemouth until Heathrow was built. From there BLAA
wanted to fly over the Cherbourg peninsula and the northern part of Spain
and make its first landing at Portela airfield in Lisbon, which could handle
Avro Yorks and was going to be extended, making it suitable also for Tudors.
From Lisbon BLAA planned to fly direct to West Africa and then across the
South Atlantic to Brazil.

There were three African options on offer: Dakar in French West Africa,
Bathurst in The Gambia or Sal Island in the Cape Verde Islands, but Booth
thought that Sierra Leone might be a possibility because a suitable airfield had
been constructed there during the war. Brigadier General Critchley of BOAC
immediately denied that the airport was any good at all. He also dismissed
the facilities at the RAF airfield at Yundum in Bathurst, saying that BOAC
had rejected them, and that Yoff in Dakar was also no good as it carried a
health risk (it was in a yellow fever area), which would not be acceptable to
the Brazilian government. In his opinion, Sal Island was the obvious choice
as it was on a direct route which saved 157 miles flying from Britain and
the land was suitable for the development of an airport. Booth protested
that surface communications with Sal Island were not good; there was no
harbour and ships had to lie offshore when discharging. He felt that the lack
of facilities would greatly increase the cost of fuel. Critchley tried to counter
this argument by pointing out that if Sal Island were used the distance across
the Atlantic was 1,760 miles, a reduction of a further 106 miles over the
route via Dakar. If Booth's point about the increases to the cost of fuel had
been admitted this would surely have negated any arguments in favour of Sal
Island, but he asked Critchley to provide him with details of the island anyway
and the proposed site of the airport, which still had to be built.

Group Captain Entwistle of the Air Ministry revealed that 'a considerable
amount of valuable meteorological data regarding the South Atlantic crossing
had been assembled and that it would be possible to examine it and reach
more reliable conclusions as to the best routing for this crossing than had
been possible heretofore'. He maintained that although Dakar was situated
to the north of the area in West Africa that suffered from the worst weather,
and that an airport in Sierra Leone would enable the crossing to be made
avoiding the bad weather, this was not necessarily so. The decision of which
West African airport to use was obviously one fraught with problems and

Sir William Hildred asked Entwistle to make a report of his findings, including the recently obtained weather data, and send it to John Booth.

There were problems with the meteorological services anyway with no international organisation available at that time. If Portugal refused to continue with its current system, which was operated with both Portuguese and British personnel, and insisted on taking control of the service itself once the war ended there was doubt as to whether or not the weather data generated would be of a sufficient standard to enable the airline to fly on to West Africa. Entwistle thought that if this did happen it might be possible to persuade the Portuguese government to accept one or two British meteorological experts in a 'liaison role' at the weather station in Lisbon. Bathurst was the meteorological centre for the South Atlantic but if it proved unsuitable it would be easy to set up other facilities virtually anywhere in British West Africa and, within South America, PAA had a station in Natal, Brazil, although its services were not always reliable.

Booth said that he intended that the airline should fly via Natal and Rio de Janeiro to the River Plate but the question of which airport to use in the River Plate area was a problem. Although he expected traffic to and from Buenos Aires to be greater than that to Montevideo, Buenos Aires did not have a suitable airport. He acknowledged the fact that Uruguay was very friendly with Britain but did not want to fly directly to Montevideo as it would delay passengers who wanted to disembark in Buenos Aires. He decided therefore to try to route the flights from Rio de Janeiro to Buenos Aires and then back to Montevideo making it the terminus until a new airport at Buenos Aires had been built.

Sir William Hildred wanted to know if there were any intentions of continuing the flights onwards to Santiago in Chile. Booth thought that it was not a viable proposition using the same aircraft, but that there might be a possibility if a smaller aircraft were to be used from Buenos Aires. He thought that it might be advantageous to extend the flight from Santiago to Lima, but that it was something to be considered at a later date. George Cribbett, Acting Under Secretary at the Department of Civil Aviation, pointed out that it would be helpful if Booth could advise him what BLAA might ultimately want to do before the other governments were contacted so that provision could be made in advance for changes the airline was likely to make in the future.

Booth wanted to know if it were possible to obtain permission from the various governments to set up maintenance and other facilities at each of the transit stops with suitable staff to man them, but Critchley suggested that he might like to consider asking Shell to do the passenger handling. As Shell had to have trained staff at each airport to oversee the fuelling of aircraft, he had asked the company to look after BOAC's passengers as well and it was doing this on a trial basis at Khartoum. Booth had heard that a similar scheme had not worked too well in South America and wanted to provide his own staff for all parts of the operation.

Since there were so many options to consider and they were all being discussed well away from the area in which the arrangements were to be made, Booth thought that it would be sensible to undertake a survey flight as soon as possible to find out just what facilities already existed and which new ones would be required. As BLAA still had no fleet he asked Hildred if it would be possible to borrow an aeroplane for the survey. He suggested that a de Havilland Mosquito might suffice if it had an additional fuel tank. Critchley thought that BOAC might be able to provide an aircraft for the flight from its Development Unit and so it was decided that Hildred would only become involved if BOAC was unable to help.

Astonishingly the only civil radio organisation open to all on the routes that BLAA intended to fly was one between Britain and Portugal. The route between Britain and Natal via Dakar was served by the American authorities, and Natal to Buenos Aires was covered by PAA, although its facilities were of a pre-war standard. Critchley told Booth that PAA had offered the use of these facilities to BOAC when it was thinking of operating flights to South America and he thought that it would be happy to do the same for BLAA.

Since the resources were so poor it was agreed that the best course of action would be a diplomatic approach to the Brazilian and Argentinian authorities to ask them '. . . to implement the international obligations which had been agreed at Chicago that countries should provide radio facilities for international air services in their respective territories'. Argentina had not attended the Chicago Convention so could hardly be expected to comply readily with anything that had been agreed there. In 1946 the airline, by then called BSAA, maintained the ex-RAF radio facilities at Natal, believing they were doing this on behalf of the MCA until the Brazilian authorities could be persuaded to take them over. When accounts were submitted the MCA prevaricated, saying that the cost of maintaining ground facilities should be paid for by the airline. But shortly afterwards when BOAC offered to maintain fire services in Bathurst it was told by an official of the MCA: 'I am to place on record that the cost of overhaul, operation and maintenance will be refunded to the Corporation by the Ministry.'

* * *

Sir William Hildred was in favour of BLAA participating in the Dodero scheme and wanted to know if Booth would be interested. He explained that Dodero had suggested that there should be one company with capital distributed four ways: Argentinian government 30 per cent; Dodero Argentine Finance Group 36 per cent; British interests 17 per cent; American interests 17 per cent.

This company would provide aircraft and run the internal air services in Argentina. Hildred said that although he was keen for BLAA to be the main British participant, it was also planned to provide six de Havilland Dominie aircraft as part of the British package. This was an optimistic suggestion since in April 1945 there were no aircraft to spare for anyone, let alone an airline in which the majority of shares were held by other countries; they just hoped that they might be available when the negotiations reached an advanced stage.

Booth told the Director General that he was only willing for BLAA to participate in this scheme if Alberto Dodero was excluded from the discussions. He had already spoken to the Argentinian Ambassador and had been told by him that an American company, thought to be PAA's subsidiary Panagra, had been conducting talks behind Dodero's back and that his government believed that Dodero was too close to certain other American interests and was, therefore, no longer a reliable representative. Hildred promised to check this situation by discreet enquiries at the embassy in Buenos Aires.

In the discussion which followed Critchley expressed the opinion that 'we ought now to choose between going into partnership with PAA in approaches to all South American countries in which we are interested, or competing with them.' He felt that if BLAA was to compete it would be 'outmanoeuvred'. PAA certainly had no interest in promoting a British airline's operations in South America and, in view of the way BOAC subsequently behaved towards BLAA, one wonders who it was that Critchley thought would outmanoeuvre them.

In addition to the discussions about routes and facilities, John Booth raised the question of British West Indian Airways (BWIA). He said that he understood that the airline was in a bad way financially despite operating a modest number of routes, but that if Lord Swinton felt that the Caribbean area was one in which BLAA could become involved. BLAA would like to acquire a financial interest in the company. Lord Swinton thought that BLAA should be able to take the part that had originally been envisaged for BOAC and said that he would press the Colonial Office for its views on whether this would be acceptable. Having had to subsidise the loss-making Caribbean airline, it is hard to see how the Colonial Office could be anything but delighted with the prospect of BLAA taking over and relieving it of its financial burden.

A week after the meeting, Cheetham, the Foreign Office representative, contacted Cribbett and told him that Dodero was planning to visit England. Referring to Booth's report of his conversation with the Argentinian Ambassador, Cheetham said:

> The Counsellor of the [Argentinian] Embassy has assured us categorically that his chief could not have possibly said anything to give such an impression. The Ambassador himself subsequently rang up . . . in considerable perturbation to confirm that he had been completely misreported. He insisted that he knew practically nothing of his own government's plans and had virtually confined himself to listening to what his visitors had to say. We cannot help wondering whether the misrepresentation of his views can have been completely accidental.

Cheetham did not elaborate on his theory that Booth had deliberately lied about his meeting with the ambassador and it is difficult to see what motive he would have had for doing so. He went on to suggest that Dodero and Booth should get together and discuss plans for the coordination of the Argentinian feeder service with the BLAA long distance flights when the former arrived in London. He could then be told what British equipment and technical expertise would be available to him after VE Day. He concluded by asking Cribbett if he would arrange air transport for Dodero's visit, provided he agreed that the meetings would be of use, and told him that: 'Quite apart from his interest in British participation in Argentine air lines, he has proved himself a good friend of ours in many ways and we should like to afford him every possible facility'. There were obviously other issues to be considered about which Booth knew nothing.

Eight days after the meeting which was supposed to iron out all the difficulties involved in the setting up of BLAA's operations, the airline discovered another example of governmental policy either to keep them in the dark or decide themselves what was best for the airline. BLAA director S.W. Black, who had been at the meeting on 12 April, wrote to Sir William Hildred on 20th expressing his disquiet about what he had discovered. He told the Director General:

> . . . it has just come to our knowledge that a very large part of the radio industry has been given contracts by the MAP [Ministry of Aircraft Production] for the development of equipment likely to be of value in civil aviation and we naturally feel somewhat perturbed to find that action of this kind is being taken without our having been given an opportunity, as a future operating company, to express our views as to future requirements. I gather that these contracts are likely to keep the development resources of the whole radio industry occupied for anything up to two years in which case it is vital that such development should be undertaken along lines which will meet the requirements of the operators concerned. In these circumstances, we would be most grateful if full information could be supplied to us in regard to the proposed contracts and future development plans and if an opportunity could be afforded to us to express our views on this important subject.

While these discussions were going on and plans were being made to start the service to South America, British Embassy officials throughout the continent were busy gathering data and sending it to London to argue the merits of the new airline operating to the particular country with which they were associated. In the case of Peru, Mr Forbes at the British Embassy in Lima, sent telegrams to the Foreign Office stating that Britain used to have the monopoly in the transportation of goods from Europe to Peru and that unless they did something quickly to re-establish this monopoly in shipping and now air transport they would lose their previous advantage to the Swedes, the Dutch and the Americans. Forbes also went on to suggest that, if necessary, sacrifices should be made elsewhere to secure large government contracts with Peru. When copies of some of the telegrams were forwarded to John Booth he commented, 'This just goes to confirm the view we expressed that an extension of our service to the west coast of South America as soon as possible will be a very good thing.'

It was becoming clear that BLAA was not just the vision of a few forward-thinking shipping company directors but was regarded by the governments of a number of South American countries, and by the British officials in those countries, as vital to the future of commerce and trade between South America and Britain. However, on the part of the British government at least, progress in expediting the start of operations of the new company was slow.

Five weeks after he had written to Sir William Hildred, Black of BLAA eventually received a reply to his letter regarding the MAP contracts. In it he was told that:

. . . in order to avoid loss of valuable time, there has been no alternative but for MAP to place contracts for the development of certain types of equipment. Some of these contracts relate merely to the production of equipment for experimental trials rather than for settled adoption. In certain parts of the radio field we cannot at the present stage settle final requirements pending International agreement on proposals for standardisation.

We shall be only too happy, of course, to let you know what has been done during the past twelve months.

The letter then went on to say that there were certain security formalities that would have to be completed before anyone from BLAA was allowed to know what was going on, but that they should not take very long to complete and that the Ministry would contact BLAA as soon as everything was in place. So five weeks on from Black's agitated letter, he had received a reply which left him as much in the dark as he had been when he wrote it.

* * *

While plans were still being made to conduct the survey flight to South America, the Americans suddenly seemed to wake up to the fact that they would soon have stiff competition on the South American routes and were not pleased by the prospect. Sir William Hildred was concerned about the American attitude but, instead of contacting John Booth, he got in touch with Brigadier General Critchley at BOAC to warn him. He told him:

Feelings in the USA are running high at the moment over our alleged diversion of British produced aircraft to civil use while we continue to demand Lease/Lend transports from the USA . . . although high level action is now in train to dispel misunderstandings and bring about a more realistic attitude on the part of the Americans, we think it advisable to proceed carefully about the projected survey flight.

The discussions regarding the provision of an aircraft for the survey flight continued throughout the summer of 1945. BOAC had been prepared to lend one of its aircraft from the Development Unit, but because of problems with the Americans and the delay to the delivery of its new Avro Yorks, which were needed for the South African route, it withdrew the offer. It suggested that an approach be made to RAF Transport Command to see if one of its VIP Yorks could be made available and this was considered but finally declined because the Americans were still making a fuss about Lease/Lend arrangements. The situation was thought to have been finally resolved in August when, on the 15th, the Japanese forces surrendered and the war in the Far East was over. With the provision of military aircraft no longer a priority the British would be able to take back some control from the Americans and make their own decisions about how their resources were to be used. Despite having no aircraft for the survey flight, plans were going ahead within BLAA for the procurement of a fleet and for the staff to handle the operations to South America.

Chapter 4

The Government Decides

When setting up the complex infrastructure necessary to enable a fledgling airline such as BLAA to begin operations, its choice of aircraft was of paramount importance. It was governed by many factors, including cost, availability, economy, availability of spares and capacity. In Air Vice-Marshal Don Bennett's case there were two more factors which made his decision an easier one. Despite being Australian by birth he was passionately pro-British. This meant that unless any foreign aircraft could offer significant advantages in any of the areas mentioned above, he would choose a British product. Secondly, he intended that the nucleus of his aircrews should be drawn from RAF Bomber Command. These were men he knew, who possessed the necessary high standard of flying skills, and in most cases were experienced Avro Lancaster pilots. From then on, the decision to start operations using Avro Lancastrians was inevitable.

The Lancastrian had originated from the need to produce an interim airliner, capable of carrying passengers and freight over some of the longest air routes at the time. It had to be brought into service relatively quickly and easily to satisfy the immediate demands of airlines which were waiting for delivery of the more 'purpose designed' aircraft such as the Avro Tudor and Handley Page Hermes.

In 1942 Victory Aircraft Ltd in Canada carried out a conversion of a Lancaster III (R5727) to enable it to be used for carrying freight. The conversion involved, among other things, removing the mid-upper turret, producing wooden fairings to cover the spaces vacated by the nose and tail turrets and the addition of a row of three windows at the rear of the fuselage. Once converted, the aircraft was handed over to Trans Canada Airlines which made use of its ability to carry loads of up to 14,000lb over long distances. It was later flown back to England where A.V. Roe at Woodford made further changes to 'civilianise' it, adding ten passenger seats and extra fuel tanks to increase the still-air range to 4,000 miles. It was registered CF-CMS and used to inaugurate the Canadian Government Transatlantic Air Service on 22 July

1943 before being granted a British Certificate of Airworthiness (C of A) on 1 September 1943. Once CF-CMS had proven itself, Trans Canada Airlines then converted two more Canadian-built Lancaster Xs and re-designated them Lancaster XPPs. Later in 1944, Victory Aircraft Ltd converted five more Lancaster Xs to XPP standard, this time using a metal nose which increased the mail carrying capacity to 3.5 tons. The original aircraft, CF-CMS, was lost in a take-off accident in June 1945, but by then the concept of a civilianised Lancaster had been fully proven.

During 1944, A.V. Roe started production of an aircraft very similar to the Canadian conversions which they designated the Avro 691 Lancastrian. This was to be used by BOAC on its Australian routes. Avro allocated thirty-two aircraft from the end of the Lancaster production line to be converted for BOAC, but in the end only twenty were used. With only nine passenger seats, the BOAC Lancastrian Is were not economical, so when BSAA expressed an interest in purchasing a number of the aircraft for its inaugural South American routes, it insisted that the passenger accommodation should be upgraded for the long flights (including more windows) and that thirteen seats should be fitted to improve the operating efficiency. In consequence, these revised Lancastrians had seven forward-facing seats on the port side and six on the starboard. They also differed from the Lancastrian I in having a row of windows down both sides of the fuselage instead of just the starboard. An order was eventually placed for eighteen aircraft and when the first six Lancastrians (registered G-AGWG to G-AGWL) were delivered to BSAA between December 1945 and February 1946 they were designated Lancastrian IIIs.

The Lancastrian proved to be a reliable workhorse aircraft for BSAA. Indeed, they bought more in late 1947 to fill the gap caused by the delays in the Avro Tudor entering service. The remaining twelve from the original BSAA order were not delivered before the airline's merger with BOAC and were diverted to meet the requirements of other airlines.

While the Lancastrian gave sterling service to many airlines, it did have a few shortcomings which betrayed its military origins. Although the tremendous load-carrying ability of the Lancaster meant that the Lancastrian was also able to carry heavy loads over long distances, it did not have the fuselage capacity to turn those loads into passenger numbers. The thirteen seats fitted to the BSAA aircraft were about as many as could be fitted into the fuselage interior while still retaining a degree of seat comfort. The aircraft was unpressurised, which meant passengers and crew had to use oxygen for long periods while crossing the Andes, a situation unthinkable in today's airliners. The outlook was not much better for the cabin crew, who had to negotiate the large wing spar when taking meals between the small galley and the passenger cabin. In the cockpit, the layout was very similar to the Lancaster from which it was derived, which meant it did not have much in the way of 'modern' navigational aids. This is what made the routes to Bermuda and across the Andes to Santiago that much more challenging than routes which other airlines were operating at the time. However, this was immediately after the Second World War and large, high-capacity airliners were not yet in service. As well as providing postwar airlines with a long range transport, the Lancastrian proved to be a very useful engine test-bed due to its versatility and airframe strength. Lancastrians were flown with a variety of engines, including some of the early jets such as the Nene, Ghost and Avon. Indeed, a Lancastrian I (VH742), modified by Rolls-Royce with two Nene turbojets in place of the outer Merlins, became the first commercial airliner to fly solely on turbojet power, on 8 August 1946.

In the early days of BSAA the airline used Avro Lancasters for transporting freight. The Lancaster's narrow fuselage was not the most capacious and a plan was formulated to increase its capacity by using an under-fuselage freight pannier. The contract for the design of the pannier was let to Airtech, a company based at Thame in Oxfordshire. It came up with a solution which was fitted to BSAA's Lancaster *Star Ward* (G-AGUM) for testing. When the time came for the first air test, the unsuspecting crew duly climbed aboard and took off. In the words of an observer, the Lancaster did 'half a circuit' before coming back in to land. It was so directionally unstable that the crew had to apply full-right aileron just to stay level. They could therefore only turn left. The crew were disgusted that the aircraft had been passed as airworthy. It was rumoured at the time that BSAA had intended to sue Airtech, but then discovered there was nothing written into the contract to guarantee that the aircraft would be airworthy after the modification!

During the war, there had been an agreement between Britain and the USA that in order to rationalise aircraft production and to focus resources where they were most needed, America would be solely responsible for the production of wartime transport aircraft. This led to the extensive use by the RAF of very capable aircraft such as the Douglas DC-3, or Dakota as it was known in RAF use. While it was a reasonably successful arrangement during the war years, it meant that at the end of the war America had a sizeable lead over Britain in the knowledge and ability to produce large aircraft suitable for the growing market for civil aviation. There is no doubting the abilities and skill of the leading British aircraft designers at the time. All they lacked was experience in providing for the subtly different needs of transporting fare-paying passengers comfortably and safely rather than the ability efficiently to carry and drop bombs.

At the end of 1941, Roy Chadwick, designer of the Avro Lancaster, realised that by replacing the Lancaster fuselage he could utilise many of its proven qualities, such as its long range and impressive load-carrying ability, to build a transport aircraft suitable for carrying a relatively large number of troops. His initial idea was for an assault troop carrier capable of being belly landed in enemy territory with little damage to the strengthened fuselage, so that it could later be jacked up, the undercarriage lowered, and the aircraft flown home. This rather extreme idea was later dropped in favour of designing the aircraft as a conventional transport. Due to the agreement with the USA, there could be no government sanction of the project, so it was initially proposed as a private venture. However, when Avro discussed the project with the Air Ministry in October 1941, it was very interested and gave the encouragement needed to proceed with a formal announcement of the idea in brochure form in January 1942.

In a move perhaps not strictly within the guidelines of the unwritten agreement with the USA over production of transport aircraft, the Air Staff announced on 19 January that they wanted to proceed with a full examination of the Avro project. They suggested it could lead to production of over 200 of the new type as long as it used the major components from the Lancaster bomber. This was just the encouragement Avro needed, and Chadwick wasted no time in producing detailed drawings for the new aircraft. He submitted his drawings to the Experimental Department on 18 February and after discussion with the Ministry of Aircraft Production (MAP) over the extent of modifications required to the Lancaster wings, the Ministry sent a letter to Avro on 24 March instructing it to proceed with the production of two prototypes.

Chadwick's design used the wings, tail, undercarriage and engines from the Lancaster mated to a totally new square section fuselage. In order to provide a clean cabin area (without the intrusion from the main spar which was to prove such a handicap for the Lancastrian) he stuck with his initial high wing design for the aircraft, resulting in the fuselage having a very 'low-slung' look. Despite many of the major components and systems being shared with the Lancaster, the time from drawing board to the first flight of the prototype LV626 by H.A. 'Sam' Brown on 5 July 1942 was still a remarkably short four and a half months. The new aircraft was given the designation Avro 685 and true to the Avro tradition of naming its four-engined aircraft after cities in the north of England, it was christened the York.

Despite being a private venture, the prototype proved so successful that the Air Ministry issued a contract for Avro to build three more prototypes and a number of production aircraft. Shortly after this contract was issued, a meeting was held to discuss roles for the new transport and it was attended by representatives from BOAC. It was clearly envisaged very early in the project that it could fill a vital role as a civilian transport.

In order to speed up testing of the York in different configurations, Avro suggested it should produce six prototypes, two of which should have Hercules radial engines instead of the Merlin of the Lancaster, due to concerns over the availability of the Merlin engines. The Ministry voiced some misgivings over the suitability of the Hercules engine, but nevertheless compromised on a total of four prototypes, two of which to be powered by Rolls-Royce Merlin and two by Bristol Hercules engines. They requested that the aircraft be completed in four configurations – freighter, troop carrier, paratroop carrier and passenger transport. The requirement for a paratroop aircraft was dropped after problems with the slipstream along the fuselage meant it would be too hazardous to use the aircraft for jumping, and this was replaced by a request for a glider tug version. The Air Ministry finally issued formal Specification C1/42 on 18 August 1942 and placed a firm order for 200 aircraft on the understanding that the primary role of individual aircraft could be interchangeable within 24 hours.

Initial flights revealed a slight lack of directional stability with the standard double-fin tail from the Lancaster. After extended flight testing at A&AEE Boscombe Down, during which the option of a single very large fin was considered, it was finally decided to add a third central fin to solve the problem on production aircraft. There followed a period of great frustration for Avro, which was to prove similar to the later debacle concerning modifications to the Avro Tudor, and which was caused by a great deal of indecision by MAP. In October of 1942 the requirement for wing and tailplane de-icing was announced, as was flame damping for the engine exhausts. Again, representatives from BOAC were involved in discussions on aircraft specification and fittings. The Ministry then could not decide whether the windows should be rectangular or circular. This resulted in a delay in fitting the fuselage skins and finally led to a great deal of bitterness between MAP and Avro over what Roy Chadwick considered to be unnecessary changes resulting in serious delays to delivery dates. After many more arguments and delays, MAP finally provided Avro with a clear understanding of how many aircraft of each configuration should be produced. One wonders whether these acrimonious exchanges had any influence on the arguments over the Tudor specification a few years later.

An indication of the importance of the new aircraft (and confidence in its capabilities) was that the third prototype was produced as a VIP transport for Prime Minister Winston Churchill. After many meetings and changing requirements to specification and interior fittings, this aircraft (LV633) was eventually delivered on 25 May 1943 and given the name *Ascalon*. As well as being used to transport the Prime Minister, it was also used by King George VI when touring service units in North Africa and the Mediterranean.

Eventually, the first production aircraft were delivered at the end of 1943 and by 1944 a steady output had been established, with many of the early production aircraft being configured as VIP transports. The Avro York continued in production in various configurations until April 1948, by which time over 250 had been built.

When Don Bennett was looking for a suitable aircraft to augment his initial fleet of six Lancastrians, he turned once again to Avro. The York offered the ideal opportunity for BSAA to operate an aircraft which was again based on the Lancaster (his crews and engineers would already be familiar with the engines and many of the systems), but with greatly increased passenger capacity and therefore reduced operating costs. On 9 October 1946 a letter was sent by the Ministry of Supply to A.V. Roe on behalf of BSAA outlining requirements for modifications to the York aircraft destined for the airline, as these aircraft were originally built to meet service requirements. The modifications included the ability to operate at an all-up weight of 68,000lb. It was requested that the Merlin power plants be suitable for use in cold, temperate and tropical conditions without modification and should be installed so that engine changes could be carried out in as short a time as possible. Flame dampers were not required to be fitted. There was a careful stipulation regarding wing and tailplane de-icing, requesting a Dunlop system, and that a fluid reservoir be installed which would be capable of holding enough fluid for 6 hours of normal use. Careful attention was to be paid to fuselage sound insulation, so that 'the sound intensity shall not be greater than would be acceptable to the operating company'. An interesting requirement that concerned ditching was that the aircraft should be capable of making an emergency landing on water with the minimum risk of injury to personnel. It is hard to see how this particular request could be met, as the high-wing design of the York was fundamentally unsuitable for ditching. Additionally, the Ministry asked that cushions be provided for all crew seats in lieu of parachutes. The section on passenger accommodation asked for a total payload capacity (for a minimum range of 2,630 miles) of 5,592lb made up as follows: 21 passengers at 170lb each = 3570lb; 21 passengers' luggage at 50lb each = 1050lb; mail, freight and other cargo = 972lb.

All in all, the list of changes was lengthy and detailed and appeared to cover everything deemed necessary to modify a basic troop-carrying York to one suitable for twenty-one seat civilian use. An example of the detail covered even extended to the type of toilets fitted to the aircraft. There was clearly some disagreement between BSAA and A.V. Roe over the type of toilet seats fitted, as shown in the following letter from BSAA to the Ministry of Civil Aviation [note the irony in the address]:

F/Lt D.D. Lipman
Ministry of Civil Aviation,
Inveresk House,
Strand WC

My Dear Lipman,
I am not sure whether it is your function to attend to our YORK requirements, but there is a small point on which we must have immediate action, so if it is not your job, will you please pass it on to the person concerned.

On our YORKS the lavatories are fitted with an old fashioned type of Elsan, of which we strongly disapprove. When we raised this matter with A.V. Roe they said that it had always been intended to fit this type and seeing that we raised no objections they went right ahead. In other words, they are fitted by default on our part to criticise something of which we were not aware. We pointed out to them that the type which we require is fitted in our Lancastrians, which were delivered many months before the Yorks, and we automatically expected the same type in the later aircraft. The position at the moment is that A.V. Roe will not supply the type of Elsan required unless they receive a definite instruction from yourselves. Will you, therefore please ask the Ministry of Supply to request A.V. Roe to fit Elsan Lavatories Type P.F.A., complete with seat lid and the seat to be of plastic, not painted wood. These are urgently required to be fitted to the three YORKS still due for delivery and eight more for retrospective fitment to the YORKS which we have already received.

Yours sincerely,

(Sgd. J.W. Kenny)

Once the initial discussions over specification were resolved, the airline took delivery of its first Avro York, *Star Leader* (G-AHEW), on 27 May 1946. This was to be the first of a total of nineteen Yorks which they operated before the merger with BOAC. The York had a more spacious cabin than the Lancastrian, so was more popular with its passengers, but it did not have the latter's range or ability to fly at high altitudes. It was hoped these shortcomings would be a thing of the past when the new Avro 688 Tudor entered service. Little did they know that the Tudor was ultimately to cause them many more problems than it solved.

* * *

The July 1945 general election had brought Clement Attlee and a new Labour government to power and the ensuing changes caused more anxiety for the board of BLAA. Lord Swinton lost his position and was replaced as Minister for Civil Aviation on 4 August by Reginald Thomas Herbert Fletcher, 1st Baron Winster. The new Minister was not sure that BLAA should have been given the go-ahead to operate the services to South America at all and so, in addition to the problems regarding the aircraft, BLAA were once again uncertain if they were actually to be allowed to operate. While Winster acknowledged the urgency of making a survey flight, he favoured it being made by BOAC with no participation by BLAA.

Before the election, BOAC had been involved with the planning of the survey flight, but had brought to it no real sense of urgency since it was for the benefit of its rivals. The change in government offered it another chance and it suddenly declared itself both ready and willing to conduct the survey flight and begin operating to South America.

On 4 September John Booth and Don Bennett went to see Winster at his office in the Air Ministry. They pointed out to him that with all the delays to the survey flight and the start of operations, Britain was in danger of being completely bypassed by other European and American airlines on the South American route. Booth cited examples of French and Swedish progress in the area and also reminded the Minister that the Americans were already flying there from the United States. In addition, the Argentinian Dodero brothers, one of whom was the author of the Dodero scheme, had purchased Sunderland flying boats in which they proposed to begin a service to London.

While all the discussions over the aircraft had been taking place BLAA had hired aircrew, the first group being due to commence duty the following week with the second arriving on 20 September. They were in a position to employ ground staff as soon as they were demobbed from the RAF. The radio and meteorological arrangements which had been made in Brazil and Argentina were now satisfactory and, should they ultimately decide to fly to Santiago, it was felt that Chilean arrangements would also be acceptable. The route that BLAA proposed to take was London – Lisbon – Bathurst – Natal – Rio de Janeiro – Montevideo – Buenos Aires with an extension to Santiago at a later date.

Bennett told Winster that as they had been unable to obtain the loan of an aircraft for the survey flight he had approached Lord Knollys, chairman of BOAC, and asked if BLAA might be permitted the use of a BOAC Lancastrian for three weeks in order to make the flight. Knollys had agreed, but it was pointed out that he had no right to do so as his Lancastrians had been provided by the Air Ministry Supply Organisation (AMSO) specifically for the purpose of inaugurating a service to Australia and that if he then lent one to BLAA, objections could be raised.

Although Bennett told Winster that BLAA had already done a lot of groundwork in establishing this new airline and that if BOAC were allocated the new routes there would be a significant delay in the start of operations, there was doubt in the Air Ministry about whether BLAA would ultimately be the airline to operate the routes. In a note written by Sir William Hildred to Winster, he said:

In my own opinion, despite the urgency of the survey, we ought to wait a few days before we press for the release of a Lancastrian to do the survey. An additional reason for waiting is that for all I know BLAA might not be the leaders of such an expedition. It might be BOAC.

Discussions continued with BLAA, but behind the scenes it appeared that the government was leaning towards the view that BOAC should be the one to operate the services to South America. Ivor Thomas, Parliamentary Secretary in the Ministry of Civil Aviation, prepared a note for the Minister three days after the meeting with Booth and Bennett in which he said that there were pros and cons in letting Don Bennett make the survey flight. The 'pro' was that:

> The survey is urgently needed. If we wait until the Cabinet approves your recommendations, and then await the consequent reorganisation of the South American service, the flight may not take place this side of Christmas.

He noted that there were two 'cons', namely:

> (i) To use a Lancastrian for this trip within a fortnight from 4th September would, in the view of AMSO, imperil the Lend/Lease negotiations.
> (ii) Bennett would be going as General Manager of BLAA and in view of your recommendations to the Cabinet BLAA may not be the instrument ultimately adopted for running the South American service.

Thomas concluded his note:

> I submit for consideration the following ways of resolving these difficulties:-
> (i) To permit the release of a Lancastrian for the purpose of this survey flight on any date after September 18th.
> (ii) To invite Bennett to make this flight not as General Manager of BLAA, but on behalf of the Ministry of Civil Aviation. Whatever decisions of policy are made, there will certainly be a South American service and you will have the responsibility for it. . . .
> (iii) To emphasise the point that we are not pre-judging the future of BLAA by sending a senior official of BOAC to accompany Bennett.

On 10 September an Air Ministry memo for the Director General written by George Cribbett, then Deputy Director General, stated that:

> I know that you and the Minister are considering what arrangements can be made for an early start of the survey flight, but I would urge that if, as is proposed in CAC (45) 3, BOAC is to have the controlling interest

in the South Atlantic Corporation they must clearly have at least equal prominence with the BLAA partner in any arrangements for the survey flight. General Critchley informed me a few days ago that BOAC would be ready, if required, to make a Lancastrian available for the flight within 48 hours of receiving notice of the requirement.

If, therefore, a decision of policy could be obtained this week from the Civil Aviation Committee, there is no reason why the survey flight should not commence within a fortnight. It is also important that actual negotiations on the Governmental plane should be opened shortly. If BOAC are to be prominently associated with the survey flight I feel less qualms about the need for a representative of this Ministry with the survey party for the purpose of discussions with Governments. Indeed, if we are not exposed to the risks we feared at the time we were considering the visit as the sole responsibility of the BLAA representative, there may be positive advantages in preliminary exploratory discussions at operator level before actual negotiations between Governments are undertaken.

Although BOAC had not been able to provide an aircraft for BLAA to use on the planned survey flight, it had managed to find one that it could use, if it was to be the chosen airline to operate to South America. It also seems that the government perceived some kind of threat from BLAA. The reference to the risks and the BLAA representative could only mean Don Bennett, since he was the one who would have been making the survey flight if an aircraft had been put at his disposal. There is insufficient evidence to show just what these risks were thought to be but, in view of the way in which civil servants operated, they were possibly a little intimidated by Bennett, who arrived like a whirlwind in their midst and expected prompt action and decisiveness rather than the waffle and time-wasting that was their forte.

Meanwhile, representations were being made by British ambassadors in South America to the Foreign Office stressing the need for immediate action. Sir David Kelly, British Ambassador in Buenos Aires, sent a telegram giving more details of the services that were being planned by France, Sweden and Brazil and it was clear that the plans were in their final stages. He also quoted from the *Herald*, an English language newspaper in Buenos Aires. The article headlined 'A British Air Line – When?' said: 'It is not only national prestige that is at stake but also development of an export trade, the importance of which has never been greater than it is today.'

Sir David concluded: 'I venture to refer to many reports in which I have given illustrations in support of this view. Owing to shortage of shipping space and the impossibility of air travel for any but high priority official passengers, we are losing constant opportunities for establishing future trade connexions owing to would-be clients deciding to go to the United States.'

Whether or not this had any bearing on the government's discussions is not clear. They did, however, appear to pick up speed in their deliberations regarding the timing of the survey flight. When Bennett next went to visit Lord Winster on 20 September he was told that although there was still no decision about whether BLAA or BOAC would be operating to South America, it was recognised that the survey flight must be made without further delay. It was felt that if it was a 'high level' flight, the host countries would have to be told which company would be operating the services and since it was not known at that point, the Minister felt that it would be best to make the survey flight a purely technical one. He proposed chartering an aircraft from BOAC and sending along some technical staff to assess the conditions and facilities both in South America and en route.

Bennett was told that if he wanted BLAA to participate under these terms he should contact BOAC immediately to discuss dates, passports and inoculations. When he asked if he might be allowed to go on the flight himself, the answer was a definite 'No'.

He told the Minister that if that was his final answer he did not think that the flight would be of any use to BLAA. Since the opening of a new route was a technical matter and he was a technical man, he thought that, regardless of his position, he should be the one to make the flight. He had no intentions of relying on second-hand information and he felt sure that neither BOAC nor BLAA had anyone as technically qualified to make the flight as he was.

Winster would not budge and replied that he would leave the choice of captain to BOAC. Following the meeting, he sent a note to Lord Knollys at BOAC passing on the details of the conversation.

* * *

During August, while the future of BLAA hung in the balance, another slightly less important matter was under discussion. The board of BLAA decided that they wanted to change the company's name. Their reasons were that British Latin American Airlines Limited was a long and cumbersome name; it sounded silly in its initial form (BLAA) and it did not translate well into either Spanish or Portuguese.

Sir William Hildred asked the Foreign Office to canvas the opinion of British ambassadors in South American countries and found that they, too, thought the name was unsuitable. Suggestions were made which included Anglo-South American Airlines (ASA or Ansama), Anglo-Latin American Air Service (ALAS) whose initials Hildred thought were 'hopeless', British-African-South American Airlines, British South American Airlines (BRS or BRISA), (British) South Atlantic Airlines, Peninsular & South American Airlines and British Airline to South America (BASA).

In a note to Lord Winster, Hildred said that when BLAA had expressed a preference for British Southern Airlines and he and Lord Swinton discussed it, they both thought it sounded like a trip to Brighton. Hildred asked for Winster's comments so that he could contact both BLAA and the Board of Trade which had to be informed if the name was to be changed. It is strange that no comment was made about the less than catchy title of 'British Airline to South America' which would seem, to twenty-first century ears, to be far more cumbersome and ridiculous than British Southern Airlines.

After much discussion it was decided in September that BLAA would become British South American Airways Limited and with the change of name came a change of premises also when, on the 3rd, BSAA moved to its new offices at 19 Grafton Street, London W1.

After months of uncertainty the long-promised survey flight finally took to the air. The BOAC Lancastrian G-AGMG, *Nicosia*, under the command of legendary BOAC Captain O.P. Jones, took off from Hurn airport near Bournemouth on 9 October 1945 bound for Lisbon, Bathurst, Natal, Rio de Janeiro and Montevideo. Bennett was not on board.

Winster had a meeting with John Booth on 8 November and told him that he had decided that he wanted to set up a company separate from BOAC to operate the South American routes. At that point he felt that the only organisation he could ask to run the new company would be BOAC since no one else was in a position to start at once. BOAC was the only company that had been nationalised and could, therefore, run a subsidised service, but he did not like to put this burden on it since once the company was running, it would have to relinquish any control it had built up. Booth agreed that under the BOAC Act it was the only company able to run a subsidised service, but pointed out to the Minister that the Act did not prevent anyone running an unsubsidised service. He said that as far as BSAA was concerned no subsidy was needed whether the company was private or state run, but that he saw no reason why the government should not buy the airline, as the board was willing to sell. If that happened then BSAA could assume control as soon as the transaction was complete, as it had an efficient staff structure already in place and a very good team.

Winster said that he intended to put the matter before the Cabinet and that he would say that he wanted the new company to be a separate entity with its own board. He then asked Booth if he would like to be on the board. He wanted to make it clear that he had no intention of becoming involved in the day-to-day running of the airline himself and said that he would put all these details in a confidential letter for Booth to discuss with members of the board of BSAA. When asked about the company's finances Booth said that the authorised capital was £1,000,000 and that £7 stamp duty had been paid on that sum. The issued capital was £50,000 – £35,266 cash and £14,733 physical assets, of which £4,000 accounted for BSAA's buildings. Therefore, although the government would have to pay £50,000 it would be getting £35,000 in cash. The shipping companies behind BSAA had absorbed all development costs up to 30 June, the shareholders expected no profit and the directors would not seek any compensation for loss of office – they simply wanted to ensure that the company was allowed to operate. If the deal were to go through, the government would be getting a ready-made company for very little outlay.

Booth told Winster that he would be ready to start operating three weeks from the day he was given the go-ahead. He had ten complete crews in place, but he wanted the Minister to be clear that these crews were available only to BSAA. If the operating rights to South America were given to BOAC then the crews would not fly for them. They had been recruited by Don Bennett and were loyal to him; they would rather return to the RAF than work for BOAC. He also pointed out that if, as an interim measure, BOAC were to start the service to South America it would probably want to use flying boats across the South Atlantic. But there were no facilities for flying boats and BSAA did not have any flying boat pilots. It would require another survey flight to be conducted which would cause further delays and he thought that 'it would be a disaster to lose the unity, spirit and enthusiasm of the small group that had been got together'. As Sir William Hildred said, 'There was no secrecy about the fact that the BSAA Board was fighting hard to see that the Government should utilise as best it could the Board's services, and the nucleus of staff which had been gathered.'

In December 1945 another White Paper was presented to Parliament by Winster. It said that His Majesty's Government proposed to establish three separate corporations with responsibility for: routes between the United Kingdom and other Commonwealth countries, the United States and the Far East (the existing BOAC); routes between the United Kingdom and the Continent and internal routes in the United Kingdom; and routes between the United Kingdom and South America.

The corporations were not going to compete with each other on the same routes. They were to be managed by their own boards and would operate with capital provided entirely by the government. It would be the policy of the government that all three corporations would be required to use British aircraft for their operations. The White Paper further stated: 'The policy set out in this White Paper will be put into effect at the earliest possible moment, but will require legislation. No delay in starting British air services, however, will be countenanced. Interim arrangements have been made to this end but supply of aircraft is the governing factor.'

By the beginning of 1946 the Air Transport Bill was being debated in the House of Commons; Ivor Thomas MP spoke for the government:

A further aspect of the problem in this interim period is that arrangements must be made for the time when the European and South American Corporations will 'hive off' from BOAC. The method by which this 'hiving off' is to be done differs in the two cases. Under the Swinton plan, it had been proposed that the South American Corporation should be formed by British South American Airways Ltd, a consortium of shipping companies, and BOAC, and a small but valuable nucleus had been brought together for this purpose. Mr John Booth was to have been chairman of the corporation and the distinguished old Imperial Airways pilot, Air Vice-Marshal Bennett, who showed his qualities in founding the Atlantic Ferry service and the Pathfinder Force, was to have been its chief executive officer. We are availing ourselves of this nucleus of skilled persons. The entire shareholding of British South American Airways Ltd, is to be bought by BOAC, so that its capital will be wholly provided out of public funds. A new board will then be appointed. Subject to the directions of the Minister of Civil Aviation on general policy, this board will have sole responsibility for the work of the company, which will operate entirely independently of BOAC. Mr Booth has severed his active connection with the shipping world and has accepted my Noble Friend's invitation to become chairman; the other appointments will be announced in due course. Air Vice-Marshal Bennett will remain chief executive officer. When the Air Transport Bill receives the Royal Assent, the statutory corporation therein to be set up, will purchase British South American Airways Ltd from BOAC and, under the name of British South American Airways, will be responsible for all services between the United Kingdom and South America.

And so, after nearly a year of discussions, anxiety and fears that BOAC would succeed in its efforts to stop BSAA from operating on its chosen routes, it received the news, for the second time, that it was to be the government's choice to fly to South America after all.

Chapter 5

The People Behind the Airline

If anyone had been looking down from an aircraft flying over Heath Row in Middlesex on a cold, damp and misty New Year's Day in 1946, they would have witnessed a curious scene. The whole area south of the Great West Road consisted of freshly laid concrete with bulldozers, tractors and large piles of building materials still dotted about. In the middle of this gigantic building site was a solitary aircraft. It was a large aircraft by the standards of the day, but seemed tiny against a backdrop of acre upon acre of concrete. Alongside the aircraft was a small gathering of people, wrapped up in warm coats, being filmed and recorded as speeches were made. It was an event of great significance for British aviation. At the centre of the crowd was Lord Winster, the Minister of Civil Aviation. His speech contained the words: 'On this first day of the New Year, this proving flight starts off from Heath Row, which will be the future civil airport of London and it takes off from the finest runway in the world.'

The crew and passengers climbed aboard, the door was closed and one by one the four Rolls-Royce engines were started. The aircraft slowly taxied across to the end of the 3,000yd runway, which had only been cleared for use three days previously. As the polished silver Avro Lancastrian named *Star Light* gathered speed down the huge new runway, the small crowd applauded. They were witnessing the first international departure of an airliner from London's new Heathrow airport.

The British South American Airways Lancastrian was leaving on a proving flight to Buenos Aires with eight crew and ten passengers on board. It was to follow a gruelling schedule over the next fifteen days, including many official receptions and nearly 61 hours in the air. The crew for the historic flight was led by Air Vice-Marshal Don Bennett with Wing Commander D.A. Cracknell as his First Officer, and Wing Commander R.C. Alabaster as Second Officer. The other members of the crew were First Radio Officer J.A. McGillivray, Second Radio Officer R.W. Chandler, First Engineer Tom Campbell, Second Engineer Gordon Rees and Stewardess (known in BSAA as 'Stargirl') Mary Guthrie.

The passenger list for the outbound flight was as follows: Signor Falcão, Signora Marroquim, Signor Marroquim, D. Edwards, Wing Commander Lawson, Wing Commander Hall, Squadron Leader Colby, Squadron Leader Stevens, Flight Lieutenant Skillman and Colonel Stirling-Wylie.

Some of the passengers were to be the new BSAA Station Managers at locations en route and were not therefore on the return flight to London.

With Donald Bennett at the controls, the aircraft took off into the mist at 12.05 and headed for the first stop in Lisbon, 5 hours 20 minutes away. Mary Guthrie was the first of a group of five Stargirls to join BSAA. She was herself a qualified pilot, having served in the Air Transport Auxiliary (ATA) until the previous September, but her experience as a pilot in the ATA could not equip her for the difficulties of preparing meals for passengers in the confined space of the Lancastrian galley. Once the meals were prepared her problems were not over as she then had to negotiate the main spar while carrying trays of food and drink. There was only one seat for the radio officer, occupied on the first leg by 'Mac' McGillivray, therefore Second Radio Officer Bob Chandler had to crouch in the confined space of the galley on the flight to Lisbon. In his autobiography he describes how Mary Guthrie did her best to serve a four-course lunch to the passengers, but by the time Lisbon was reached the galley was a shambles and knee-deep in dirty dishes. Bob rolled up his sleeves and helped her with the washing up so that when the time came to take off from Lisbon everything was neat and tidy.

After stops at Bathurst and Natal, 32 hours and 17 minutes after leaving London, *Star Light*, in the hands of Donald Bennett, made an impressive landing on the short runway at Santos Dumont airport in Rio de Janeiro. It had been in the air for a total of 28 hours and 46 minutes. The crew must have been absolutely exhausted, but there was no time to relax. There was a magnificent welcome awaiting them as they stepped down from the aircraft. Bob Chandler later commented that it felt as though half the city had turned out to greet them. After being taken to a comfortable hotel where they were wined and dined at a reception held in their honour, the crew were airborne again only 13 hours later for the 5½-hour flight to Montevideo. Another warm welcome was awaiting them at Montevideo's Carrasco airport and parties and receptions had again been arranged. This time there was the chance for a little relaxation as the stay at the Beach Hotel in Montevideo was for three days. On 6 January they flew on to Buenos Aires and were accommodated in the City Hotel, where they had another three-day stay.

On 9 January *Star Light* took off from Buenos Aires for the return flight to England. The route home was similar to the route out, with the addition of a refuelling stop in Dakar between the landings in Bathurst and Lisbon. They arrived back at Heathrow airport on the afternoon of 15 January and were back at work in Grafton Street the following morning.

On their return to London the crew set about writing operational procedures and training manuals based on the information they had gathered from the trip. The many radio facilities were documented, as were the details of the various contacts and agents at all the stations down the route. The technical information about the performance and fuel consumption of the aircraft was documented, and negotiations were held on the use of engineering facilities for aircraft maintenance. Though hectic, the fifteen-day trip had served its purpose by laying the foundations for the airline's first scheduled service to South America.

* * *

Through all the uncertainty of 1945, work had continued, putting in place the staff and facilities that would allow BSAA to operate.

Don Bennett acquired a secretary in June when Eileen Gummer came to work for him, earning a wage of £5 per week, and on 1 August Bernard Porter, a long-time employee of the Royal Mail Steam Packet company and the Royal Mail Lines, joined BLAA as its Chief Accountant. In November he was appointed Company Secretary to the renamed BSAA.

In September the airline gained a very experienced Commercial Manager, Leonard Hough. He had worked for Imperial Airways both in London and at Croydon airport before being transferred to Kampala in Uganda as Station Manager. When he left Uganda he became Station Manager in Baghdad and then in Alexandria before going on to Cairo and then Paris where he was Assistant Manager. In 1940 he went to Lisbon to start the operations of the newly formed BOAC and finally became BOAC's Traffic Superintendent in Baltimore before returning to Britain to join BLAA, where his salary was £1,200.

The Technical Manager, James W. Kenny, also joined the company in September 1945, having spent eleven years working in aircraft design and construction with Armstrong-Whitworth and Short Brothers. John C. Rose was appointed Supply Manager in September 1945. He had been in the RAF, but before the war had worked for the London travel agents Dean and Dawson where his final position had been as publicity and supplies manager. He ended his RAF service as Group Equipment Officer with the Pathfinder Force, a position that earned him the MBE.

In a very short time BSAA had gained a number of highly experienced people, but many more staff were needed. At the end of the war, with many ex-RAF pilots, navigators, radio operators and engineers wanting to leave service life and take up careers in civil aviation, there were plenty of qualified people available, but Don Bennett was after a particular type of person. He recognised that in order to make a profit, the company could not afford to take on large numbers of staff to cover every eventuality and so wanted to have employees who would be good at their own jobs, but would also not object to helping out with other tasks as well if the need arose. He often said that he would never ask a member of staff to do anything that he would not be prepared to do himself. His enthusiasm and boundless energy made him a hard act to follow, but he was as good as his word and could often be found helping out when an extra pair of hands was needed.

When he had been offered the position of chief executive, Bennett had asked to have at least six pilots with experience of flying the Atlantic. In the end he got only two – Gordon Store and David Brice.

Gordon Store had been with Bennett during the Atlantic Ferry operations and before that had flown for Imperial Airways. In the early 1930s he had been a flying instructor at the London Aeroplane Club. In 1931 he, along with 19-year-old debutante Peggy Salaman, had flown a Puss Moth called *Good Hope* to his native South Africa from England in the record time of 5 days, 6 hours and 38 minutes. Although Salaman had financed the trip and owned the aeroplane, it was 25-year-old Store who was the main pilot and at the end of their epic flight Salaman said of him, 'He threaded his way through Africa as easily as a taxi-man in London.'

Store was appointed Operations Manager for BSAA, joining the company in October 1945 at an initial salary of £2,000 per annum. Although he and Bennett respected each other's abilities, they were not close and had very different characters. Store, a fine pilot, was a quiet plodder who liked to do everything by the book; Bennett was innovative and daring. It may have been that Store was, perhaps, a little jealous of the charismatic Australian. While they were not personal friends they each had something to bring to BSAA and Store's quiet composure balanced Bennett's impetuosity very well.

The position of Chief Pilot went to David Brice, ex-Imperial Airways and RAF Coastal Command, who was also an Atlantic Ferry pilot. He flew with

BOAC from 1941 until he joined BSAA in 1945 at a salary of £1,400 per annum. In 1947, unhappy with the very different style of management from that which he had been used to, Brice left BSAA and worked for short periods for both Silver City Airways and Skyways before rejoining BOAC to fly Stratocruisers on the North Atlantic route.

Bennett had made it a rule that all pilots had to have both a Civilian Pilot 'B' licence and a First Class Navigator's licence as he did not want to waste resources on navigators who could not fly or pilots who could not navigate. So, having joined BSAA, the pilots, many of them elite ex-Pathfinders, had to sit down and study for their new licences. Some were outraged that what had been good enough for their country in a time of war was not considered sufficient for a civilian airline, but Bennett was adamant and so they studied.

BSAA's radio superintendent, J.M. 'Mac' McGillivray, had also been an employee of Imperial Airways. He began his employment with BSAA on 5 December 1945 and was given the task of employing other radio operators. With Gordon Store he interviewed Bob Chandler who had begun his career in the Merchant Navy, but had been bitten by the flying bug and had transferred to aircraft. He, too, was ex-Imperial Airways and had served on the Atlantic Ferry. Despite being offered jobs by several other airlines he chose to accept the offer made by BSAA, impressed with the challenge the new company presented and the enthusiasm of the staff already working for it.

* * *

In the same way that the Blue Star Shipping Line had used the word 'Star' in naming its ships, BSAA decided that its aircraft would have names and that the prefix would be 'Star' with the aircraft being known as Starliners. The airline's call-sign was Starline, the stewardesses were known as Stargirls and one in particular was also affectionately known, for obvious reasons, as *Star Bottom*; a name which followed her when she went to work for BOAC after the demise of BSAA. Even a small crane used by the maintenance staff was jokingly referred to as *Star Hoist*. To complete the corporate image the airline's logo, designed by artist Norman Rissen in the summer of 1945, was a 'speedman' which graced the side of its silver and blue aircraft.

* * *

Don Bennett, although he did not always interview prospective employees, did try to have a short meeting with them once they had been offered employment. Keith Hayward went to BSAA as a traffic apprentice in November 1945 at the age of 16 and met the Chief Executive at the company's Grafton Street office. He recalled that Bennett had a wall-chart, rather like a family tree, on which he wrote the names of each employee. He told the young apprentice exactly what he expected of him and left him with the impression that he would have to work extremely hard and learn very fast if he wanted to keep his job. Hayward did work hard and enjoyed his job. He retains warm memories of his time with BSAA to this day.

One of Keith Hayward's responsibilities was to deal with the flight crews' papers, checking that passports were in order and that the visas needed in South America had been obtained. Once operations began the flight papers required by the South American countries were seemingly endless. Despite attempts to reduce the amount, it was still so much that the airline had to issue staff with lists detailing the type, quantity and distribution. Keith spent many hours waiting at the passport office and at various South American embassies dealing with the documentation. When asked for his opinion of Don Bennett he says that he had great respect for him but that, as a 16-year-old boy, he was terrified of him too.

The Grafton Street office had a commissionaire named Max at the entrance. In the basement was a canteen, also used by the staff of the hairdressing salon next door, which belonged to the rather camp 'celebrity hairdresser' Mr 'Teasey Weasy'. May Cox worked in the canteen and remembered the colourful people she used to serve. She said that Don Bennett did not seem to care for long lunch breaks in fancy restaurants and regularly came down to the canteen and ate his lunch with the staff.

At Heathrow airport the first BSAA Station Manager was Wing Commander Dennis Milson, a hard taskmaster and stickler for punctuality. Keith Hayward recalled that when an aircraft was due to depart Milson would make the staff line up alongside and, as it began to taxi, he would come to attention and salute smartly. Keith also says:

. . . it was necessary on those tailwheelers to provide a fairly heavy burst of power on one of the outer [engines] to obtain a 90° turn, and the consequent violent slipstream would often cause the band of erect dispatching staff to scatter in a most undisciplined manner. It could be embarrassing for the rather 'top drawer' traffic girls at a time when female modesty of dress was still in vogue.

Modesty of dress was a problem for the Stargirls as well as the traffic staff. Because of the difficulty in having to negotiate the main spar of the Lancastrian, the Stargirls who worked on these aircraft were given culottes, then called divided skirts, to preserve their modesty as they climbed over to reach the galley. One Stargirl was heard to remark that it was a pity that the Lancastrian had 'not yet been properly converted' as there was still a 'large lump' between the cockpit and the passenger compartment. She did not seem to appreciate that this 'large lump' was what held the aircraft together.

The first Stargirl, Mary Guthrie, went off to Buenos Aires on BSAA's maiden flight on 1 January 1946, wearing her Air Transport Auxiliary (ATA) uniform. She arrived back in England, following the successful flight of *Star Light*, to a big welcome from the press. Not only was she the first Stargirl to work for BSAA, she was the first stewardess of any airline to cross the South Atlantic and the photographers turned out in force to record the event. Photographs of her clutching a large pineapple appeared in national newspapers, along with interviews in which she declared that she had had £25 with her but that there was so much to buy in the shops in Buenos Aires and the other cities that she visited, that she could easily have spent £2,500. Years later, away from the glare of the press she admitted: 'It was all such fun; we were pioneering and, after six years of war, landing in a land of plenty for me at any rate, was too much. I over ate and had a bilious attack! It was wonderfully happy. The spirit was terrific; everybody helped one another and wished to succeed; memorable, exciting days.'

Four other ATA pilots, Cecily Power, Zoë Jenner, Ruth Helen Kerly (known as Helen) and Rita Baines, were also employed as Stargirls. They were soon supplied with their uniform divided skirts; better than conventional skirts but less practical than the trousers they had worn when flying with the ATA. The uniform retained a military look – a double-breasted jacket, metal buttons and a shirt and tie. Later, to coincide with the arrival of the Avro Tudor, it was changed to a collarless navy blue single-breasted jacket with plastic buttons – apparently some of the first to be used in airline uniforms – and an A-line skirt. Under the jacket, which had a 'speedman' badge above the pocket, and a pale blue ring around each sleeve, the girls wore pale blue blouses with small collars. The look was completed with a cap which had a badge with the letters BSAA beneath a pair of wings, dark gloves and high-heeled shoes. This uniform was made by Debenham and Freebody in a crepe-type fabric and surprisingly, considering recent wartime shortages and rationing, was very stylish.

Rita Baines, one of the ATA girls, married David Colby, a BSAA pilot and former Pathfinder, who was First Officer on the ill-fated flight of *Star Tiger* in January 1948. Tragically, at the time of her husband's death Rita was pregnant with their first child.

Although Stargirls were employed as flight crew, they were also given duties when on the ground. They sometimes worked on staff rosters or acted as secretaries to various senior members of staff. One Stargirl, Priscilla Vinyals, remembered how she used to be given letters to type by the radio superintendent. He would begin dictating and then give up, expecting her to know what he wanted to say and to complete the letter for him.

Priscilla, the daughter of an English mother and a Spanish father, was a fluent Spanish speaker and had worked alongside her father for the BBC World Service. The sister of one of their colleagues had become a Stargirl and was really enjoying herself so the colleague suggested that Priscilla might also like to fly. She applied and was immediately interviewed and accepted. Her pay was £4 10s per week and she also received an additional 7s 6d for speaking Spanish. At her interview with Don Bennett, she and another Stargirl were given a lecture by the Chief Executive in which he rambled rather a lot and did not seem to be making any point that they readily understood. It was only towards the end when he told them that they had to look after themselves and were not to have anything to do with the passengers 'that way' that the truth dawned and they realised the subject of their pep talk had been the 'birds and the bees'. In spite of a rather clumsy approach, he was trying to protect the Stargirls from the more amorous passengers. He had less luck with amorous crew members. On Christmas Eve 1946 a captain, radio officer and Stargirl (not Priscilla) were found together in a hotel room in Santiago. The airline coyly described the event as 'prejudicial conduct' and, following a disciplinary hearing at the beginning of 1947, all three were dismissed.

The maintenance of BSAA's aircraft was the responsibility of Wing Commander William W. Warner who was appointed Maintenance Supervisor in September 1945, and F.G. Gold who joined the company in the spring of 1946 as Overhaul Superintendent, earning £950. Towards the end of 1946, when he was released from the RAF, Group Captain Charles F. Sarsby, who had been with the Pathfinder Force as its Chief Engineer and with 229 Group Transport Command in India, became BSAA's Technical Manager; a post which paid £1,200 per annum. He was joined by 'Wilbur' Wright as Chief Engineer and Bill Forsyth as Line Maintenance Manager.

In December 1946, 21-year-old Frank Price was sitting on the top deck of a bus. Having recently left the RAF he was heading for Heathrow to look for a job with BOAC. He had worked on Avro Lincolns and had both engine and airframe licences as well as some electrical qualifications. His former commanding officer had given him a letter of recommendation and advised him to apply to BOAC, but as the bus passed a building on which was written 'British South American Airways' he decided that it sounded far more interesting than BOAC. So he got off the bus and went to see if BSAA had any vacancies. He was interviewed by Bill Forsyth and, in view of his qualifications, immediately offered a job. Frank went on to become an electrical inspector for the airline and then took a posting to Montevideo.

Frank recalled that in the early days BSAA lacked electrical equipment for testing generators. When he spoke to his boss about it he was advised to 'go and ask Bennett to buy some test equipment'. He did so, realising too late that his boss had not really meant him to speak to the chief executive. Bennett pointed to an aircraft outside the hangar and said, 'You've got four perfectly good test beds over there already.' Frank voiced the opinion that it was not efficient to fit overhauled generators to the aircraft, find that they did not work and have to dismantle them again. He offered to search for some second hand equipment to buy, saying that it would ultimately save time and money and eventually found an ex-RAF magneto/generator test rig for £40. Bennett was delighted and congratulated him on his initiative and time-saving ideas.

Aubrey Dare was with Skyways until he joined BSAA as an electrician. Both he and Frank Price remember Don Bennett as being 'a terrific leader'. Frank said he led by example and the staff had great respect for him because they knew his capabilities and knew that he wholeheartedly believed in everything he did.

When Fred Whitworth left the RAF and returned to his home town of Nottingham he found a job working on luxury cars. From there he went to A.V. Roe to work on Lincolns before coming to London airport and BSAA, working in No. 1 hangar at the Hatton Cross end of the airport. He was offered accommodation at a hostel in Iver, Buckinghamshire. The hostel, Bangors, a big house with extensive grounds, had once been the home of British Fascist Oswald Mosley's aunt. Knowing that housing would be difficult for some of its staff after the war, BSAA had bought the house and converted it to accommodate thirty to forty men. It had a resident warden and a house committee, with a chairman named Lucas, which saw to its smooth running. Fred enjoyed living at Bangors. Most weekends there were house parties, also attended by some of the Stargirls and, on summer Sundays, tennis matches and afternoon tea on the lawn.

John Silver, as Station Engineer at Heathrow, was Fred Whitworth's boss. He too had housing problems, exacerbated by the fact that he was already married with a family. When BSAA heard of his difficulties he was told that if he could find a suitable house, the airline would buy it and rent it back to him. He found one in nearby Hayes and BSAA became his employer and his landlord.

* * *

As a result of BOAC's endeavours to stop BSAA becoming the airline to serve the South American routes, and its refusal to allow the smaller corporation any hangar space or other maintenance facilities at any of its bases, Bennett had made an arrangement with the Hawker Aircraft Company to use its facilities at Langley airfield, 5 miles to the west of Heathrow.

The airfield had been built just before the war on land bought by the government with a compulsory purchase order from Parlaunt Park Farm. It was intended as a base for training RAF Volunteer Reserve personnel, but plans changed and in 1937 building of a 600,000sq ft factory began; it cost £775,000 and was where Hawker built Hurricane fighters, the first being delivered in October 1939. With the increasing demands for aircraft, the site was extended to include new factory space and a hangar and it eventually covered an area of 750,000sq ft. It was here that BSAA set up its own maintenance base where it undertook all major engineering work. When an aeroplane was ready to depart on a scheduled flight it was ferried to Heathrow to pick up its crew, passengers, baggage, cargo and mail. It was a rather strange arrangement, in the wartime spirit of 'make do and mend', but one that seemed to work well. Engineering apprentices Richard Enser, Keith Johnstone and Graham Phipps used to put their bikes on board the York that operated out of Heathrow on a Saturday and were then allowed to cadge a ride on the positioning flight the evening before. All three lived further away from Heathrow than they did from Langley, but enjoyed the treat of a weekly flight and were happy to cycle the extra distance for the privilege. Richard felt that the happy atmosphere at Langley was largely due to Bennett, as when you had someone at the top who was willing to get some overalls on, it was good for the morale of the rest of the workers: 'He was an inspiration to everyone at Langley, a great fellow, a natural gentleman.'

At the end of March 1947 21-year-old Reg Ottaway kicked a tyre on an RAF aircraft, declaring it to be the last he would ever work on, and prepared to return to England. Three years before, his mother had been very ill and Reg, the only one of her four sons to survive beyond his teens, had applied for a compassionate posting to be nearer his mother and two sisters. The RAF's idea of compassion was to post him to India. Now that the war had been over for nearly two years he just wanted to go home. He had a very good service record; his skill in his trade, flight mechanic airframes, was noted as being superior and his commanding officer had added the remark: 'Has carved out his work in his service trade in admirable fashion'.

He sailed for England on board HMT *Queen of Bermuda* and eventually reached his Surrey home on 18 April 1947. The following day he went to meet Muriel Payne, who had been his pen friend for all the time he had been stationed in India. Although their respective homes in England were no more than 3 miles apart, they had never met. Three weeks after that first meeting Reg and Muriel became engaged. They married in July the following year and spent forty-seven happy years together until Reg's death in 1995.

After being demobbed, Reg went looking for work and, despite his vow never to work on another aeroplane, found himself a temporary job with Hawker at Langley airfield. By the middle of July he was working for BSAA, where he was reacquainted with Group Captain Sarsby from RAF Palam, Delhi.

Reg looked back on his time with the airline with great affection. It was a great experience; he enjoyed the work and the camaraderie in the young, go-ahead company. BSAA had a flourishing cricket team which Reg joined and Muriel, also a fan of the sport, did the scoring for the team's matches. He had great respect for Don Bennett, appreciating the way the boss would roll up his sleeves and help out when needed.

Albert Axten, an upholsterer with BSAA at Langley, remembered Bennett's habit of helping out too. He was happy to have been working for him and was lucky to have been offered a flight by Bennett when he positioned *Star Light* to Heathrow for its departure on 1 January 1946. He had not known at the time that this would be the first aircraft to fly out of Heathrow. After they landed Albert had to catch a bus back to Langley to resume his duties.

Ly Bennett, incidentally, was less appreciative of her husband's habit of 'mucking in' with the boys. Arriving at Langley one evening, dressed for a gala event of some sort, she found him up on a gantry, covered in grease and working on an engine. Understandably, she was not pleased.

Aubrey Dare and Frank Price recalled that Bennett had a ritual when closing the hangar door at Langley if he was the last to leave. He would: 'start his car (which was parked in the hangar) and press the button to close the electric hangar doors. He would then walk back to his car, take off his jacket, put it in the car with his hat and umbrella, then get in and drive out of the hangar with inches to spare on either side of the car as the doors were closing.'

Although the standard of work at Langley was good, many procedures were not done 'by the book'. One day a Lancastrian was in the hangar having a major overhaul. One side of the aircraft was supported by jacks as a wheel had been removed. All the engines and their ancillary components had also been taken off as complete units and one of the engineers was washing the used engine oil from the bulkheads with 100 octane fuel. Unfortunately a live wire at the bulkhead shorted and caused a fire. It quickly took hold and burning debris fell into a drip tray under a nacelle setting this ablaze too. In the ensuing panic someone attached a rope to the aircraft and was about to tow it out of the hangar when he remembered that it only had a wheel on one side. Happily a more quick-thinking engineer grabbed a fire extinguisher and doused the fire before it spread out of control.

Eileen Gunnell, secretary to the Station Manager at Heathrow, used to come to Langley once a week to deliver the engineers' pay packets. She thought that Don Bennett was 'a bit of a rebel', but one with a sense of humour. He drove a fast car, an Armstrong Siddeley Hurricane, and would always drive into the gateway marked 'Exit' when arriving at Langley.

Because Bennett's secretary was also named Eileen she was called Eileen One. Eileen Gunnell was Eileen Two and stayed with BSAA until just before the birth of her son. She says of her time with the airline that she 'absolutely loved it'. She used her staff concessions only once when she flew to Lisbon for a short holiday. Since staff were only permitted on board if there were spare seats and were not allowed to book places for themselves, her holiday lasted twice as long as it should have when she was offloaded from her return flight due to the aircraft being full.

Ted Hayden had memories of BSAA at Langley, too, although he did not work for the airline. He was an employee of Hawker and recalled an occasion when Bennett delivered an aircraft from Langley to Heathrow because no other pilots would do it. It had been raining heavily and the grass runway at Langley airfield, which was prone to flooding, was a quagmire. Fearing that if they taxied the aircraft out to the runway it would become stuck in the mud no one wanted to take a chance and so it was trapped in the hangar. Hayden described what happened next:

In due course a car (an Armstrong Siddeley) streaked onto the apron and out got AVM Bennett. This was my first view of this incredible man. Looking at him it was difficult to believe he was the much decorated airman from the Second World War. Fairly tall and slim in build, he struck me as an Oxford don or some other academic.

Bennett ordered the hangar doors to be opened and the aircraft to be placed at the entrance. Hayden continued:

He then boarded the aircraft and the engines were started. With brakes applied, full throttle was selected on the four Merlins and the brakes were released. The York shot forward across the apron; luckily the weight was off the oleos by the time it reached the marshy ground. It then shot across the runway, diagonally, and became airborne; a real aircraft carrier take-off.

Hayden was not the only one to remember this incident. Paddy Cormican said that Bennett had another pilot, Bernard Patrick, with him. He asked him to lower the flaps to 15 degrees *after* they started to roll, to get the maximum acceleration. Cormican recalled a similar incident when Bennett had taken off in a Lancastrian from part of the perimeter road when the airfield was covered in snow and slush.

Paddy joined BSAA in February 1947, having come from the Air Ministry attached to 41 Group RAF Maintenance Command where he was an instrument maker. He was employed by BSAA in the same role, initially to carry out compass swings which had to be done every time an engine was changed. Merlin engines had a life of only about 300 hours so Cormican was kept busy and would often do the compass swings while the aircraft was being flown on an air test. Distant Reading Compasses (DRC) were used which were complicated and contained a gyroscope revolving at 3,600rpm. They were positioned in the tail of the aircraft as far away as possible from the major magnetic disturbances. The magnets aligned the gyro with magnetic north and it took some time for the gyro to react to changes. This was a trap many inexperienced people fell into when carrying out the compass swings. They would make the adjustments, then the gyro would 'catch up' and they would have to make the adjustments all over again.

Cormican said that Langley was a 'happy environment to work in' and that there was a good spirit there. He also remembered that in the terrible winter of 1947 a woman would come around each morning bringing the workers cups of hot Bovril, which they found most welcome as the conditions were icy. To address this problem Bennett arranged to have several large trees in his garden felled and chopped into logs to provide heating for the staff.

Bill Jewitt was the Senior Instrument Inspector with BSAA at the time and encouraged Paddy to study for his licences. He eventually got an engineers', a navigators' and a radio licence. He said that the airline was keen for its staff to obtain as many qualifications as possible and there was always encouragement to do so from the management. He emphatically denied that there was any cost cutting on spares and maintenance saying, 'When we needed new instruments, we got them.'

Cormican was later transferred to the line maintenance section at Heathrow and, while there, he got his instrument licence for the overhaul of mechanical and electrically operated instruments, and his compass licence. He related how, from his 'lowly position in the airline' he looked up to Don Bennett and tried to emulate him. He thought him to be a 'superb pilot and navigator, and a licensed engineer as well who thought nothing of swinging a compass and who believed that his pilots should do the same'.

Working in Hut 43 in the Duty Navigator section when not flying, were pilots Maurice Aries and his deputy, Robin Macilwaine. The Route Intelligence Officer was Angus Brooks who produced the navigation charts covering the routes flown by BSAA. The work was complicated and fine in its detail, involving cutting and pasting together several charts for some of the routes, with important features being highlighted in red. Cormican remembered the charts being produced to a very high standard. He also worked in the Duty Navigator section along with some Stargirls, fulfilling their 'land' roles between flights and recalled that one, Evette Huntley-Flindt, had been an actress and dancer on the London stage before joining BSAA. But it was not through her acting that Eve became famous. When she left the airline it was to marry Ted Branson and some years later their son, Richard, founded his Virgin music empire and then went into the airline business himself with Virgin Atlantic. In a rather strange case of history repeating itself, Virgin Atlantic, another young dynamic company with a charismatic boss, found itself the victim of a dirty tricks campaign by British Airways, the airline which had, in part, been formed by BOAC.

Chapter 6

Ministry Interference

Despite the successful arrangements at Langley, some facilities were needed at Heathrow and Bennett contacted Sir William Hildred at the Ministry of Civil Aviation (MCA) on 20 October 1945 asking for his help in securing a small amount of space there.

Bennett attended a meeting on 1 December to discuss what facilities could be provided and Hildred wrote on 12 December apologising for the delay in giving an official response and saying that he was glad to hear that:

> . . . reasonably satisfactory arrangements were agreed at a meeting which you attended on the site.
>
> I should like it to be clearly understood that this use of Heathrow applies only to survey flights. The use of Heathrow for commercial purposes is a very different matter. I should be grateful if you would as far as possible, avoid publicity for the survey flights.

On 10 January 1946, ten days after Lancastrian *Star Light* had left for Buenos Aires, BSAA received a letter setting out the conditions more formally and informing the airline which facilities would be available for it to use. Fuel for the flights would be supplied by means of a mobile bowser, meteorological reports would be sent from Hurn via Heston, there would be no radio facilities and an air traffic control officer would be sent from Uxbridge when required, no control by any visual methods being available. It concluded by informing the airline that: 'A small amount of office accommodation of a temporary nature has been made available to your company on the understanding that this shall be vacated at any time if it is required by the Department for other purposes.'

Gordon Store replied, saying that its contents had been noted and that certain aspects would be the subject of discussion in the near future.

There was much to be discussed. Although the MCA was reluctant to allocate permanent facilities to a state-owned airline, operating with the full approval of the government, it was not as reluctant to start levying charges for the scant services it did provide. As soon as BSAA began to operate its proving flights from Heathrow it started to receive bills from acting airport manager G. Moody for landing and housing fees. They were sent to Dennis Milson, but when Bennett heard about it he contacted Moody himself. In a letter dated 18 March 1946 he said:

> In your letter of 23rd February, you refer to housing fees for aircraft and attach a table of charges. . . . These charges are applicable to an aerodrome on which certain facilities exist, and it could not, by any stretch of imagination, be said that these normal facilities have been provided. It would appear, therefore, that the rates do not apply. Moreover, it is pointed out that the 50% charge for standing in the open is applicable only when the use of hangarage is optional, and this percentage is simply on the basis that the alternative accommodation is erected and is standing by ready for use should it be required. The aircraft owner then has the option of paying the full charge to be under cover or the 50% charge to be in the open and, under normal circumstances an aircraft is often moved into the open in order to save the cost of hangarage when work is not being performed on it. We have no such facility, and we strongly object to the idea of paying 50% of the standard charge. We suggest that there should be no charge for housing at Heathrow in view of the circumstances.

The letter was forwarded to the MCA in London and a series of discussions ensued between it and the acting airport manager. The upshot of these exchanges was that Moody felt that he had been quite within his rights to charge 50 per cent of the housing fees, reflecting the position that the aircraft would be kept in the open but ignoring the fact that there was simply no alternative.

Bennett had a genuine grievance in being expected to pay charges that had been formulated for a time when the airport was fully operational and had all its facilities in place, while having to operate in what was, at that time, little more than a giant building site. But his stance did not endear him to the airport authorities and he never really managed to establish a very harmonious relationship with the MCA.

On several occasions John Booth had also been exasperated with the way the Ministry worked. He was particularly annoyed at being told that the MCA would decide which passengers could be carried on proving flights, although it would have seemed logical that a proving flight was the ideal opportunity to move staff down the line to take up their jobs rather than have to lay on extra flights for them. Even on scheduled flights the Ministry declared that it would decide who should be carried first and any seats that it did not require could be allocated at BSAA's discretion. In view of the fact that Lord Winster had made it clear that he had no intention of becoming involved in the day-to-day running of the airline, one wonders how BSAA could possibly have coped if the Minister *had* decided to involve himself. With his active participation and the day-to-day ministerial interference, the management of BSAA would have had little or no involvement at all. Yet in spite of all this, BSAA was expected to make a profit.

* * *

One of the offices that had been allocated to BSAA at Heathrow was a hut known as Building 41, which was used as its central stores. On 3 May 1946 Moody sent a note to the MCA in London to say that a request for a partition to be erected in the hut had been made by BSAA and an estimate for the cost of work involved was given as £12 10s, which the airline expected to pay. Then, on 7 May, BSAA received a letter from an official at the Ministry which said:

I am now to inform you that it is proposed to open the airport at an early date for use by International Airline Operators and it will therefore be necessary to reallocate all the space on the aerodrome. . . . In the meantime, I am to request you to take steps to vacate those huts now occupied by you for storage purposes, as these comprise the only available accommodation for allocation to the Airline Operators who will be using the Airport initially.

A month after the request was made for the partition BSAA was told that it could still build it, if it wanted to, but that it could no longer have Building 41 for its stores as it had been allocated to BOAC. It is easy to see why Bennett became so frustrated with the treatment handed out to BSAA in those early days and it is difficult to understand why the airline was treated so shabbily and why BOAC was always given priority. Not only did BOAC have priority, BSAA also had to give up some of its office space for an American airline's use – one of the 'international airline operators' – as if it were merely a squatter on the airfield, not the government's chosen company to operate the important services to South America. Since the airport was newly built, why was the office space so limited?

BSAA decided to move its stores to Langley. Years later, long after BSAA had ceased to exist, it was said that a few items, including some engineers' overalls, were found in an underground bunker on the airfield, still tagged with BSAA labels. Since the airfield at Langley also no longer exists, but has been replaced with a business park, it is difficult to know exactly where this bunker was located but it is believed to still be there somewhere, perhaps still housing some long forgotten items that once belonged to BSAA.

* * *

From the start BSAA tried to run its operations as if it were a private rather than a state-owned company. Its aim was to offer a good service, with reliable British aircraft, and to make a profit. It also wanted to look after its staff.

Not realising that it was expected to ask permission of the government for almost everything it did, a BSAA pension scheme was set up. On 22 January 1946 a circular was sent to all staff detailing the proposed scheme and attaching an application form. The scheme was to be backdated to 1 January 1946, the date that the airline made its first flight, and had been well thought out. In some respects it was better than that already being operated by BOAC, especially for aircrew. BSAA pilots, having completed the minimum qualifying period of ten years, the same as that for BOAC, could retire at the age of 37, three years earlier than those of BOAC and the 'death by accident' benefits were higher in the BSAA scheme, as were the disablement benefits and general death benefits for all staff. Staff began joining the scheme but by the middle of March Bernard Porter, the Company Secretary, had to write to them explaining that the government had decided that a combined pension was to be set up for the staff of all three state airlines. BSAA had to make arrangements for the money already contributed to be put into a holding account until it could be re-invested in the government scheme – yet another irritating interference in the running of the airline by the government, which added no value but caused a lot of extra work. Perhaps the government was guarding against the day it knew it would be closing the airline.

On 15 March 1946, BSAA inaugurated what would become a twice-weekly service to South America with a route that covered Lisbon, Bathurst, Natal, Rio de Janeiro, Montevideo and Buenos Aires. The aircraft used on the first flight was Lancastrian G-AGWK *Star Trail* and the passenger list, with destinations, was as follows: Mr Johnson (Lisbon), Mr Scotchbrooke (Natal), Mr Adams (Rio de Janeiro), Mr Lloyd-Jones (Rio de Janeiro), Mr Nisbet (Rio de Janeiro), Miss Holmes (Rio de Janeiro), Mr Wilson (Montevideo), Mr & Mrs Carlisle (Buenos Aires), Mrs & Miss Dixon (Buenos Aires) and Mrs Baker (Buenos Aires).

Just over two weeks later BSAA introduced what it called a 'fast service', reaching Buenos Aires in two days and returning to London in three.

On 22 April Don Bennett was the pilot on another proving flight. At 06.58 GMT, Lancastrian G-AGWI *Star Land* took off from Heathrow for Buenos Aires. This trip was made to check facilities in South America and the Caribbean and, as well as the Argentinian capital, Bennett visited Santiago, Lima, Bogota, Caracas, Port-of-Spain and Natal, discovering problems with ground transportation in some of the cities, lack of English speakers in air traffic control in Chile, difficulties with diversion plans at Santiago and no suitable accommodation in Lima. The Queens Park Hotel in Port-of-Spain was old-fashioned but acceptable, although the food was not very good. On a more optimistic note the food from the BWIA Terminal Building Restaurant was good and could be provided for BSAA flights at a cost of 10s per person.

There were serious problems with weather forecasting. Although the American airline Panagra produced weather reports it refused to supply them for BSAA flights, presumably because it regarded the airline as a competitor. Bennett could not even get them to supply the forecasts for the proving flight. Later on, similar problems were encountered with Pan American Airways (PAA) who, although willing to provide forecasts, charged such exorbitant fees and put up so many obstacles that BSAA's pilots were often only able to get the weather data by asking favours of friendly PAA pilots.

In Bennett's report of the proving flight he made the following decision regarding the Andes: 'The Andes must be crossed in clear conditions unless it is certain that no large Cumulus or Cumulo Nimbus are likely and that the wind at high level is less than 30 knots. Large Cumulus and Cumulo Nimbus must be avoided completely without fail.' So much for the claims of some journalists that pilots were instructed to cross the mountains by the shortest possible route whatever the weather.

The visit to Santiago was covered extensively. The British Ambassador met the aircraft at Los Cerrillos airport and Bennett remarked about the visit: 'The reception in Chile was friendly. Cooperation from all quarters and the officials with whom contact was made appeared to be free from all complications and were natural. It is not anticipated that any great difficulty should arise with regard to the operation of our airline.'

How those words must have come back to haunt him, for the British Ambassador was none other than John Leche, friend and acolyte of Lowell Yerex whose involvement with BSAA had been rejected by the board in favour of Air Vice-Marshal Don Bennett. Leche, unable to promote Yerex in this instance, began taking spiteful sideswipes at Bennett and BSAA with unsubstantiated claims of reckless fuel economies and drunken air crew. He may even have used his diplomatic status to influence others, as very similar uncorroborated claims later surfaced in Bermuda.

While in Trinidad Bennett had meetings with the Governor, Sir Bede Clifford, and Sir Lennox O'Reilly of BWIA. There was much talk of BSAA taking over the smaller airline and Bennett felt it could be advantageous, but that it required careful handling as the share prices were inflated and the company was making big losses. He thought that if it could be liquidated and then re-formed with its assets acquired by BSAA, it might work.

* * *

On 31 May 1946 Heathrow airport was officially opened as the new London airport, although commercial flights had departed before this date.

When Heathrow was functioning fully, BSAA had the use of what was known as 'the bungalow' for the engineers seeing the aircraft away and for some of the technical administration staff. Curiously this building was one of the only original dwellings that had been left when the area was cleared for the new airport and was a much more substantial structure than the assortment of huts that would comprise the rest of the airport facilities for quite a few years to come. The original passenger facilities were not even buildings, but tents with duckboards to stop the passengers sliding into the mud that was a constant feature of Heathrow in the early days.

Soon after starting scheduled operations BSAA also did some charter flights, some to South America but others transporting fruit and vegetables from Paris to London on a regular basis, and in June 1946 the airline made two special flights to Athens carrying supplies for the United Nations Relief and Rehabilitation Administration (UNRRA). Later a charter flight was made from Greece to New Zealand to take twenty-one Greek seamen to pick up a ship and return it to Athens. Because of the difficulties in finding extra Stargirls to crew the flight, Don Bennett turned to his wife, Ly, and his secretary, Eileen Gummer, and both agreed to become Stargirls for the return flight.

Another unusual flight was a pleasure trip for a group of children, who were shown around the aircraft by the crew, then took their seats for the flight during which they were looked after by two Stargirls. Once back at the airport one of the little boys was allowed into the cockpit where the pilot, Captain Cracknell, explained how it all worked and answered his questions. The whole trip was captured on film by British Pathé News.

In June 1946 BSAA started using the Avro York on its routes with one service a week terminating in Santiago. Stargirl Priscilla Vinyals remembered one flight that she made in a York very well. At the back of the galley was a fridge containing, among other things, an open tin of condensed milk. South Americans apparently liked very sweet things and so the fruit juice that was served was sweetened. On one side of the galley was a water heater and on the other an oven. Priscilla had just made coffee when the aircraft hit some bad turbulence. She lost her balance and fell over. Coffee and water tipped over her and, as the aircraft was buffeted about, two large flasks containing fruit juice fell over, the fridge door opened spilling the condensed milk and a bag of sugar fell to the floor. By the time the aircraft was flying normally again and Priscilla had tried to get to her feet, she found she was stuck and had to call a passenger to help prise her out of the sticky mess.

Food preparation on board the aircraft was much more labour intensive than it is today. BOAC used ready cooked meals, stored in large vacuum flasks to keep the food warm until a meal service was required, but BSAA wanted food that was freshly cooked and so went to caterers J. Lyons. Although the Stargirls had to make side dishes such as salads themselves, the main meals, known as 'Frood', were heated in the galley ovens from frozen. The menus were not elaborate, but most had more flavour than food that had been kept hot for hours on end. One or two meals were very bland and following a complaint Priscilla spoke to the catering manager about them and was sent to J. Lyons to see how the 'Frood' was prepared. The complaint was about a meal consisting of boiled chicken, served with either boiled potatoes or rice and a white sauce. It tasted all right but looked very unappetising and Priscilla thought that they could at least serve a few peas to brighten it up a bit.

A typical BSAA meal consisted of roast beef, cooked and carved in the galley, with potatoes, mixed vegetables and gravy, then fruit salad and cream, cheese and biscuits to follow. Because the aisles on the aircraft were too narrow for trolleys the Stargirl had to place the cutlery on the passengers' tables and then fetch the plates on a tray and serve the food. Priscilla thought it might be easier if they wrapped the cutlery in a napkin and suggested as much, but was firmly told that it 'wasn't the proper way to do things'. She also suggested that they show films to reduce the boredom of the very long flights. BSAA had contemplated this and had begun an in-flight movie service at the beginning of 1947. A projector was set up at the back of the cabin with a speaker hooked up on a bulkhead behind the passengers. It all went well but then the airline was told by the MCA that it would have to stop showing the films as the stand on which the projector was placed might prevent escape through the doors if there was an emergency.

Since air travel was very expensive, especially on the long routes to South America, passengers were rich and used to a luxurious lifestyle. There were some, however, who for various reasons had to reach their destinations quickly, sometimes being financed by their employers, but who were not used to air travel and did not feel at home in an aeroplane. One such passenger was a woman who was sitting alongside a child with her mother. The flight was not full and the mother and daughter asked if they could move to other seats. Priscilla asked if there was a problem and was told that there was an unpleasant smell where they were sitting that was making them both feel nauseous. She moved them and a little later saw that the woman who had been sitting beside them was trying to tidy her hair using a very dirty comb. She tactfully suggested that the woman might be more comfortable if she were to freshen up in the lavatory where there was a mirror. The woman looked at Priscilla with a puzzled expression and asked 'What lavatory?' She had not realised that there were any such facilities on the aircraft and the reason for the unpleasant smell immediately became apparent.

Sometimes passengers not only felt uncomfortable in the unfamiliar atmosphere of a long distance flight; there were occasions when they should not have been travelling at all. John Brennan, who joined BSAA in June 1946 as a radio engineer, recalled that on a proving flight between Kingston and Bermuda, a stowaway had been found. The man had served with the army during the war and wanted to start a new life in England. He had not made any proper arrangements and lacked the funds to buy himself a ticket so had sneaked aboard in the hope that he would be allowed to travel to Britain. Once the aircraft was airborne he came out of his hiding place, frightening the life out of Stargirl

'Poppy' Hagerston. When she heard his story she felt sorry for him and gave him some food. On arrival in Bermuda the police were called because the man did not have any paperwork. Arthur from the White Horse Tavern said that he would take the man in, but the police decided that he should be sent back to Jamaica. The stowaway himself was embarrassed by all the attention he received and the fact that he was not looking his best. John Brennan remembered him saying that if he had known he would be the centre of attention he would have made sure that his boots were polished. There were other stowaways, too, including two staff members from Dakar and a young Portuguese man.

In his role as radio engineer, Brennan sometimes flew as supernumerary engineer. During one flight the radio officer was having some problems with the radar equipment. Knowing that Cynthia Arpthorp, the Stargirl on the flight that day, had been a radar mechanic with the Fleet Air Arm during the war, the captain suggested that she might be able to help. Cynthia fixed the problem in no time at all. When the Radio Superintendent, McGillivray, heard about it back in London he was furious with the poor radio officer and very nearly sacked him.

Cynthia was herself helped by Brennan and a pilot named Jones when she injured her finger and was unable to continue her duties. Both men assumed the roles of Stargirls and between them served the passengers a meal, cleared up the dishes and washed them, allowing Cynthia to rest her hand. Brennan reckoned that they did pretty well, considering it was a full flight.

He remembered another occasion when some impromptu maintenance was required in the cockpit. He was on board a York one day when he encountered a problem with the radio. By chance Bennett was also on the aircraft and, hearing of the problem, asked how he intended mending it. Brennan pulled a small rubber hammer out of his flight bag and tapped the radio. It burst into life immediately and Bennett congratulated him on fixing it. He then opened his own flight bag and pulled out an identical hammer which he kept for exactly the same purpose.

Brennan told an amusing tale of life for a radio officer on board a BSAA aircraft. It had been a long flight and the captain, wanting some weather information, called out to the radio officer. Receiving no reply and suspecting, correctly, that the man might be dozing, the captain asked Brennan to give him a prod and wake him up. The ensuing conversation went like this:

Captain: 'Radio, you were asleep.'
Radio Officer: 'No, I wasn't, Captain.'

Captain: 'Yes you were. You had your eyes closed.'
Radio Officer: 'Well, I don't need my bloody eyes open to hear the radio, do I?'

Brennan married a pretty Stargirl with the very British name of Jean Macfarlane even though she came from Chile where her father worked for the Coates Cotton Company. There were other crew members from South America, too. Stargirl Mary Browne's full name was Maria Teresa del Soconne Browne and she came from either Argentina or Chile; and pilot Archie Jackson was a native of Chile where several generations of his family had lived after emigrating from Wakefield in Yorkshire to start a nitrate business in South America.

From the start of its operations BSAA had only employed women as cabin staff, but in 1948 that changed and it was decided to take on stewards as well. This caused a lot of concern among the Stargirls, especially those who had the most seniority as they were worried that they would become junior to the men.

Tom Harmer had been a chief steward with the Blue Star Line. During one shore leave he received a telegram from a Mr Denman, with whom he had worked at the Blue Star Line. The telegram asked him to contact Denman and gave the address as a building on the north side of Heathrow airport. Tom was curious and went along to see his former colleague who was, by then, the Catering Manager of BSAA. Denman asked him if he would like to become a steward for the airline and Tom agreed. When he became engaged to his girlfriend, Patricia, she told him that if he were to go back to sea she would not marry him and so he stayed with aviation for the rest of his working life. He was happy with BSAA and told Patricia that it was a fun company to work for and that morale was high.

Priscilla Vinyals also remembered Denman. He was not popular with the Stargirls as he made it clear that he expected them to bring him 'goodies'. If there was nothing left on the aircraft for him to collect the Stargirl concerned was given a hard time.

Denman had employed a woman to wash the dirty dishes from the aircraft when they returned to London, but the Stargirls usually had to do the washing up themselves as this woman was invariably found with her feet up on Denman's desk, smoking and chatting to him.

It is easy to see why Denman wanted the little luxuries. The end of the war had brought more rationing of some items than during the conflict itself and the temptation to grab what one could must have been great. It was just a shame that he expected the Stargirls to provide these luxuries for him. Others, who also craved extravagant extras, did at least pay for them and the girls were often able to supplement their incomes with items such as 'Lisbon baskets' – little shopping baskets that brought a splash of colour to austere postwar Britain.

* * *

Behind the scenes the correspondence between the airline and the Ministry regarding landing fees and the way they were calculated continued for much of the rest of 1946 and into 1947. Every time BSAA wanted to operate a flight out of Heathrow the aircraft had to be positioned there from Langley and so incurred extra landing charges. It was decided that these positioning flights could be regarded as training flights but then the Ministry decided to charge the landing fees for training flights as well. By the end of August it had been agreed that BSAA could have a contract rate which would enable them to make a number of landings for a set fee and then pay half rates above that figure. The airline was asked to estimate how many flights it thought it might make on a monthly basis and when this figure was slightly exceeded was told that the rates would have to be reviewed and would probably be increased. When the bill for landing fees was received it was discovered that the way in which the fees were calculated was by the maximum take-off weight of the aircraft rather than the landing weight. By February 1947 an exasperated Bennett, referring to the training flights, declared:

> We would point out that these landings are 'something for nothing' as far as London airport is concerned in that they are of second priority to all other flights. They are stopped whenever there is any other traffic and only take place if the area is completely free. We would moreover point out that the Minister's policy to encourage air transport to operate at a reasonable cost to the travelling public is becoming increasingly difficult to achieve. To place an additional burden on us, therefore, will of course only be reflected in higher costs to the travelling public to the detriment of the trade and commerce of the nation. It is hoped, therefore, that you will view this problem and incidentally the obvious effect on safety which it might incur with the sympathy and reasonableness with which we are sure the Minister's policy would be in keeping.

Frantic work continued to set up the airline's infrastructure and overseas facilities. While many of the airports were available because they had been used by various air forces during the war, there was a lack of suitable accommodation for both passengers and crew at the transit points along BSAA's proposed route to South America.

In Lisbon they stayed at the Palace Hotel which had a casino and was very pleasant, but the first stop on the mainland of Africa, Yundum airport at Bathurst in The Gambia, lacked any accommodation and initially it was proposed that the BOAC rest house at nearby Fajara should be used. This was done for a while, but did not prove to be popular as the washroom facilities were filthy and the passengers were constantly bothered by boys seeking tips. At Yundum itself, the only refreshment offered was lukewarm stewed tea. Ultimately BSAA wanted its own facilities and the MCA contacted the Air Ministry on its behalf to ask if a hut could be erected on the airfield. This would provide facilities for customs, immigration, a passenger lounge, dining room, kitchen, toilets and sleeping accommodation for twenty passengers (eight women and twelve men). It was thought that it would be possible to provide this building for around £3,000 but the superintending engineer at the airport felt that he might be able to reduce the costs if he used a hut that already existed on another part of Yundum airfield and had it dismantled and reconstructed in an appropriate place. By doing this he could reduce the cost to BSAA to around £2,000. The airline agreed; it even managed to have the costs reduced to £1,500 and by the beginning of April 1946 work had begun on the building.

On 8 April a 'top secret' telegram arrived at the Foreign Office from Buenos Aires. It had been sent on behalf of Dunnett of the MCA, who was on a visit to Argentina, and was addressed to George Cribbett at the Ministry. The telegram said that Dunnett had seen a letter from BOAC:

. . . asking for authority to construct [a] building at Yundum (repeat Yundum), airport at approximate cost of £10,000 (repeat £10,000). BOAC stated that this was to meet their requirements and those of British South American Airways. I asked Booth at Yundum where this building was to be situated and he expressed complete ignorance of the whole project. He said that approval had already been obtained for the construction of [a] smaller building at [a] cost of £1,500 (repeat £1,500) to meet all British South American Airways requirements, and this building is now under construction. . . . BOAC's request would seem to be completely unjustified.

Since BOAC was scaling down its use of Bathurst and, in any case, already had the rest house at Fajara, there seems to have been no justification for the request of £10,000 at all, especially when the airline was using BSAA's name to enhance its claim. It prompted Foreign Secretary Ernest Bevin to write to the Minister asking for his observations. Lord Winster told Bevin that although it was usually up to individual airlines to arrange for their own accommodation, 'so long as BOAC continue to operate under my directions in accordance with the wartime provisions of Section 32 of the British Overseas Airways Act, I exercise a greater degree of control, especially financial.' BOAC did not get the money it had requested, but it is peculiar that the Minister did not question why it was requesting these funds for a building that it did not need and was stating that it was doing so, in part, on behalf of a company over which it had no jurisdiction and who did not require either the building or BOAC's intervention.

Happily the provision of accommodation in other cities did not create any more contentious situations. In Buenos Aires they stayed at the City Hotel and in Santiago, the Carrera. In Santa Maria accommodation was reserved for them at the Terra Nova, which was at the airport and had been converted from some huts that had been erected on the airfield during the war.

When, in September 1946, a regular service was started to Caracas via Santa Maria, Bermuda and Kingston, Jamaica, they found a home from home in Arthur's White Horse Tavern in Bermuda. Situated in St Georges, it was run by a British couple, Arthur and Rosy, who treated the airline staff like family. If a flight was late arriving in Bermuda, Arthur would wait up for the crew, lying on a mattress on the veranda. On more than one occasion he fell asleep while smoking a cigarette, set fire to his mattress and had to fling it into the sea to put out the fire.

Although Arthur was fond of the BSAA crews, as they were of him, his sometimes rather juvenile, practical jokes were not always appreciated, especially when they involved him jumping out from behind a pillar and squirting them from a soda siphon. Airline uniforms were difficult to dry in a hurry.

Accommodation in Jamaica was also first-rate. The crews stayed at the Myrtle Bank Hotel, which was usually referred to as the Turtle Tank and served a very good planter's punch.

The hotel in Rio de Janeiro, the Serrador, was new; it was a tower block of twenty floors with a nightclub, the Night and Day, where the crews used to eat. The rooms had very heavy curtains and some of them used to play silly games, swinging on the curtains out of the window and back in again until one crew member died after a fall.

The city had two airports. Santos Dumont was the most practical, being close to the centre of the city, but it was too small to accommodate the aircraft used on this route and its runway was only long enough for aircraft no bigger than DC-3s. The alternative was the new military airport at Governor's Island. When it was first built it did not have a bridge to link it to the mainland and although BSAA obtained permission to use the airport, there was no transport provided to get the passengers off the island and into the city. Through the offices of the Royal Mail Shipping Company they hired a tug which was waiting at the island whenever a flight was due and took the passengers onto the mainland. It was not ideal; the tug, owned by a former pirate, shipped water in rough seas and kept breaking down. Bennett thought about how he could improve the service to the passengers and decided to buy a boat which would be kept permanently in Rio.

In the summer of 1946 he purchased a 112ft-long ex-Navy motor launch and decided to sail it to Rio himself with the help of a few crew borrowed from the staff of BSAA. He tried to get John Booth, himself a master mariner, to come along on the trip but the chairman sensibly refused. He then tried Bob Chandler who had begun his career in the Merchant Navy. He also declined, at which point Bennett is said to have yelled at him in frustration 'You're fired'. This abrupt dismissal was immediately countered by Booth who had overheard the conversation and so Bennett had to look further afield. He eventually assembled a crew comprising two engineers from Langley, two catering staff, Captain Allcock as second in command, a cabin boy and Bennett's wife and children. They departed from a jetty along the Thames near to Tower Bridge and almost immediately ran into trouble when they narrowly missed being hit by a large cargo vessel as they were busily waving goodbye to the little party that had assembled to see them on their way.

Despite having promised to keep in touch with head office every day, nothing was heard from the launch which, in keeping with the airline tradition, was named *Star Haven*. Then, a few days after it had left, a message was received saying that it had been taken in tow by a French fishing boat near Brest after the entire crew was found to have been totally incapacitated by seasickness. When they set off again they got as far as the Bay of Biscay before *mal de mer* and a faulty engine stopped them once again. They abandoned the attempt altogether and returned to England. In April the following year *Star Haven* was sold and eventually the Brazilians built a bridge between the island and the mainland.

The purchase of *Star Haven* had not been Bennett's best idea, but his inability to sail her to Brazil had been one of the only times he had failed in a task he had set himself. Wisely, the trip was rarely mentioned again.

Despite the difficulties with boats and hotel accommodation the first few months of BSAA's operations went very well. John Cheetham of the Foreign Office made a trip through a number of cities served by BSAA and spoke to passengers to ask their opinions of the service they had received. All the people he spoke to were very impressed with the standards of technical efficiency and courtesy on the flights, which Cheetham said were 'in sharp contrast to the casual treatment meted out to travellers by Pan American Airways'. The service on the ground spoiled the general impressions of excellence but was, to an extent, dependent on others such as hotel staff and locally employed personnel. As time went on BSAA was able to put more trained employees in place to address the problems with its own offices.

* * *

On 30 August 1946, BSAA suffered its first aircraft loss. The Avro Lancastrian III G-AGWJ *Star Glow* was taking off from Bathurst, The Gambia, when a swing developed which the pilot was unable to control due to the unstable nature of the runway. The aircraft partially left the metal runway, the main undercarriage collapsed and the aircraft was damaged sufficiently to be written off. Of the seventeen people on board (five crew and twelve passengers) six were injured, with one of the crew and one passenger suffering serious injuries. The captain of the aircraft was New Zealander Brian W. McMillan (later to lose his life as captain of the ill-fated Avro Tudor *Star Tiger*), although it was being flown at the time of the accident by the First Officer W. Harrison.

The aircraft was taking off from a Pierced Steel Planking (PSP) runway, which is a structure consisting of interlocking strips of metal, laid on a bed of sand. It was difficult material to handle because of its size and incredible weight, coming as it did in bundles of thirty planks which weighed around one ton. As an example, to cover a 150ft wide runway of 6,000ft in length would take over 2,300 tons of PSP. It is believed that in this case the sand on which the PSP was laid was rather loose. As the aircraft started to swing on its take-off run the metal strips forming the runway started to roll up under the main wheels and halted the aircraft very abruptly, causing the undercarriage to collapse. When word of the accident reached England, Bennett himself flew a replacement Lancastrian out to Bathurst to allow Captain McMillan to carry on with the service.

Just over a week after this loss, Bathurst was the scene of a far more serious accident. It was Saturday 7 September 1946 when Avro York G-AHEW *Star Leader* was scheduled to operate the third leg of service AS60, the thrice-weekly flight from London to Buenos Aires via Lisbon, Bathurst, Natal and Rio de Janeiro. The aircraft had left London at 11 a.m. on 6 September with twenty passengers and four crew on board. After a refuelling stop at Lisbon, it arrived at Yundum airport in Bathurst at 02.43 on Saturday 7th. Captain Frank Griffin reported that the aircraft was carrying no defects from the previous sector and a new crew was assigned to take the aircraft on the next leg of the journey, across the South Atlantic to Natal. Its captain was 30-year-old J.N.S. Cumming, who had piloted a BSAA Lancastrian service into Yundum two days previously.

John Cumming was an ex-RAF squadron leader who had been awarded a DFC and bar for his wartime service in Bomber Command. He was married with two children. His wife was expecting their third child (a son, who was to be born on 25 January 1947). The First Officer was 25-year-old Michael G. Wade. Both men had considerable flying experience in the RAF prior to joining BSAA. The radio officer was Ernest D. Slater and the Stargirl was Mrs Miriam W. Herrington, the widow of an RAF officer for whom sadly this was her first, and last, flight as a BSAA air hostess.

The aircraft was refuelled with 2,248 gallons and a routine technical inspection was carried out which revealed no faults. The passengers would have taken the opportunity to stretch their legs while the aircraft was being prepared, but now they reboarded and took their seats for the engines to be started and the aircraft to leave the ramp an hour after it had landed. After waiting for another aircraft to land and taxi in, *Star Leader* reached the end of the active runway (runway 23) at just before 04.10.

The aircraft was watched from the control tower as it commenced its take-off run, which was estimated to be approximately 1,500yds. After witnesses lost sight of the aircraft, a glow was seen to the south accompanied by the sounds of explosions. It is estimated that the aircraft had impacted the ground between one and a half and two minutes after the start of its take-off run. With the exception of one 23-year-old female passenger, who died later, all on board were killed instantly. Howard Webb, a BSAA radio officer, was standing on the tarmac next to the Lancastrian *Star Land* (which had just landed, and in which he was shortly to leave for Lisbon) and he witnessed the take-off and the start of the subsequent climb. He felt that it was normal, but was convinced that the aircraft had initiated a turn to the left to return to the airfield due to some technical difficulty, and was equally sure that there was no fire before it came down. Another witness, A. Johnson, a BSAA ground engineer at Bathurst, had started working on the Lancastrian and was standing on the wing when he watched *Star Leader* take off. He stated that he believed the aircraft had become airborne sooner than expected and seemed to climb rather more steeply than normal.

Star Leader had been built by A.V. Roe & Company Ltd in 1946. It was issued with its C of A on 27 May and delivered to BSAA at its home base of Langley on 21 June. It was a new aircraft, with only 453 flying hours in its logs by the time of the accident. The only significant maintenance required during the short life of the aircraft was the replacement of the starboard inner engine as a result of problems with the reduction gear. This was carried out during routine maintenance the day before the aircraft left London.

The investigation into the accident was carried out by the MCA. Apart from its usual thorough examination of the wreckage, which ascertained that the aircraft had been banked steeply to port when it hit the ground and was on a heading of approximately 110 degrees compared with the 227 degrees runway heading, it focused on two particular areas, the weight of the aircraft and the relevant experience of the Captain. The weather was considered fair at the time with a very light wind and a cloud base of 1,500ft so was not considered to be a factor in the accident. Similarly, the investigation of the wreckage found no evidence of any pre-existing failures in the aircraft before the accident and it was considered, somewhat controversially, that all four engines had been operating under considerable power at the time of the initial impact. Photographs of the wreckage show the characteristic bending of the propeller blades which indicates an engine under power at impact, but the blades were bent to differing degrees of severity (with the port outer blades bent significantly less than the port inner) so it is hard to be sure that all engines were under considerable power at the time.

The weight at take-off was calculated to be 68,770lb and the centre of gravity (CG) was well within limits. BSAA imposed a company limit on the take-off weight for the Avro York of 69,000lb even though the authorised maximum weight for this aircraft on the C of A was 71,000lb. This implies that BSAA wished to add its own safety margin within the absolute limits of the C of A. It is significant that despite the take-off weight being within both the company and the legal limits it was still a very heavily loaded aircraft.

The examination of the licensing and experience of the crew highlighted an anomaly. It was discovered that while the First Officer had 1,355 hours of flying time in the RAF (of which 95 were at night), his Class 'B' Pilot's Licence, although valid, was not endorsed for the Avro York. His flying time on Yorks was however 36 hours 10 minutes by day and 4 hours 48 minutes at night. Due to the fact the investigation did not comment further on this anomaly, and indeed stated that it had no bearing on the accident, it must be concluded that they were satisfied that Captain Cumming was the handling pilot at the time. Captain Cumming's experience was examined more closely. He held a valid Class 'B' Pilot's Licence, including a validation for the Avro York, in addition to a First Class Navigator's Licence. He had built up a total of 2,760 flying hours in the RAF, including 400 hours at night. Since joining BSAA he had flown over 300 hours as first officer on Lancaster and Lancastrian aircraft and nearly 21 hours as first officer on Yorks. His experience as a captain was considerably less, amounting to 25 hours on Lancasters and Lancastrians. On Yorks, he had flown only 3 hours 52 minutes by day and 1 hour 3 minutes by night as captain, none of which was on scheduled services. It became apparent therefore that this was Captain Cumming's first flight in command on a scheduled York service. It also emerged that the flight was his first take-off (by day or night) in a York loaded to more than 65,000lb.

Sadly, this was an accident for which the investigators could establish no clear cause. The evidence suggested that the aircraft was fully serviceable, the weight and balance was within limits, there was no suggestion that the freight had shifted and caused the CG to move, there was no material evidence of fire in the air and no evidence of any structural failure. The report highlighted the lack of experience of the handling pilot on this type of aircraft and at this weight. The official conclusion was stated as follows: 'The accident occurred as a result of the Captain losing control of the aircraft very shortly after it had left the ground. The cause of the loss of control cannot be determined with certainty, but that it was due to a mishandling of the controls by the Captain is the most likely explanation.'

The Air Registration Board made the recommendation shortly afterwards that operators of Avro York aircraft should impose a reduced take-off weight limit of 68,000lb.

In reviewing the circumstances of the accident, it seems possible that the acceleration of the aircraft was slower than the Captain was expecting, due to the weight being heavier than he was used to. As a result, it is possible that he may have pulled the aircraft into the air at a more extreme angle of attack and lower airspeed than was normal and it stalled, rolled to the left and impacted the trees a mile or so from the runway. If this was the case, the altitude of the aircraft when it stalled would have been far too low to effect a recovery.

BSAA carried out its own investigation into the accident. In his summary report Bennett felt that the opinion of the official report that the accident was due to 'mishandling of the controls by the Captain' was most unfair. He thought it was far more likely that there had been a failure (or significant reduction in power) of the port outer engine, resulting in the aircraft entering a turn to the left and a semi-stalled condition from which it did not recover.

After the publication of the official report, the Air Safety and Technical Committee of the British Air Line Pilots Association (BALPA) issued a statement criticising the findings. It took 'strong exception' to the opinion expressed in the report that the pilot lost control of the aircraft. It considered that the failure of the port outer engine fitted the circumstances more closely, and noted that 'the Ministry is quite prepared to condemn by implication a pilot as being inexperienced on a type when, at the same time, by its own regulations, it accepts that a pilot is fit to fly for hire or reward with a very limited number of hours and without requiring proof of night flying on that type'. The statement also suggested that the accident could have been the result of an instrument failure, but that the official investigation had not considered this possibility. They believed it to be very unlikely that the captain would have attempted such a tight turn to the left at low altitude if the aircraft was handling normally.

It was surely no coincidence, following so soon after the loss of *Star Leader* and the take-off accident which wrote off Lancastrian *Star Glow* at Bathurst just over a week earlier, that on 18 September Bennett issued an addition to the BSAA 'Operations Standing Orders' which discussed the 'finer points of flying' and placed the emphasis on safety. In particular, he made the following statements:

Cockpit drill must be such as to minimise the danger of mishandling of flap and undercarriage lever and of reducing power incorrectly, and in particular it must be such as to cope in the case of an engine failure. In this respect, Aircraft Officers are reminded that if an outer engine cuts at or just after unstick speed or in the early stages of the climb, it is necessary to throttle the opposite (good) outer engine slightly in order to maintain rudder control, and also perhaps to pull the boost control cut-out and to take override maximum power on the inner engine on the failed side.

An outer engine failure at night just after take-off particularly requires quick and instant action on the above lines.

He also made the following recommendation: 'Aircraft Officers are reminded that, due to the difference of ground angle, the swing tendency on a Lancastrian is worse than on a York; on a Tudor I is worse than on a Tudor II. The tail should therefore not be raised too quickly.'

Nowadays it seems incredible that an accident report which places the probability of blame on the captain of the aircraft, should also reveal such a lack of crew experience of scheduled flying on the particular type being flown. However, for a balanced view of the circumstances sixty years ago, we should compare BSAA with other airlines of the period.

An interesting article appeared in *The Aeroplane* in May 1947 which highlighted the problems of inadequate crew training and experience. It focused on the outcome of six accident investigations covering accidents to civilian airliners between August 1946 and January 1947 (including the accident to *Star Leader*). The airlines discussed included BOAC, BEA and Scottish Airways. The purpose of aircraft accident investigations and the resulting reports published by the MCA (and latterly the Accident Investigation Branch and Air Accident Investigation Branch respectively – AIB and AAIB) has always been to discover the actual cause of accidents, not specifically to apportion blame or be critical of individuals, but rather to share the findings with as wide an audience as possible so that lessons will be learned and the same type of accident will be prevented from happening again. Consequently, the article noted that although the probable cause of most of the accidents listed was lack of experience, lack of crew training and improper technique, the main responsibility for avoiding accidents such as these in the future should rest with the airlines themselves. The author was also of the opinion that the greatest measure of company responsibility of all the accidents discussed concerned the accident to a BOAC DC-3 at Stowting in Kent, as the investigation revealed that all but one of the flight crew was unfamiliar with the route being flown. Clearly BSAA's problems were by no means unusual in 1946.

The aviation press at the time reported that it had been a very bad week for airline travel as, in addition to the BSAA accident, Air France had suffered two serious accidents involving significant loss of life on two consecutive days. On 3 September an Air France DC-3 crashed near Copenhagen killing all twenty-two people on board, and the following day another Air France DC-3 crashed, this time shortly after take-off from Paris on a flight to London, resulting in the deaths of twenty of the twenty-six people on board.

* * *

Following the two accidents in The Gambia, BSAA decided to use the Senegalese capital Dakar as its transit stop in West Africa. Dakar, however, was as bad as Bathurst.

BSAA did, at least, find a hotel, the Majestic, for the inbound crews, but it was a terrible place. It was always overcrowded and the only crew member who could be guaranteed a room to herself was the Stargirl. The male crew members had to share, sometimes as many as three to a room, and their rest was disrupted when one person had to leave to take an outbound flight while others were arriving at the end of an inbound. The overcrowding was so bad that there were always people sleeping in the corridors and, in addition, the water was only turned on twice a day for an hour at a time. It was often cut off mid-shower leaving the crews covered in soap and shampoo and, consequently, there was always a mad rush for the bathroom when the water was switched on. The hotel lacked basic items such as toilet paper which the crews had to bring with them from home.

Dakar was not well-liked by BSAA staff and the following year it would be even less popular, making the airline wonder if it had not made a big mistake in moving from Bathurst.

* * *

A month after the loss of *Star Leader*, the Minister of Civil Aviation, Lord Winster, was given the job of Governor of Cyprus and was replaced by Lord Nathan of Churt. It is hard to understand the logic behind Prime Minister Attlee's decision to appoint Nathan and the Parliamentary Secretary, George Lindgren, to the MCA. According to an article in *The Aeroplane* magazine at the time, the Minister and the Parliamentary Secretary 'have not a clue about aerial transport'. Even Nathan's biographer, H. Montgomery Hyde, describing his subject's suitability for the position at the MCA, said, 'Admittedly Nathan did not know very much about its work, although he had managed to pick up a few pointers from Lord Londonderry, a former Air Minister and enthusiastic amateur pilot.' His inexperience was evident. Of the four ministers of civil aviation under whom the airline operated, Nathan would be the one with the least relevant knowledge, who interfered most in the running of the airline and whose appointment would create many of the situations that ultimately ensured the demise of BSAA.

Chapter 7

A Bad Year For Safety

By 1947 the airline had added Sao Paulo, Nassau, Port-of-Spain, Barranquilla and Lima to its routing and the following year included Miami, Havana and Mexico City. There were also scheduled refuelling stops at Gander, Stephenville, Keflavik and Shannon.

Despite BSAA's continually expanding route network, the remainder of 1946 passed without any further incidents. However, 1947 was to prove a bad year for safety. On Saturday 12 April 1947, Avro York G-AHEZ *Star Speed* took off from Lisbon on the estimated 8-hour flight to Dakar, French West Africa. On board were nine passengers and a crew of six, led by Captain Godfrey J. Earnshaw. Captain Earnshaw was an experienced pilot with over 2,160 hours in his logbooks. He had flown BSAA Yorks for 330 hours and had already made ten landings at Dakar, eight of which were in the York and seven of those at night. The other crew members were First Officer F. Beard, Navigator C. Ellison, Radio Officer D. G. Stott and two Stargirls, Lynn Clayton and Margaret Bray.

The aircraft had taken off at 16.30 with 2,176 gallons of fuel in its tanks, although the figure shown on the flight plan which Captain Earnshaw handed to the BSAA Station Manager at Lisbon was 2,356 gallons, the difference being enough to increase the predicted endurance of the York from 10 hours 10 minutes to 12 hours 30 minutes. This flight plan was duly transmitted to Dakar, leading the controllers there to believe that the aircraft had enough fuel on board to keep it in the air until 05.00 on 13 April. They were also given an ETA at Dakar of 00:30, whereas in fact it did not arrive over the airfield until 01.30 with only enough fuel on board for another 1 hour 10 minutes flying time.

The disparity between the ETA and the actual arrival time overhead Dakar is explained by an inconsistency in the weather forecast used to prepare the flight plan in Lisbon. The surface winds in the Western Sahara were stronger and more southerly than forecast. Additionally, the forecast had been prepared for a direct course at a cruising altitude of 10,000ft. The aircraft actually changed course slightly when flying over land and flew at an altitude of 12,000ft. This resulted in the winds being far less favourable, the difference in wind speed being in the order of 12 to 18mph. Although this explains the late arrival over Dakar, it highlights another strange anomaly with the flight plan. The additional headwinds at 12,000ft would have been enough to account for the aircraft taking 8 hours 46 minutes to cover the distance from Lisbon to Dakar. However, having examined the meteorological reports available at Lisbon, the First Officer entered an estimated flight time of 7 hours 50 minutes on the BSAA flight plan, yet the Captain of the aircraft entered an estimated flight time of 8 hours 30 minutes on the flight plan in the Lisbon Control Centre.

The airfield at Dakar was still in the process of being taken over by the French from the Americans in April 1947 and consequently the French authorities had not yet been able to install any up-to-date radio landing aids or even adequate approach and runway lighting. Had they done so, this accident may have been avoided. Significantly, Captain Earnshaw was aware of the Notice to Airmen, or NOTAM, which stated that runway 120 (the only runway along the track of the radio range and, significantly, the longer of the two runways) was temporarily out of use.

When the aircraft arrived over the airfield the visibility was poor and a thin layer of mist was starting to form about 300ft above the ground. Despite the poor visibility, the runway lights, although not bright, could still be seen from the aircraft so Captain Earnshaw attempted to land. Before he arrived at the runway threshold he lost sight of it and when he saw it again he was already over it and misaligned with the runway centreline. He immediately opened the throttles fully to go around. He made two more attempts at landing, both with the same result. It was reported that kerosene lamps had been lit at the runway threshold, but during one approach the pilot, thinking he was heading for one of these lamps, nearly collided with the marine light at the Les Mamelles semaphore station. This is an indication of how poor the visibility had become.

By this time, there were two other aircraft holding over the airfield and a fourth shortly to arrive. The repeated attempts to land had compromised the already marginal endurance of the aircraft. Inevitably, when an aircraft attempts a landing, the engine power is cut back to allow the airspeed to reduce to a suitable approach and landing speed. If the aircraft then has to abort the landing, the throttles are opened wide to quickly regain enough flying speed to safely climb away. This process uses far more fuel than an aircraft in cruising flight or even in a holding pattern. Therefore as each attempt at landing failed, it was making the fuel situation very much more precarious.

The primary diversion airfield stated in the flight plan was Bathurst, and with the fuel available it should have been possible to divert there any time up to 01.55 at the very latest, providing accurate details of the Bathurst weather were made available to the crew. At 01.47 the Radio Officer attempted to make contact with Bathurst but received no reply. It was only after 02.00, when the diversion to Bathurst was no longer possible, that he received a transmission giving the current meteorological situation there.

At 01.55 the crew were asked by the Dakar tower controller to state the aircraft's endurance, to which they responded that it had only one hour of fuel remaining. As it was therefore too dangerous to consider a diversion to Bathurst, the controller ordered them to divert to Thiès, which is only 37 miles away. The crew responded that they did not know Thiès and that they were having difficulty understanding the communication from the tower. The BSAA Station Manager, Mr Glenny, who was in the tower at the time, took the microphone and transmitted the magnetic course (090°) and distance (37 miles) to the crew.

After a few more minutes, during which presumably the crew were considering their limited options and looking for an airfield plan for Thiès, Captain Earnshaw decided he had no alternative but to make a 'crash landing'. By this time it was 02.40 and the fuel was nearly exhausted. The aircraft was turned in the direction of the closed runway 120, however the pilot lined up on the lights of a taxiway to the side of the runway, presumably believing this would give him the longest distance in which to stop the aircraft. He made a careful approach and cut the throttles before touching down on a bearing of 160°, but 170yds later hit a large pile of stones left as a result of work on the runway, causing the underside of the fuselage to split open. The aircraft skidded and progressively broke up over the next 650yds before hitting a large ant hill. Just over 100yds beyond the ant hill the starboard outer engine collided with a baobab tree and was torn from the wing, resulting in the rear fuselage and tail breaking away from the rest of the aircraft and coming to rest a short distance from the main wreckage, which by now had spun round and had come to a standstill on a heading of 273°.

Nobody on the airfield had heard the noise of the crash, and the personnel in the tower were only made aware that the aircraft was on the ground when one of the injured members of the crew struggled to the tower from the wreckage to look for help. When helpers arrived at the scene of the accident, they found that six of the passengers had died when the fuselage split open and one had suffered serious injuries. The remaining two passengers and two members of the crew had suffered minor injuries.

BSAA immediately assigned its Operations Manager, Captain Gordon Store, to carry out an investigation into the complex circumstances surrounding the accident in parallel with the official investigation. He looked into the fuel status of the aircraft, the possibility of an earlier decision to divert to Bathurst and the communication difficulties encountered when information was being passed from the air traffic controllers in the tower. His findings, published on 26 April 1947 (and which were not mentioned in the subsequent full report) were that the Airport Authority had 'a poorly qualified girl operator on sole duty in the tower, [who] had absolutely no organisation for making available Thiès, Bathurst, or anywhere else as immediate Diversion Aerodromes'. It was apparent from Captain Store's report that BSAA had made repeated requests to the Airport Authority over the previous six months to organise regular communication between Dakar (YOFF) and either Bathurst or Thiès with a view to making these airfields available and open without notice for emergency diversions. He suggested that a pilot in possession of such information would have been able to utilise one of these diversion aerodromes without hesitation. Presumably if these arrangements had been put in place, all BSAA pilots would have been briefed on the location of Thiès. He also stated that the local Air Traffic Control had 'no up to date orders on local control or diversionary procedure'.

The report goes into some detail regarding the fuel situation on the York, but does not offer any explanation for the discrepancies in the flight plan estimates of the aircraft endurance. Why the Captain should enter a figure of 2,356 gallons in the flight plan when there were only 2,176 gallons in the tanks is a mystery. Perhaps it was a simple arithmetical error, but this explanation was never put forward.

In addition to the report by Captain Store, a confidential report was compiled by the air attaché in Rio de Janeiro and sent to the Air Ministry in London. It was most scathing in its assessment of the facilities at Dakar at the time of the accident. The report consisted of the testimonies of three American captains of Panair, the Brazilian airline. The first, Captain Jones, was their chief instructor and had taken off from Dakar shortly before *Star Speed* arrived. The second, Captain Biggers, was another Panair instructor and he had arrived over Dakar in a Constellation ten minutes after the York. He had to circle the airfield for two hours and while doing so had listened to the whole of the radio conversation between *Star Speed* and the tower. The third Panair pilot, Captain Chase, was technical adviser to the airline. It is evident that all three men were very experienced pilots and they were forthright and unequivocal in their condemnation of the facilities at Dakar. They stated that 'the French girl tower operators are worse than useless', quoting an example of a conversation between the tower operator and the crew of a York when the co-pilot said, 'You are only confusing us, give us landing conditions and leave us alone, we only have 200 gallons of gas left', to which the tower girl replied 'You are already cleared to 200 feet'! They pointed out that a few days previously there had been a mid-air collision in the area due to inadequate control from the personnel in the tower. Of the organisation and emergency procedures at Dakar they made the alarming statement 'there is none'. The report went on to add that the flares released to aid Captain Earnshaw in his attempts to land were released far too early, while the York was on its downwind leg, and were out before the aircraft could make its approach. In summary they concluded that the runway markings and lighting were totally inadequate, as were the radio facilities, and the possibility of using Sal Island in the Cape Verdes instead of Dakar should be explored at the earliest opportunity.

In a present-day accident investigation the investigating authority will publish their findings so that lessons can be learnt to prevent a similar type of accident happening again. They do not seek to apportion blame for the sake of it, but only when it is essential as part of their recommendations for future accident prevention. In the case of the accident to *Star Speed*, however, there were several parties with a keen interest in the outcome of the investigation and for whom the apportioning of blame was beneficial if it absolved them of direct responsibility. In the weeks following the accident, there was a great deal of discussion surrounding the reasons why Captain Earnshaw did not attempt to divert to Bathurst when he was still able to do so. This culminated in the BSAA Chairman John Booth writing a letter to the Ministry of Civil Aviation on 8 July reinforcing the statement by Captain Store in his report, that had Bathurst been open and available as a diversion airfield, the accident would not have happened. The Minister replied to this letter by commenting that Captain Store's report did not include any evidence that Captain Earnshaw had attempted to contact Bathurst in time to make arrangements to divert there. Curiously, the BSAA Chairman replied the following day, apologising that he had not included the section of Captain Store's report containing details of attempts made by *Star Speed* to get in touch with Bathurst. He therefore included this section of the report in his letter, which included the following statement, under the heading 'Diversionary Action':

At 0147z G-AHEZ's Radio Officer called Bathurst with the intention of asking for Bathurst weather. Although G-AHEZ and G-AHFA (another BSAA York) had both worked Bathurst satisfactorily, and all the evidence indicates that the operator of the HF/DF station MRO was wide awake – no reply was received to calls.

He also stated that:

Dakar did not attempt to contact Bathurst by W/T, though this was nominated on the Flight Plan message as alternative.

When the report of the official accident investigation was published on 22 September 1947 it listed a number of contributory causes, including:

Errors in the flight plan ETA
Errors in the stated endurance
Lack of decision on the part of the pilot
Inadequate runway lighting
No approach lights
No radio facilities for landing in bad visibility
Difficulties in radio telephony exchanges between the control tower and the
    aircraft
Insufficient knowledge of the English language by the controllers in the tower
Slight nervousness of the crew during the attempts to land

The report concluded with the possibility that the radio range which is placed in the direction of runway 120 and which was temporarily out of operation would not have given a sufficiently accurate indication for landing. It also noted rather ironically that, had the aircraft proceeded to Thiès when it was instructed to do so, it would not have found the runway lit, owing to telephone difficulties between Dakar and Thiès on the night of the accident.

This accident highlighted all too well the difficulties in routing scheduled flights through airfields where the infrastructure compared very poorly to the best European airports at the time. There is also some irony in the fact that the crew had been criticised for not diverting to Thiès when instructed, yet had they done so, the outcome may well have been the same, or worse, due to the Thiès runway not being lit. As is so often the case in aircraft accidents, there is not one single cause. Most accidents are the result of a number of contributory factors which individually are not dangerous, but which when added together result in a tragic outcome.

* * *

Nearly two months after the accident to *Star Speed*, and before the final report was published, an incident occurred which is arguably the most regrettable in BSAA's short history, not least because it could easily have been avoided with the use of some common sense and diplomacy.

On the morning of 4 June 1947 two men walked into the British Embassy in Lisbon asking to see the Ambassador, Charles Stirling, on an important matter concerning the accident. They were Dr Costa Pinheiro, a lawyer from Oporto, and his son who was also a lawyer and the head of a secretariat in the Ministry for the Interior. They were informed that it would not be possible for them to see the Ambassador that day, but they would be seen by the Air Attaché, Wing Commander Clayton, the following day. When they returned the next morning and explained to the Air Attaché who they were, the reason for their visit became apparent.

Dr Pinheiro explained that one of his sons, Fernando de Sousa Costa Pinheiro, was one of the six passengers killed in the accident to *Star Speed* and that he wished to present a memorandum to the Ambassador strongly criticising BSAA for the way they had handled the matter of the transportation of his son's body from Dakar back to Lisbon.

His memorandum is as follows:

BSAA aircraft *Starspeed* left Lisbon on the 12th April 1947 and crashed at Dakar in the early hours of the morning on the 13th April. On the afternoon of the 14th April I was informed by telegram from the BSAA. Office in Lisbon that my son who was one of the passengers had been killed in the crash.

On the 17th April a meeting was held in Oporto at which were present W/Cdr. Hall, Manager of B.S.A.A., a Doctor and a Magistrate of the City, and myself. At this meeting W/Cdr. Hall promised that my son's body would be brought from Dakar to Lisbon in a B.S.A.A. aircraft. This would be done as soon as necessary official formalities in Dakar and Lisbon had been completed, and would be without charge to the families of the victims.

After this meeting my son was in daily contact with the British South American Airways Agency, and when it had been ascertained that all the formalities for removing the body from Dakar had been completed, we asked when the body would be brought to Lisbon. We were given evasive answers such as that the British government were sending an R.A.F. aircraft for the bodies.

On the 19th May at a meeting in Oporto between myself, my son and brother in law and a Mr. Johnson who is now acting as Manager during the absence in England on leave of W/Cdr. Hall, we were again promised that B.S.A.A. were bringing the bodies from Dakar in one of the Company's aircraft and at the Company's expense. Johnson explained at the same time that certain difficulties were being encountered, as though the coffins of the two children killed in the accident [would fit], the coffins containing the two men were too big for the freight compartment.

We asked whether it was possible that a large British government Company authorised to carry international traffic, did not have a single spare aircraft with which to collect the bodies of victims from the scene of a crash. In answer to our question concerning this supposed shortage of aircraft, Johnson said that he was extremely sorry and hoped that we would understand the Company's position. He added that they were studying the possibility of freighting the bodies from Dakar by any one of the International Air Lines which called there, and also of obtaining the only B.S.A.A. freight aircraft available, which happened at that time to be in South America. In any case he guaranteed that everything would be arranged within a very short while, 15 to 30 days at the maximum.

After the meeting on the 19th May we enquired daily if any action was being taken, and were informed each time that nothing had been settled, or that it was up to Head Office in London, or that London did not reply to their enquiries etc.

Now, two months after the accident and after having given solemn promises that the bodies would be brought back to Lisbon by air in a few days, we are informed that the company are unable to implement their original promises and that they are endeavouring to get the bodies brought by sea. This latter expedient is unlikely to succeed as ships which call at Dakar rarely call at Lisbon, in any case I strongly protest at this suggestion and I think I have the right to demand that the Company honour its promises and transport my son's body directly from Dakar to Lisbon by air.

A Company of the size and importance of B.S.A.A. should not count only the material costs on an occasion like this. It is incomprehensible to us that the Company should try to dishonour the promises which they originally made.

As well as handing over the memorandum to the Air Attaché, Dr Costa Pinheiro reiterated the substance to him verbally. He also told him that he had been informed by a member of BSAA staff in Lisbon that if he wished to charter an aircraft at his own expense, he could of course get his son's body back to Lisbon immediately.

Wing Commander Clayton must have passed on the details of Dr Costa Pinheiro's visit urgently to the Ambassador as on 7 June he wrote a letter to Mr Hoyer-Millar at the Foreign Office in London explaining the seriousness of the issue. He stated that according to the BSAA local manager, the airline had promised the family they would return the body to Lisbon, but had not agreed to bring it back by air. They had established that it was impossible to fit the large coffin through the passenger door of one of their Avro York aircraft and the Head Office in London had refused to use one of its freighters or to charter an aircraft specifically for the task. It seems that even when the local BSAA representative in Lisbon had warned of the adverse publicity being generated, the airline had refused to comply with Dr Costa Pinheiro's wishes, partly on the grounds of cost and partly because they felt that it would imply an admission of liability for the accident. The Ambassador stressed the gravity of the situation in his letter by stating:

The Costa Pinheiros are a large and influential family in the North of Portugal and have stirred up a good deal of feeling about this matter, which is one to which the Portuguese attach great religious and sentimental importance. We should have thought that at a moment when we are anxious to build up our position in civil aviation we ought to do everything in our power to establish a reputation for courtesy and consideration, and that from the point of view of good-will it would pay B.S.A.A. well in the long run to be more forthcoming, rather than to take their present quite legitimate, but slightly 'bureaucratic' attitude.

He finished with:

> If you agree with us, therefore, you may feel disposed to approach the Corporation with a view to getting them to reconsider their position and make arrangements to fly the bodies home.

The Air Attaché also attempted to emphasise the importance of the situation by writing a letter on 11 June to the Assistant Chief of Air Staff at the Air Ministry in London to inform him of Dr Costa Pinheiro's visit. He also warned that Dr Costa Pinheiro belonged to an influential Portuguese family and was determined to 'do as much harm to the prestige of British South American Airways as possible', stating that the Lisbon evening paper *Republica* had carried an article the previous evening attacking BSAA for the handling of the affair and warning that other national daily newspapers were preparing to run similar articles. This was followed by a telegram to the Foreign Office from the British Embassy on 13 June (originally classified 'Restricted' but stamped 'SECRET'), warning that the press campaign would be particularly damaging not only to BSAA but to British civil aviation as a whole if left unchecked and stating that the Press Attaché had managed to persuade the main newspapers to delay printing their articles for a few days.

On 17 June the Foreign Office responded to the Ambassador's letter by forwarding it to the MCA with a covering letter suggesting it would be more appropriate if the Ministry approached the airline to resolve the issue rather than the Foreign Office. It seems this plea came too late to prevent the newspaper *Jornal de Noticias* from publishing a long article bitterly attacking the airline, in which it included the slightly questionable statement that 'the Company [BSAA] was not the victim of a fortuitous accident. The accident was the result of the pilot's incompetence, and of the lack of organisation, training and discipline of the personnel of the rescue services.' BSAA's reluctance to fly the bodies of the Portuguese passengers back to Lisbon was out of concern that the act of doing so would be seen as an admission of liability; however it did not prevent the Portuguese press from forming their own opinions on liability and making them widely known.

Finally, on 5 July the MCA passed on the contents of the letters it had received from the Foreign Office to Air Vice-Marshal Bennett at BSAA. The Foreign Office again wrote to the Ministry on 6 August to say that the family of the dead man had once more visited the Embassy in Lisbon on 17 July and threatened to launch a full press campaign which would be very damaging to British interests in Portugal. Despite Bennett responding to the Ministry on 14 August (presumably exhausted after spending long days flying over the Andes searching for Lancastrian *Star Dust*) with the somewhat astonishing view that the family's behaviour was 'ridiculous and disgusting', the whole affair was brought to a close when it was announced by the Foreign Office on 13 September that the bodies of the Portuguese victims of the *Star Speed* accident had been delivered to Lisbon at BSAA's expense and that a representative of the British Embassy in Lisbon had attended the funeral.

This was clearly an unnecessarily long and extremely damaging incident which caused a great deal of hostility towards BSAA in Portugal. It is hard to see why it was not resolved much sooner. In a written summary of the affair, the MCA stated that the British Ambassador to Portugal believed Bennett's later goodwill visit to Lisbon with the Avro Tudor IV was boycotted by the press as a direct result. It is possible that BSAA's reputation in Portugal never fully recovered.

Chapter 8

A Very Suspicious Death

It is a sad fact that in civil aviation there are sometimes fatalities, but they are not always as the result of an air crash. Sometimes accidents or illness can be the culprits; sometimes the cause can be more sinister.

On 26 January 1947, 29-year-old Jagwida Irena Orosz and her husband Stanislaw, both displaced persons of Polish origin, boarded BSAA Lancastrian *Star Guide* under the command of Captain Cliff Alabaster at Heathrow for flight PW15, on the first leg of their trip to Bogota, Columbia. There was a slight delay because trouble with one of the engines caused the aircraft to return to the stand for maintenance work to be carried out. Once it was airborne, it ran into bad weather over France and the passengers had a bumpy, uncomfortable ride. The engine trouble resurfaced when the Lancastrian was 30 minutes flying time away from its first transit stop at Santa Maria in the Azores, necessitating further maintenance.

During the course of the journey Mrs Orosz felt ill and fainted. She was given oxygen from the aircraft's emergency supply and appeared to recover. Upon arrival in Santa Maria she was taken to the airport hotel and a doctor was called. He advised bed rest and gave her a series of injections; the final injection caused convulsions and made her much worse, and she died in the early hours of the following morning. The BSAA Station Manager at Santa Maria, Mr Collins, helped to arrange for her body to be returned to England for burial, as per the wishes of her husband, and there the story may have ended. However, it was to take a series of bizarre turns that, even now, cannot be properly explained.

One of the other passengers on board the same flight was an official from the Foreign Office, Robert Urquhart, who was travelling to Caracas. Fifty-year-old Urquhart, a married man with four daughters, had been a diplomat all his working life and, by 1945, had become Inspector General of HM Consular Establishment.

Observing the collapse of Mrs Orosz he decided, four days later in Natal, to telegraph a complaint about the way the crew had behaved, not to BSAA but to the Foreign Office in London, with a request to send it on to the MCA.

Mr Freese-Pennefather of the Foreign Office telephoned Mr Simpson at the MCA to inform him of the incident and sent him a copy of the telegram on 3 February. Simpson contacted BSAA on 4 February in a brief note, written to Wing Commander L.D. Groom, Bennett's PA, telling him that, according to Urquhart, 'the prevailing opinion among the passengers, which apparently he shared, was that the aircraft ought to have put back to London when it was clear that the woman's life was in danger'. One wonders how Urquhart came to the conclusion that Mrs Orosz's life was in danger when all she did on the flight was faint. As the days went by, more and more information was passed back and forth between the various departments of the Foreign Office, MCA and BSAA, and two detailed but vastly different pictures of what had happened began to emerge.

BSAA's Station Manager in Santa Maria made a report in which he said:

The passenger (Mrs Orosz, with husband, both Poles and displaced persons) who had fainted soon after take-off but recovered, was taken by ambulance with the medical officer to the airport hotel and put to bed. The husband showed no anxiety and did not accompany her to the hotel but stayed for one hour at the airport after the other passengers had left, checking his baggage.

Mrs Orosz was given several injections by the Airport doctor, about six in all. She died at 270300z [03.00 GMT on 27 January]. The doctor refused to give a certificate of death. The husband, who was not with her when she died but had been in her room during the doctor's first visit, refused to allow the Airport doctor to conduct a post mortem, at which the doctor appeared most relieved.

Mr Orosz, the husband, at first desired to have her buried at Santa Maria but later wished to take the body to Poland, and compromised with Huddersfield.

. . . I have now persuaded the airport doctor to issue a death certificate for Mrs Orosz and have obtained the authority the husband requires to take the body to UK.

Mrs Orosz's body arrived in England on 3 February. The police and the coroner were informed and took over the formalities, one of which was the arrangement for a post mortem. The final part of Collins's report disclosed some disturbing facts for the airline:

I think an autopsy on arrival would be to the advantage of the Corporation
as the husband threatens action against BSAA. He blames the height and
the food alternatively. All the other passengers ate the same food and the
place he was taking his tuberculous wife to was Bogota, 7,000ft or more
above sea-level.

The Captain reduced height immediately to 3,000ft after she fainted in
flight and the oxygen supplied was sufficient for 32,000ft, throughout the
remainder of the voyage. There was no question of turning back as she had
apparently recovered so much that the husband lit a cigarette and resumed
his seat at the rear of the aircraft.

Wing Commander Groom sent the details of the report to Simpson at the
MCA with the comments:

With regard to the foregoing I think you will agree with me that the whole
affair strikes one as odd, particularly so when we consider the nonchalant
and apparently casually indifferent attitude taken by the husband in flight,
and also his subsequent attitude and the 'round robin' received by you.
I should appreciate a copy of this 'round robin' together with copies of any
other letters referring to this accident you may have received from a public
source, although now that the English post mortem is going to be held
I think that the potentiality of harmful publicity is now lessened.

I hope the foregoing will be sufficient for you to answer any adverse
comments that come your way.

Groom received a reply from Simpson to his letter two days later and was
surprised to learn that there had been no other communications about Mrs
Orosz's death, despite Urquhart's claim that all the other passengers agreed
with his assessment of the situation. Simpson said that he had forwarded a
copy of the telegram to the BSAA secretary, Bernard Porter.

A week later BSAA received a letter from London solicitors Hilder Thomson
& Dunn which informed the airline that they were acting for Mr Orosz. The
letter claimed that Mrs Orosz had been medically examined before the flight
and was fit to travel. It also stated that when she asked the Stargirl for help
after feeling faint all that could be done for her was to give her 'three bottles
of oxygen which were used up in a few minutes'. It alleged that there were
no medical supplies on board the aircraft except for some smelling salts and

whisky and that when Mr Orosz asked the pilot to make a landing in France, he refused. The letter continued: 'In these circumstances, it seems clear that the death of Mrs Orosz was due to the negligence of your Company and we shall be glad to hear that you admit liability.'

In reply to this communication Porter compiled the following report on 28 February:

Reports have been received from the Captain of the aircraft and from the Stargirl, and have been submitted to the company's medical adviser. The death certificate has also been obtained from Santa Maria. It is understood that a post mortem was carried out on the return of the body to this country, and application has been made for a copy of the pathologist's report. This has not yet been received.

After reading the reports of the Captain and Stargirl, the Company's medical adviser stated he was convinced that no claim could possibly be maintained against the Company in respect of this death, which, according to the death certificate, was due to pulmonary tuberculosis and heart trouble.

A Foreign Office official, Mr Urquhart, who was a passenger on the aircraft, cabled to the Foreign Office (for transmission to the Ministry of Civil Aviation) the following message:

'Fellow passengers in British South American Airways service to Azores January 26th deplore circumstances of death of Polish woman (Orosz). They hope that Court of Enquiry will (?decide) whether it was not a mistake to continue flying when it was apparently at a stage that Polish woman's life was in danger.

'Arrived Azores woman was given number of injections and died in convulsions after a specially stiff one.

'Husband has received permission from Portuguese authorities to take back body to England. Amongst passengers is a hospital nurse. Her narrative follows.'

(Narrative not included)

With reference to this cable, the following comments may be made:

(1) The Captain states categorically that at no time was it suggested to him that the aircraft should put back. He himself spoke to the husband of the deceased passenger when the aircraft was approximately over Finisterre in order to decide whether to continue or to put into Lisbon, and at this stage he was assured by the husband that Mrs Orosz was recovering.

(2) The statement that at the Azores a number of injections were given and that the passenger died following convulsions after a specially stiff injection is purely hearsay evidence seeing that no-one but the doctor was present when the injections were made. In any case, what happened when Mrs Orosz was under the doctor's care is no responsibility of the Company.

The Solicitors acting on behalf of the husband have written attributing the woman's death to negligence on the Company's part, and they have also called to see me. All question of liability has been repudiated, and I am convinced that the Solicitors themselves realise the weakness of their case. I have informed the husband and the Solicitors that so long as they contend that the Company is in any way liable for what has occurred, the Company must also take up a strictly legal attitude.

Apart from the note in the telegram saying that the nurse's narrative follows, there is no record of any 'narrative' from a nurse existing and no one seems to have either seen it or known anything about it except Urquhart.

By the end of April Urquhart had returned from Caracas and had been posted, as Minister Plenipotentiary, to the British Embassy in Washington from where he contacted a Mr W. Evans at the MCA, telling him:

Edden told me that you would welcome a word with me about the BSAA flight of January 26th last, in the course of which a Polish woman suffered a seizure and died later in the Azores. I rang your office several times, but you were away at meetings and so forth, and in the result I had to rush off without discussing the affair with you.

I will admit frankly from the outset that I feel somewhat strongly about what happened, as did most of my fellow passengers. When the trouble first began I held aloof, regarding it as a matter for the pilot, as captain of the ship, and his officers to cope with; but it was presently evident to most of us that they failed to rise to the occasion, and, what was worse, there was evidence of desire to hush it all up and suppress any fact which might be unpleasant. This is more than the average British citizen with a normal sense of public spirit could endure, and it was only my assurance to certain other passengers that the case would, I felt sure, be carefully gone into by the proper officials, which restrained them from taking action themselves. I should like to feel sure that I have not in any way misled these other passengers.

I gather that the pilot has been exonerated on the ground that he was not at any time asked to put down to ground. The distraught husband, as a matter of fact, was begging all and sundry in broken English, French and German to have the plane go down, since, as he rightly said, it would be dreadful for his wife to be left in that condition for the further 8 hours of the flight to the Azores. What the pilot was actually asked to do, I do not know. I do know that the stewardess several times ran forward to the cockpit with every sign of consternation on her face, and she later spontaneously said to me that she really thought the woman was dead at one stage. I cannot believe that she failed to say as much to the pilot. Now it is an extraordinary fact that the pilot did not at the material time leave his cockpit and come back to see for himself what was happening. He did not appear among the passengers until he went to the lavatory at the rear of the plane, which was a very long time after the crisis had passed, and even then he did not give his first attention to the prostrate passenger. He passed her by on his way aft without a glance and then worked his way forward, exchanging a few words with each passenger in the conventional way. It was only when he came to the hospital nurse, sitting over the gangway from the unconscious woman, and asked her how she felt that he got the sharp retort that she was all right, but there was a woman seriously ill on the other side of him. The nurse commented on this later in terms of great indignation. There is no doubt that he was a weak man who shrank from facts which might compel him to make a decision to go down. He took a chance hoping that the woman wasn't really ill and his evasion may easily have cost her her life.

If a pilot can get by with the excuse that 'nobody asked me to go down', when he knows that one of his passengers is in sudden danger of dying, then our standards are low indeed. I may add that the Station Manager at the Azores, commenting on this aspect of the affair, said that of course there were a score of places where the pilot could have come down in France.

I understand also that the deceased woman was described as abnormal, having tuberculosis and what not. A strong effort was made at the Azores to get us to say that she had appeared abnormal, but as I happened to be the one to help her into the plane I know that she showed every sign of normality as she went in and was not in the least excited. I agree, of course, that I know nothing of the state, for example, of her lungs, but is it really the case that the Portuguese doctor can cover up his gross incompetence like this? In my telegram I mentioned that the body was being taken to

England so that an independent examination could be made (I am assuming that my information is correct and no such independent examination was, in fact, made). I quote the Station Manager at the Azores again; he himself agreed that the Portuguese doctor was no good and one only has to hear the husband's account to know how grossly incompetent he was, even when due allowance is made for the exaggeration and bias of the husband. The hospital nurse was there offering to help and give information about what she observed on the flight, but no attempt was made to question her. All this makes it the more deplorable that the pilot did not land in France, where medical facilities would have been better than in the Azores.

The affair really stinks and many people, including foreigners, have smelled it. We all know that the BSAA are facing great difficulties and shortages, but I do suggest that it will not help them in the long run if an affair of this kind is glossed over.

If I have misstated anything I apologise in advance. I have not been informed in detail of what has been decided and it may be that the affair is not in the slightest danger of being 'glossed over'.

The man from the Foreign Office had another card up his sleeve in what now appeared to be a vendetta against BSAA. Obviously annoyed that his complaints had not resulted in some sort of action being taken against Captain Alabaster or the airline, he wrote to BSAA in April demanding a refund of his air fare. Don Bennett was furious; so furious that he dashed off a letter to the MCA advising the contents of Urquhart's letter and saying:

The reason for drawing your attention to this is that the passenger in question R. W. Urquhart is in the Foreign Office and appears to have taken advantage of his position to do as much damage to this Air Line as possible.

He was on a service which had a maximum of misfortunes in the way of weather, of technical difficulties and in addition one of the passengers died while on the ground at the Azores. The circumstances of this death have been investigated in an entirely proper manner and the causes are entirely unassociated with flying or with anything done by BSAA.

Mr Urquhart while on the trip assumed a position of antagonism to BSAA and did his best to damage our good name in every way possible. He interfered in matters of which he had no knowledge and spread rumours amongst the passengers quite unfounded on fact.

All of this might very well have been overlooked but we have now received a letter on official Foreign Office paper demanding a refund of the fare paid by the Foreign Office for his passage. Obviously as he was carried to his destination there is no question of a refund but as it appears that Mr Urquhart is determined to damage this Air Line to the maximum we feel we should draw your attention to his action. You may care to make enquiries at the Foreign Office.

His grounds incidentally for the refund of the fare are that he contracted pneumonia and for reasons of which we are not quite clear he assumes that it is the responsibility of BSAA. While appreciating that in this instance the passenger suffered considerable discomfort and inconvenience due to weather and technical difficulties and while apologising to him for these factors, we feel it is most regrettable that a member of the Foreign Office should take up the attitude which Mr Urquhart has adopted. It is for this reason that we wish to draw the attention of the MCA to this case.

Sixty years after the event it is difficult to see why Urquhart reacted so vehemently to what had happened. Perhaps it was just because, as a husband and a father of girls, he was upset at having witnessed the illness and untimely death of such a young woman. But that does not explain why, three months after the death of Mrs Orosz, he was still actively trying to apportion blame in a situation where he was not in possession of all the facts. Several things in his account of the flight do not seem to add up.

If he really was as outraged as he maintained and wanted to do something about the airline and the crew that he felt were to blame, why did he wait until he reached Natal to dispatch his complaint, when the facilities in Santa Maria were perfectly adequate for him to send a telegram immediately? In his initial report he mentioned the nurse who, he said, had also made a report which was supposed to have followed his. If she did do this, what happened to it and why does it not appear with all the other official records of the case? He also maintained that most of the other passengers felt as strongly as he did but this claim does not seem to be borne out, as no other passenger made a complaint about the conduct of the crew or the fact that the aircraft flew on to its intended transit stop rather than make an intermediate landing. Although Urquhart said that there was an attempt to hush up and suppress any unpleasant facts, no one else has ever spoken officially about any such attempt. Surely if the other passengers felt as outraged as he says they did there would be some evidence of this? His own complaints have been noted and filed; where are those of the other passengers?

Then there is the question of the crew. If Urquhart is to be believed then the captain, the Stargirl and the BSAA Station Manager at Santa Maria all must have lied. Since Mrs Orosz had tuberculosis and heart problems and did not die until after she had received treatment from a doctor, whose only link to BSAA was that he was the airport doctor at a place to which the airline operated, why would any of them have needed to lie about the circumstances of her death? Perhaps Urquhart merely took their comments out of context. Perhaps when he said that the Stargirl thought at one stage that Mrs Orosz was dead, he was speaking the truth; the passenger had, after all, fainted. When Mr Orosz went and sat down and smoked a cigarette, it would be reasonable to assume that the Stargirl then believed that Mrs Orosz was feeling better. The detail about the cigarette is contained in the Station Manager's report, but he was on the ground in Santa Maria at the time that this incident occurred, so must have been told about it either by the Stargirl or by another passenger. He may even have been told by Captain Alabaster since, despite Urquhart's allegation that he did not come and see how Mrs Orosz was himself, the Station Manager's report says that the pilot spoke to the passenger's husband while the aircraft was overhead Finisterre and that he had been assured that Mrs Orosz was recovering. He did, however, reduce height to allow her to breathe more easily. When he then went to the lavatory and stopped to exchange pleasantries with the passengers, it would not have been unusual for him to bypass the 'unconscious woman', merely believing her to be asleep. Urquhart's comments about the pilot being a weak man are simply bizarre. How could he form this judgement of a man who *he* says stayed in his cockpit and only emerged to visit the lavatory and chat to a few passengers? He does not even seem to have known Captain Alabaster's name; it was not mentioned once in either his telegram or the subsequent lengthy report he made from Washington.

Why did Urquhart not think it strange that a man, who he claimed was frantic about his wife's health, sat down next to her and lit a cigarette, knowing that she had tuberculosis and breathing problems? He appeared to believe that the fact that Mrs Orosz had 'tuberculosis and what not', whatever he meant by 'what not', had no relevance to her death and not only blamed BSAA and the crew, but the Portuguese doctor as well. One wonders on what he based his opinions of Portuguese medical facilities. He could not have made an impartial judgement on the actual doctor concerned anyway since he was not present when the examination of Mrs Orosz took place.

Perhaps the most curious of all Urquhart's comments was the one in which he said: 'The affair really stinks and many people, including foreigners, have smelled it. We all know that the BSAA are facing great difficulties and shortages, but I do suggest that it will not help them in the long run if an affair of this kind is glossed over.'

BSAA had, of course, had difficulties. In common with many other airlines of the time there had been accidents as well as problems with BOAC, PAA and with the attitude of the government, but how would Urquhart have known about these unless someone had tipped him off about them? In the beginning of 1947, the airline was doing rather well. When its financial results were published the following year it would be shown that, in contrast to both BOAC and BEA, BSAA had actually made a profit for the period ending 31 March 1947.

Mr Evans at the MCA, the recipient of the report from Washington, also seems to have been puzzled about Urquhart's attitude. In a note that he wrote in May 1947 to accompany all the paperwork that had so far been collected about the case he said:

> I am at a loss to know how to deal with Mr Urquhart's letter. We cannot be the judge between his story and that of the captain. In any case, Mr Urquhart was travelling only as an ordinary member of the public and the question of how the matter should be handled by BSAA is one for their management and not for us. I think, however, that we might put the case to A/VM Bennett for his comments, but for the fact that Mr Urquhart's letter might amount to libel, and I do not think we should send a copy of it to BSAA (particularly with A/VM Bennett in his present mood on the question) unless we have legal advice on whether it constitutes a libel or not.

Urquhart may have been right when he said that the 'affair stinks'. A closer examination of Jagwida Orosz's husband, Stanislaw, revealed that he also was trying to damage BSAA but for a rather different reason. Following his return from Santa Maria with his wife's body, he had been busy. Having eventually decided, while in the Azores, that he wanted his wife to be buried in Huddersfield (presumably the place where they were living before embarking on the flight) he changed his mind and had her body taken back to Poland by ship. He then engaged his first solicitor but, realising he had a weak case against BSAA, he consulted another London solicitor, Henry Snowman.

Snowman wrote to Urquhart in May 1947 addressing his letter to the MCA, believing that he worked there. He said he understood that Urquhart had a memorandum signed by all the passengers and requested him to call and arrange a meeting. He was quickly informed by the Ministry that Urquhart was at the British Embassy in Washington.

By July 1947 Orosz had engaged another London solicitor, Evill & Coleman. They wrote to the MCA to say that they were now acting on behalf of Mr Orosz and giving details of the complaint against the airline which included the 'facts' that the aircraft only had enough oxygen on board for a few minutes and that the pilot refused to land. Evill & Coleman did not get any satisfactory results and Orosz sacked them, engaging Wildman & Co.

Lawrence J. Wildman met R. Stuart Kinsey, an MCA official, on 5 December and, as a result, Kinsey made an allegation of unprofessional conduct against the solicitor. Since Kinsey had not been involved with the case from the beginning he requested that all the paperwork be brought to his office for the meeting. While he was waiting for it to arrive he slipped out of his office for a moment. When he returned he found that the papers had been delivered and Wildman had rifled through them, reading the report made by Urquhart from Washington. Kinsey believed that if Wildman had not been able to look at these papers, which were marked confidential, he would never have known about the report. Knowing that the papers were confidential it was also rather remiss of Kinsey to leave the solicitor in a situation where he had unsupervised access to them, unless he wanted him to take a look. A few days after this meeting Wildman sent a letter to the MCA requesting a copy of the report. The request was denied.

Obviously encouraged by his discovery, Wildman wrote on 20 February 1948 to the Attorney General, the Right Honourable Sir Hartley Shawcross, apprising him of what he considered were the facts and asking for his assistance in obtaining the names and addresses of the other passengers, the protest signed in the Azores and the 'allegation of criminal negligence sent by Mr Urquhart to the Ministry of Civil Aviation'. He informed him that he had been invited by the Coroner for St Pancras to make this request on his behalf. Something about the letter troubled the Attorney General as he sent a copy of it to the MCA asking that it be forwarded to the coroner, Mr (later Sir) Bentley Purchase, for clarification. The MCA, in a covering letter to Bentley Purchase, tried to distance itself by stating that its 'attention has only been brought to the case by the receipt of Mr Urquhart's report'.

In view of some of the patently ridiculous suggestions made in Wildman's letter it is no wonder that Shawcross was troubled. Wildman alleged that:

The plane was not airworthy in so far as the four engines were defective, the supports to the wings were not adequate, the oxygen apparatus was broken, there were no medical supplies on the plane, and it was not possible for the plane to come down over water.

He also stated that:

. . . the deceased complained of lack of air and was unable to breathe. The husband requested the Piolot [*sic*] to come down but this he refused to do and continued with the flight until he reached Azores.

On arrival at Azores the passengers were sent to a hotel for 5 hours and four new engines arrived, having been flown out from England. The four new engines were fitted to the plane before it was able to continue the journey.

The passengers held a Protest Meeting and all signed a protest against the criminally negligent manner in which the plane was manipulated, as during the flight the plane was continually gaining and losing height with such frequency as to cause alarm to the passengers. Furthermore the visible movement of the wings caused them fear and alarm.

. . . The body was flown back to England and a Post Mortem examination was held some seven days after the death. . . . The examination was conducted in a hurried manner and Mr Orosz being unable to explain himself adequately in English was much dissatisfied with the failure to hold an Inquest or Enquiry whereat verbal evidence could be taken as to the cause of death.

Subsequently Mr Orosz obtained translations of Medical Evidence dealing with the condition of the deceased prior to making the journey which establishes she was in good health. A further medical report which has now been forwarded to the Coroner, Mr Bentley Purchase, disclosed that the death was due to the effects of the ordeal in the plane.

Our client has requested us to respectfully point out that in his opinion the death was entirely due to the fact that the pilot refused to bring the plane to land on a French airfield. It is submitted that his apprehension that the defects in the plane would be discovered to the disadvantage of the company on a foreign airfield was not sufficient justification for his refusal to assist a woman in extremis.

The letter concluded with the solicitor referring to his client as 'Mr Stanislaw Azores'.

It is almost incredible that a supposedly educated man such as a solicitor could have written such drivel about the state of the aeroplane. It had not needed four new engines but one. Engine changes are sometimes necessary, then and, indeed, now; wings do flex somewhat – without that flexing they would break off – and it is hardly surprising that the aircraft could not 'come down over water'; it was a Lancastrian not a flying boat. His comments about Mrs Orosz being in good health, when her death certificate stated that she had died of pulmonary tuberculosis and heart problems, would suggest that his knowledge of medical matters was as poor as his knowledge of aviation.

The lack of an inquest leads one to believe that Bentley Purchase, a coroner with an impeccable reputation, was also not taken in by the ridiculous allegations and must have been satisfied with the reasons shown on the death certificate and the subsequent findings of the post mortem.

On the same day that Wildman wrote his preposterous letter, 20 February 1948, an article appeared in the *Daily Express* under the headline 'Woman Dies: Airline gets a Writ'. More correspondence was exchanged between all the various departments concerned and these were joined by BSAA's solicitor, Beaumont & Son, seeking information for the impending proceedings. By the beginning of May, however, everything seems to have ground to a halt.

In view of the next development in this bizarre affair it is strange that Stanislaw Orosz made such a fuss and drew so much attention to himself in the year following his wife's death. It is also odd that no one thought to question how a displaced person, supposedly with little knowledge of the English language, managed to afford and instruct no less than four London solicitors, unless he had help from someone.

Sometime in early 1948 Captain Cliff Alabaster received a visit from a Scotland Yard detective investigating the death of Mrs Orosz. He was not investigating the case against the airline, however. On the contrary, the investigation centred on the possible murder of Mrs Orosz by her husband. It emerged that Orosz had been married before and his first wife had also had tuberculosis, contracted while living in a camp during the latter days of the war. Orosz saw the illness as a way to make money and decided to take his first wife on an aircraft where he knew the altitude would affect her breathing. The poor woman had died as a result of this flight and her husband had picked up a big insurance cheque.

Finding the second Mrs Orosz also had tuberculosis (or perhaps seeking a sufferer of tuberculosis for his second wife) Orosz bought tickets to Bogota, a city 8,600ft above sea level where even the fittest of people can be affected by the altitude. He boarded the aircraft with his sick wife knowing that if the flight did not kill her, the altitude in Bogota almost certainly would. This seems to explain his attitude on the aircraft, his first request to have his wife buried in the Azores and his refusal to allow a post mortem; if the airport doctor had suspected any of this perhaps it explains his initial refusal to issue a death certificate and his relief that there was no post mortem held in Santa Maria.

Although expecting to hear the outcome of the police enquiry, no more news filtered through to Captain Alabaster. BSAA was not sued by Orosz and his own fate remains unclear as the police file on the case has not survived.

Bob Urquhart, as he was known to friends and colleagues at the time, was knighted in 1950 and retired in 1955, ending his diplomatic career as Ambassador Extraordinary and Plenipotentiary in Venezuela. He died in 1983 and there appears to be no further official record of his involvement in the case of the death of Mrs Orosz either.

Other records concerning Urquhart do exist. In his dealings with others in his own job he seems to have been far more cautious than his behaviour with BSAA would suggest. One of his letters, written to a colleague, said, 'More important, of course, than merely getting evidence is getting at the facts.' He does not appear to have felt any such constraints in the matter of BSAA and Mrs Orosz. Could it have been because he knew that he did not need the facts in this case; he merely needed to make a fuss? Were his actions taken out of concern for the sick woman and her devious husband or was he prompted by something or someone else to damage the airline? It seems that we will never know for sure.

Chapter 9

STENDEC

In 1934 Sir Alan Cobham had founded his new company, Flight Refuelling Ltd (FRL), to explore and test the possibilities of in-flight refuelling. Several trials had been made including those in which Don Bennett and Gordon Store had participated, flying at the time for Imperial Airways.

In 1946 more trials were considered by the MCA and Ministry of Supply and BSAA was asked if it would cooperate. Seeing how beneficial in-flight refuelling could be to the airline, the company agreed. The aircraft which would be used by BSAA were two Lancasters belonging to FRL, based at Ford in Sussex, which had been converted to receiver aircraft; two more were changed to tankers.

The initial trials were conducted between July and October over the English Channel and the Home Counties and proved to be successful. It was then decided that they were ready to test the system under operational conditions and, at the end of January 1947, J.W. Kenny, Don Bennett's technical assistant, contacted the MCA to ask for its help in arranging permission from the Brazilian government to operate weekly flight trials commencing in April and continuing for approximately three months. It was proposed to fly the aircraft direct from London to Natal, crossing the South Atlantic at its narrowest point, and to refuel them from tanker aircraft which would be based in Dakar. BSAA did not intend to carry either passengers or freight on these flights, but left open the possibility of transporting company stores and spare parts.

Two weeks later Sir Alan Cobham contacted the MCA himself to advise it of a change in plans. Rather than test the refuelling system over the South Atlantic they had decided to fly the North Atlantic route, refuelling the aircraft between Santa Maria in the Azores and Bermuda, thus allowing a non-stop flight between London and Bermuda.

Due to complications in setting up the tanker base in the Azores and in getting the aircraft ready, the trials were delayed until the end of May. The first flight took place on 28 May with Bennett piloting the receiver aircraft

and David Prowse of Flight Refuelling at the controls of the tanker. On board
the receiver, in addition to the Air Vice-Marshal, were John Wheatley as First
Officer, Radio Operator Bob Chandler, an engineer from FRL named Chalky
White, two more radio operators and Sir Alan Cobham.

The aircraft took off from London at 09.00 and headed for Bermuda. It
was planned to rendezvous with the tanker off Lagens on the island of Flores
in the Azores. When the receiver aircraft was within range of the island
Chandler waited anxiously for a signal to let him know that the tanker had
left its base at Santa Maria and was delighted to hear that it was on time
and on course for the rendezvous. He soon picked up a blip on the Rebecca
cathode ray tube which announced that the tanker was nearby. Soon it was
flying overhead; the fuel hose was connected to it by Chalky White and the
transfer of fuel began. On that first flight 2,000 gallons were transferred
taking just 35 minutes, with the aircraft flying at a height of 8,000ft. The
extra fuel was stored in a special belly tank and was pumped up to the wing
tanks when they began to empty.

According to Bob Chandler in his book *Off the Beam*:

> . . . the AVM had been transferring fuel from the belly tank to the wing
> tanks and found that things were not going well. I found that we had
> burned out both generators. Everything electrical was switched off to save
> the aircraft accumulators to drive the transfer pump to empty the belly tank
> into the wing tanks. This was done and we finished with a dead flat battery.
> The AVM set himself to navigate by astro but we soon ran under cover of
> high cloud and were reduced to dead reckoning.

Bennett proved himself to be an excellent navigator because, despite the
difficulties and although somewhat late, the crew spotted the Cooks Point
lighthouse in Bermuda and landed safely at Kindley Field 20 hours after
leaving London. The tanker aircraft had only needed to be away from its
home base for 1 hour and 34 minutes. Although this was much quicker than
the normal time taken between London and Bermuda, one of the test flights
produced an amazing time of 13 hours 59 minutes, achieved by taking a
direct route between the two airports which entailed the tanker aircraft flying
out to meet it 450 miles from its base at Santa Maria.

Eleven return trips were made and of the twenty-two single sectors only two
were unsuccessful. Once the receiver aircraft developed engine trouble and

had to divert to Santa Maria without having attempted a refuelling; on the other trip it diverted after the two aircraft failed to find each other in time for the refuelling to take place.

The actual procedures used were quite simple. The receiver aircraft's flight plan was signalled to the tanker base before take-off and during flight it signalled position reports, its estimated time of arrival at the rendezvous point and the amount of fuel it needed. When the aircraft was approximately 300 miles away it established wireless contact with the tanker and at a distance of between 70 to 100 miles VHF contact was established. The final contact was made with Eureka/Rebecca radar equipment and by visual sightings. On the westbound flights where the distance still to be travelled was much greater, the amount of fuel transferred was usually around 2,000 gallons which took anything up to 40 minutes. On the return eastbound trip only 1,000 gallons was needed and this transfer could be accomplished in as little as 19 minutes.

The trials were deemed to have been a great success and were well publicised as several of the flights had carried both British and foreign press. The BSAA crews who took part in the trials were varied but the consensus of opinion was that the refuelled flights, although longer than those done in two hops, were much less tiring due to not having to make intermediate landings with all the attendant formalities they had to deal with. Although the payload could not be increased with in-flight refuelling it was felt that the procedure would be worthwhile for the speed and convenience that it afforded both passengers and airline alike.

Later, in 1948, BOAC also took part in trials which were encouraged by the MCA and BSAA asked for modifications to be made to the Tudor V so that in-flight refuelling could be done with this aircraft type also. The company later changed its mind when it began using Tudor IVs in preference to the Tudor V and the procedure was never taken up for the commercial flights of either company.

Although the refuelling trials had been successful and the airline was beginning to recover after the events at Dakar in the spring, the company was hit by yet another tragedy in the summer of 1947.

* * *

Three of the aircraft lost by BSAA resulted in their complete disappearance, presenting accident investigators with the almost impossible task of trying to ascertain what happened, without any evidence from wreckage to help them. Two of these aircraft were the Avro Tudors *Star Tiger* and *Star Ariel*; the third was the Avro Lancastrian G-AGWH *Star Dust*, which was to make newspaper headlines nearly fifty-three years later when, remarkably, wreckage was discovered on Mount Tupungato, high in the Andes.

The publicity generated by the discovery of the wreckage in early 2000 was both good and bad. The good thing was that it brought BSAA to the attention of many people who until then had only a passing interest in aviation, and for some it made them curious to find out more about this pioneering airline. The downside was that it also attracted the attention of many journalists who spotted the opportunity to publish material about the airline which was embellished with enough sensationalism to sell their work, but which in some cases showed scant regard for the facts in order to do so. Consequently, many people who have only read about BSAA in some of the more far-fetched stories about *Star Dust* will not see beyond the exaggerations to the real truth about the airline, its generally highly competent crews and its forward-thinking and talented chief executive.

* * *

In 1947 the BSAA route for passengers wishing to travel to Santiago, Chile was from London to Lisbon (5 hours 10 minutes flying time), Lisbon to Dakar (8 hours 40 minutes), the long crossing from Dakar to Natal (9 hours 10 minutes) then Natal to Rio de Janeiro (6 hours 35 minutes). There followed an overnight stop in Rio before the flight resumed at midday the following day for the 5 hours 50 minutes leg to Montevideo. Leaving Montevideo at 18.40, the flight was scheduled to arrive in Buenos Aires 1 hour and 15 minutes later, where the aircraft would be changed in preparation for the approximately 4 hours 30 minutes final leg to Santiago, leaving on the following day at 13.55. By today's standards this was a long and gruelling flight, but in 1947 the alternative means of travel were so much slower (surface travel to Santiago took 22 days) that the passengers were willing to pay the £352 16s 0d return fare (the equivalent of over £9,200 today) to travel by air. The high cost of airline tickets in the late 1940s, relative to today's very cheap fares, meant that typically BSAA passengers tended to be businessmen, government officials or wealthy families; such was the case with *Star Dust*.

The passenger list for BSAA service CS59 on 2 August 1947 was as follows: Paul Simpson, King's Messenger, carrying a diplomatic bag (embarked at

Buenos Aires); Martha Limpert, elderly German lady who had been held by the British after the war and was returning home to her family in Chile; Peter Young, British businessman (embarked at Buenos Aires); Casis Said Atallah, Palestinian businessman; Harald Pagh, Swiss businessman; Eric John Gooderham, British businessman (embarked at Buenos Aires).

There was a crew of five on board *Star Dust*, comprising Captain Reginald James Cook, First Officer Norman Hilton Cook, Second Officer Donald S. Checklin, Radio Officer Dennis B. Harmer and Stargirl Iris Moreen Evans. Captain Cook was 29 years old and, like many of the BSAA pilots, had previously served as a pilot in the RAF. He had joined BSAA fifteen months earlier in May 1946. His total flying time was 1,971 hours during which he had flown many types including the Mosquito, Lancaster, Viking, Lancastrian and York. His total time on the Lancastrian was just under 438 hours, of which 39 hours were as captain, all of them on a flight-refuelled service from London direct to Bermuda and return, with refuelling taking place off the Azores. Flight CS59 was Reginald Cook's last flight from London to Buenos Aires as captain of a York, and his first flight as captain of a trans-Andean Lancastrian, although he had crossed the Andes eight times before as a first officer. In addition to his pilot's licence, Captain Cook held a First Class Navigator's licence.

Norman Cook, the First Officer, was 30 years old and was also an ex-RAF pilot. He had a total of 2,129 flying hours in his logbook and like the Captain held a valid First Class Navigator's licence. His flying time in Lancastrians was 127 hours and this was to be his first Andes crossing. The Second Officer, Donald Checklin, was a 27-year-old ex-RAF pilot who had a total of 2,074 hours in his logbook, of which only 34 hours were in Lancastrians, although he had already made the Andes crossing four times. The three pilots aboard *Star Dust* had a combined total flying time of nearly 6,200 hours, which considering their comparative youth, made them experienced pilots.

Although Flight CS59 from London to Buenos Aires was flown by an Avro York, the final leg from Morón airport in Buenos Aires to Santiago was always operated by an Avro Lancastrian, due to the type being more suitable for the high altitude crossing of the Andes. The only area in which the Lancastrian was poorly equipped for this route was in radio navigation equipment. There was a Eureka beacon at Los Cerrillos airport in Santiago, consisting of a small box near the control tower transmitting a signal for incoming aircraft to home on to, but apart from this basic navigational aid the BSAA crews flying the

Andes had to rely on their radio compass and the accuracy of their dead reckoning navigation. Unfortunately this needs clear sight of the ground to calculate the wind speed and drift, a luxury the crew of *Star Dust* did not have. It is also known that HF radio communication was almost impossible in the weather conditions *Star Dust* encountered, therefore the crew communicated solely using Morse.

Captain Cook and his crew had brought in York *Star Venture* from London the previous day and, with the same crew, Lancastrian *Star Dust* lifted off from the Buenos Aires runway at 13.46 GMT on 2 August, bound for Santiago. Although some rumours have circulated that BSAA aircraft made the Andes crossing with the bare minimum of fuel, *Star Dust* took off with 1,380 gallons in its tanks, enough for a duration of over 6 hours 30 minutes. The flight plan estimated a flight time of only 3 hours 50 minutes.

There were three recognised routes in 1947 for making the westbound Andes crossing. These were the central (direct) route which was either via or slightly south of Mendoza, the northern route via San Juan and the southern route via Planchón. The decision of which of the three routes to take was always made by the captain, but only after a careful study of the predicted weather in the mountains. Crews were always briefed to avoid the central route in the event of bad weather and wherever possible to avoid flying into cloud over the mountains due to the extreme turbulence often encountered in the cloud tops. The weather forecast given to Captain Cook was based on the synoptic chart for 20.00 on the previous day augmented by the Buenos Aires forecast timed at 13.00 on the day of the flight. It painted a picture of clear weather from Buenos Aires as far as Mendoza, but thereafter the cloud base was down to zero in the mountain passes with very limited horizontal visibility. Once clear of the Andes on the western side, the clouds would be more scattered for the final leg of the flight into Santiago. The forecast also warned of snowstorms in the mountains with moderate to intense turbulence. Crucially, the forecast for the upper winds was given as: 'W. 17/22 knots rotating to N.W. 17 knots towards Mendoza: S.W. 33 knots in the passes.'

The actual weather at Mendoza at 18.00 was stated as 'overcast with blue holes'. There was a large layer of cloud between 10,000ft and 20,000ft and it is believed that due to the weather conditions at the time, Captain Cook would not have been able to see the ground at Mendoza at all. The actual weather on the central (direct) route at the El Cristo Pass for the period 12.00–18.00 was that the pass was in cloud and it was snowing. A 33 knots gale had started at 12.00 and increased to 45 knots by 20.00. There were gusts of wind during that period of around 60 knots. The actual weather at Santiago around the time contact with the aircraft was lost was eight-tenths cloud with bases between 10,000ft and 20,000ft. Visibility was said to be 5 to 8 miles and improving, with light winds from the south-south-west. A forecast and weather report was sent to *Star Dust* from Santiago at 16.45 and it was acknowledged by the aircraft. The only difference between this report and those given previously was that the cloud tops were estimated as being at 23,000ft.

It has been suggested that Captain Cook, as a result of this 16.45 forecast, may have decided to fly above the cloud tops in clear air. Furthermore, if he had been unable to break clear of cloud, meteorologists believe that the aircraft would have been in icing conditions. This is a possibility, but unlikely to have been a contributory factor in the accident.

The Lancastrian aircraft was fitted at the factory with a de-icing system on the propellers, wings and tail surfaces. In the case of the propellers, this consisted of two tanks of de-icing fluid (one in each wheel well) and electric pumps which drew the fluid from the tanks to 'slinger' rings mounted on the rear of each propeller hub. The effect of these rings was to deliver de-icing fluid by centrifugal force along the leading edge of each propeller blade so that it would be naturally spread across the surface. The system for delivering de-icing fluid to the wings and tail surfaces was a Dunlop design, which consisted of a broad strip of fabric wick which was covered with a fine metal gauze and cemented to the leading edges of the aerofoils before being further strengthened by metal strips riveted in place. The de-icing fluid was pumped to various points along the leading edges of the wings, tailplane and fins, where it would seep slowly through the gauze and be blown back by the slipstream over the entire surface, including the ailerons, elevators and rudders. The fluid for the flying surfaces was supplied from a 20-gallon tank in the centre section of the aircraft. This system was proven to be effective in not only preventing ice-build up, but in loosening ice which had already adhered to the wings by slowly creeping under the surface of the ice and allowing it to be removed by the slipstream. The fluid was capable of being delivered either automatically, or via a manual switch. The automatic system was triggered by the use of a small pitot head device mounted under the nose of the aircraft. As soon as this started to ice-up, the pump operated and a green light illuminated on the instrument panel. It would be very surprising if Captain Cook had not armed the automatic system before climbing to altitude to make the Andes crossing. Even if this simple precaution had been overlooked, there was an emergency switch to be used when ice had built up to such an extent that it was affecting the handling of the aircraft. If used in this mode, the system was capable of shifting ice a quarter of an inch thick. The fluid in the tank was sufficient for 5½ hours use in normal mode, or up to 1 hour 5 minutes in emergency mode. As none of the radio messages transmitted from *Star Dust* mentioned any icing problems it seems very unlikely that airframe icing contributed to the loss of the aircraft.

The following position reports were received from the aircraft:

15.07   33° 55' S. 62° 33' W. Height 10,000ft, course 286°, speed 196 knots, ETA Santiago 17.30

16.00   33° 25' S. 65° 30' W. Height 10,000ft, course 282°, speed 196 knots, ETA Santiago 17.30

17.00   32° 50' S. 68° 30' W. Height 20,000ft, ascending to 24,000ft, speed 194 knots, ETA Santiago 17.43

17.33   ETA Santiago 17.45

17.41   ETA Santiago 17.45. STENDEC

Clearly when the last message was sent at 17.41 the crew believed they were only four minutes from Santiago. They never arrived. After repeated attempts to contact the aircraft, the alarm was raised at 18.15 by the air traffic controller at Los Cerrillos and was relayed to BSAA via the controller at Mendoza. By 20.15 the aircraft was known to be down somewhere as by then its tanks would have been empty. The question was, where? Both Chilean and Argentine armies sent search parties into the mountains along the border between the two countries. The ground search was also joined by hundreds of civilians who ventured into the Andes on foot and on skis, hoping to find survivors from the Lancastrian. The Argentine Air Force initiated the aerial search the following day and were assisted by civilian aircraft of the American airline Panagra and the Chilean national airline LAN. The Chilean Air Force joined the search on 5 August.

As soon as the news of the disappearance reached London, Don Bennett gathered together as many off-duty BSAA flight crew as he could muster in

1. With speeches made, Air Vice-Marshal Donald Bennett shakes hands with Lord Winster on 1 January 1946 before boarding *Star Light*. A smiling Mrs Bennett can be seen just to the left of Lord Winster. *(Torix Bennett)*

2. With its engines running, *Star Light* is filmed by news crews just before its historic departure from Heathrow. *(Torix Bennett)*

3. A portrait of Air Vice-Marshal Donald Bennett while still a wing commander with 77 Squadron in 1941. *(Torix Bennett)*

4. A rare aerial shot of *Star Light*, on the first international departure from the newly built Heathrow Airport, New Year's Day 1946. *(Torix Bennett)*

5. Company hack Percival Proctor 3 G-AGTH *Star Pixie*, photographed in 1950 when flown by B.F. Collins in the *Daily Express* Air Race. Notice it still retained its BSAA name and 'speedman' logo. This aircraft ended its days in Morocco. *(Authors' collection)*

6. Lancastrian *Star Trail* being loaded with air mail in the specially adapted nose compartment during 1946. (Aeroplane Monthly *via Richard Riding)*

7. Lancastrian G-AGWJ *Star Glow* after its accident while attempting to take off from a poorly laid PSP runway at Bathurst on 30 August 1946. *(Authors' collection)*

8. Avro York G-AHFH *Star Glitter*, was registered with BSAA in March 1946. It was transferred to BOAC at the time of the merger and ended its days in a landing accident in Saudi Arabia in 1962. *(A.J. Jackson collection, Roger Jackson)*

9. A dramatic shot of Avro York G-AHFD *Star Mist* landing at BSAA's maintenance base at Langley. *(British Airways Museum)*

10. Lancastrian G-AGWI *Star Land* which was delivered to BSAA in January 1946. A Stargirl watches as freight is stowed in the nose. Note the chute at the side of the steps, for the swift unloading of freight, and the flag extended through the cockpit window. The aircraft was sold to Flight Refuelling Ltd at the beginning of 1949 and was used on the Berlin Airlift. *(British Airways Museum)*

11. Avro 683 Lancaster I freighter G-AGUL *Star Watch* provides the backdrop for the photo of the BSAA engineering staff at Langley. The aircraft was written off at Heathrow Airport following an accident on landing after a training flight in October 1947. *(via Reg Ottaway)*

12. The interior of an Avro York, showing the comfortable seats and the overhead coat racks. It was decorated in light blue and silver. Note the reading lamps above the windows. *(Avro Heritage Centre)*

13. Avro Tudor IV G-AHNJ *Star Lion*, shortly before being renamed *Star Panther* in the summer of 1947. The second Tudor IV to be delivered to BSAA (G-AHNK) then became *Star Lion*. *(via Richard Riding)*

14. Lancastrian G–AGWK *Star Trail* after striking a radio mast when forced to make a landing attempt during a heavy thunderstorm in Bermuda on 5 September 1947. *(Authors' collection)*

15. The surprisingly spacious and comfortable interior of an Avro Tudor IV. The width of the seats and size of the aisle compare favourably with many modern airliners. *(Torix Bennett)*

16. Lancastrian III G-AGWH *Star Dust* which was lost in the Andes on 2 August 1947. *(via Richard Riding)*

17. Fine study of Avro Tudor IV G-AHNK *Star Lion* at Langley in late 1947. Notice the contemporary cars in the background. *(Authors' collection)*

18. An Avro Lancastrian interior showing the comfortable reclining seats, meal tables, curtains and washroom door at the rear of the cabin; a far cry from the Lancaster bomber from which it was developed. *(Avro Heritage Centre)*

19. The cockpit of an Avro Lancastrian. The RF Indicator and DR Compass Repeater should be shown on the top of the panel just below the windows, but they are missing in this photo. *(Avro Heritage Centre)*

20. Avro York G-AHFC *Star Dew* with BSAA engineers at Langley. Left to right: Jack Hunt, Tim McGarry, Tom Sheridan, Jim Cook, Reg Ottaway and Larry Chaves. *(via Reg Ottaway)*

21. BSAA engineers working on Lancastrian G-AGWJ *Star Glow* in the hangar at Langley in 1946. *(British Airways Museum)*

22. An air to air shot of Avro Tudor IV G-AHNK *Star Lion* on its maiden flight from Woodford on 29 September 1947. *(via Richard Riding)*

23. Stargirl Celia Hepworth welcomes passengers disembarking on a BSAA Lancastrian. (*British Airways Museum*)

24. Two Lancasters belonging to Sir Alan Cobham's Flight Refuelling Ltd. In cooperation with BSAA, successful in-flight refuelling trials were conducted between the Azores and Bermuda in 1947 using the 'looped hose' system. *(Avro Heritage Centre)*

25. Despite having been fitted with a Lancastrian nose cone, the blunt tail of G-AGUM *Star Ward* identifies it as an Avro Lancaster. It was bought by BSAA in 1947 for use as a freighter. *(A.J. Jackson Collection, Roger Jackson)*

26. Lancaster G-AGUM *Star Ward* taxiing back to the hangar at Langley following its near disastrous test flight as a result of fitting the large and ungainly Airtech freight pannier. *(Richard Beddoes)*

27. Air Vice-Marshal Bennett at the controls of Avro Lancaster G-AHJV at the start of the flight refuelling trials to Bermuda on 28 May 1947. (*Torix Bennett*)

28. Tudor V G-AKCC *Star Swift*. Notice the much longer fuselage and blunt nose of the Tudor V compared with the smaller Tudor IVs *Star Leopard* and *Star Panther* parked alongside. (*Richard Riding*)

29. Tudor IV G-AHNN *Star Leopard* in the typical BSAA Tudor IV markings of a large Union Jack on the fin and pale blue cheat line above the cabin windows. (*Richard Riding*)

30. A rare photograph taken in early 1949 of Tudor IVB G-AGRF in BSAA markings, but still displaying its original name *Elizabeth of England*. This aircraft was intended to be the flagship of the BOAC Tudor I fleet, but never entered passenger service with that airline. (*Authors' collection*)

31. A sad end for Lancastrian G-AGWG *Star Light* at Kindley Field, Bermuda. It came to grief during a three-engined emergency landing on 13 November 1947 as a result of an engine fire. (*Authors' collection*)

32. Avro York G-AHFE *Star Vista* on the ground in Lima after belly landing on 13 March 1949. It is a tribute to the smooth touchdown by Captain John Wright that the aircraft suffered relatively little damage. (*Authors' collection*)

33. The unusual and distinctive fuselage markings on Lancastrian II G-AKTB *Star Glory* were painted dark blue. This nine-passenger version of the Lancastrian only served with BSAA for a short period before being sold to Flight Refuelling Ltd. *(Authors' collection)*

34. Tudor V G-AKBZ *Star Falcon* on the Berlin Airlift. Note the fuel pipes trailing from the rear door. These pipes were connected to the 2,300 gallon fuselage tanks as soon as the aircraft landed, allowing the precious cargo of fuel to be loaded and unloaded quickly. *(Roy Day)*

35. In the cockpit of a Tudor V on the Berlin Airlift. By the end of the Airlift, BSAA Tudor Vs had carried out 2,331 flights, transporting over 19,800 tons of fuel into the city. *(Roy Day)*

36. Stargirls Celia Hepworth (left) and Priscilla Vinyals (right) pose in front of a BSAA Avro York. *(British Airways Museum)*

37. Avro York G-AHFG *Star Haze* on the ground at Porto Alegre in Brazil. The aircraft was badly damaged by hailstones during a violent storm and the pilot, Captain 'Wyn' Fieldson received cuts and bruises while struggling with the elements to bring the aircraft safely to the ground. *(Captain E.D. 'Wyn' Fieldson)*

38. Company communications aircraft Avro XIX Anson G-AIKM *Star Visitant* photographed before its forced landing in a field near Luton as a result of fuel starvation on 21 April 1949. *(Authors' collection)*

39. Airspeed Consul G-AIUX *Star Master* used by BSAA in 1949 to evaluate the Sperry Zero Reader. *(A.J. Jackson collection, Roger Jackson)*

40. The BSAA bus bringing passengers from the aircraft to the terminal at the end of their journey. Stargirl Celia Hepworth looks on. *(British Airways Museum)*

41. BSAA crews form a guard of honour as the coffin of their late Chief Executive, Herbert Brackley, is placed in the Avro York G-AHFD *Star Mist* to be flown to his home in Norfolk for burial. *(British Airways Museum)*

42. BSAA staff help passengers to board the Avro Tudor that will take them to South America. Note the size of the doorway which was small as the aircraft was pressurised. The Tudor was the first British airliner with a pressurised passenger cabin. *(British Airways Museum)*

order to mount a search for the missing aircraft. He flew out to Buenos Aires in another Lancastrian and with crew staring intently out of the Lancastrian's windows he spent days flying very low over the mountains, including Tupungato, along valleys barely wider than the wingspan of his aircraft, in a vain search for any sign of *Star Dust* and its crew. He maintained a punishing schedule of flights in order to try and find them, barely stopping for food and rest. Indeed, some of the crew who accompanied him felt it was a futile exercise and they were convinced that they would find no sign of life even if they spotted wreckage, but for Bennett it was a case of continuing regardless until he was absolutely certain that he had done all he possibly could for the crew of *Star Dust* and their passengers.

There was an unusual addition to the aerial search in the form of a privately owned photo-reconnaissance Spitfire XI. The reason for this Spitfire being in Argentina in 1947 is an interesting one. In early 1947 Captain Jaime Storey, an Argentinian volunteer pilot in the RAF during the war, had decided to form a new company specialising in aerial photography. He had recognised that due to the rapid expansion of industry and agriculture in Argentina after the war, there would be a growing market for oblique and vertical aerial photography of agricultural and industrial sites for the purposes of advertising and development. At the time, government mapping projects were being handled by the Argentinian cartographic agency Institute Geografico Militar and it was stipulated that any commercial aerial photography companies must be staffed entirely by Argentinian subjects in the interests of national security.

Captain Storey realised that a large part of his potential work would involve high altitude flights, much of it over the Andes themselves. He knew that hangar space would be at a premium, maintenance costs needed to be low, and he would be operating from small airfields, so he decided that the only aircraft for the job would be a photo-reconnaissance Spitfire. The decision was made easier for him due to the majority of his RAF experience being on Spitfires. Another benefit was that if he procured an ex-RAF aircraft, all the problems of range, camera installation and heating and equipment for high altitude flight would already have been solved.

He obtained a suitable aircraft, a Mk XI (LV-NMZ) which had only flown 20 hours with the RAF before being put into storage, and managed to buy two old Zeiss Contessa Nettel plate cameras which, although made in 1924 were the only cameras to offer the high quality necessary for oblique advertising photographs. The aircraft was also fitted with three Williamson

F.24, F.8 cameras (two vertical and one oblique). The market in Argentina was expanding so rapidly that Captain Storey decided not to waste time in shipping his aircraft from the UK, but instead took the bold decision to fly the Spitfire to Argentina. He worked out a route which took him from Hurn to Buenos Aires via Gibraltar, Dakar, Natal, Rio de Janeiro and Montevideo. The longest leg of this route was the 1,850 mile ocean crossing from Dakar to Natal. To give the Spitfire the range to make this crossing an auxiliary 170-gallon fuel tank was fitted under the centre section and an additional 20-gallon tank was fitted in each wing. This gave a total of nearly 428 gallons of fuel available from the Spitfire's seven tanks.

Realising the flight would be fraught with danger if undertaken alone, Captain Storey approached Air Vice-Marshal Bennett for advice. Bennett kindly agreed that he could fly alongside a scheduled BSAA York service, although it was decided that in the event of bad weather, rather than closing up on the York in such a tight formation that it would cause concern for the passengers aboard the BSAA aircraft, he would break formation and continue on his own. Bennett was concerned that he would receive angry letters from passengers complaining of dangerous flying. The only radio Captain Storey planned to carry was a VHF set to enable him to communicate with the Radio Operator of the York. He estimated that the majority of the journey would be carried out at 185mph at an altitude of 10,000ft. This fitted in well with the planned speed and altitude of the York.

After procuring the aircraft from the Ministry of Supply, preparing it for the long flight and arranging all the necessary paperwork in record time (including a Certificate of Airworthiness), Captain Storey took off from Hurn at 10.50 on 29 April 1947. He flew in formation with the York for part of the way and his journey to Buenos Aires was completed without any problems.

Thus, in the days following the disappearance of *Star Dust*, Captain Storey was able to fly over the Andes, searching for the missing Lancastrian in his Spitfire. It was an ideal aircraft for the task as its manoeuvrability allowed it to search in small valleys, into which it was too dangerous for the larger search aircraft to venture, and its long range tanks meant it could stay airborne for several hours without landing to refuel. Alas, all the aerial searches proved fruitless. Not a trace was found of the missing aircraft. By 21 August the search was called off. *Star Dust* was lost.

The Minister of Civil Aviation called for a full investigation. It soon became clear that neither the Argentine nor Chilean governments at the time were willing to embark on such an enquiry unless it could be proved categorically that the aircraft came down within its borders, a task which was clearly impossible without the evidence of wreckage. Both governments promised their full support and cooperation if the British government wanted to send an investigator to South America to establish the cause of the accident. On 26 August, Major S. Stocks was sent from the Accident Investigation Branch of the MCA to Chile to piece together the final minutes of flight CS59. When his official report was published in December 1947, it was a brief document which was necessarily inconclusive. It stated that Captain Cook should not have attempted to cross by the direct route and that the possibility of severe icing could not be ignored. The actual cause of the accident remained obscure.

The final radio message from *Star Dust* has puzzled people for many years due to the inclusion of the word 'STENDEC' to end the message. The Chilean radio operator said that the reception was very clear but the message was rather hurried. As she did not understand STENDEC she asked the Radio Officer to repeat it. This he did, twice more, and each time she interpreted the same word, STENDEC. Many have assumed that as the message was sent hurriedly, the Radio Officer was dealing with an emergency, or he knew the aircraft was in serious trouble. It would seem more likely that he was hurrying because he believed they were near to Santiago and he wanted to switch to voice telephony to speak to the controller at Los Cerrillos airport. He would have been frustrated that he had to repeat the Morse code message, therefore did so hurriedly.

There have been a great many suggestions over the years from amateur radio enthusiasts and members of the public as to what was meant by Radio Officer Dennis Harmer's message that day. The theories range from the possible to the downright ridiculous. One of the letters received by the MCA (on 11 June 1948) was from A. Harmer, the brother of *Star Dust*'s Radio Officer. He suggested a slight amendment to the spacing of the letters would result in the word VALE or 'farewell' in Latin followed by a C for the last initial of the captain. Another popular theory was that STENDEC is an anagram of DESCENT and the letters were re-arranged due to Harmer suffering from hypoxia after a failure of the oxygen system. This seems highly unlikely. A person suffering hypoxia would not be expected to make the same mistake consistently three times in succession, neither would a normal message be expected to consist of the single word 'descent'.

The actual Morse code which the Chilean Operator believed she received was:

S	T	E	N	D	E	C
...	_	.	_.	_..	.	_._.

The last two letters are of interest, as a recognised sign-off or 'end of message' signal would be 'AR' (with no space between the letters). Therefore a standard signoff could be sent as the Morse '._._.' in other words EC without the space. If the messages from *Star Dust* were sent quickly it is quite conceivable that spaces could be misinterpreted. This still leaves STEND to be explained. Almost without exception, the various theories for the meaning of the message, which were submitted to the MCA at the time, involved moving spaces, or other very subtle changes to create different letters.

Some of the suggestions included:

S	O	S		I	C	E	= Self explanatory
...	___	...		..	_._.	.	

S	T		E	N	D		AR	= star
duST/END/Signoff

| ... | _ | | . | _. | _.. | | ._._. | |

S	T		E	N	D		AR	=
SanTiago/END/Signoff

| ... | _ | | . | _. | _.. | | ._._. | |

V		E	N	D		AR	= message
separator/END/Signoff

| ..._ | | . | _. | _.. | | ._._. | |

S	T	A	R	E	AR	= STandard/ARrival/
East/Signoff

| ... | _ | ._ | ._. | . | ._._. | |

It is impossible to be sure what Dennis Harmer intended his final message to mean. It was almost certainly not STENDEC. Even though the later discovery of the wreckage of *Star Dust* helped us to understand the events of that day in 1947, the word STENDEC will always remain a mystery.

It seems possible that the well publicised 'discovery' of the wreckage in January 2000 was not the first time *Star Dust* and the remains of its passengers and crew had been visited since 1947. Many stories have been circulated over the years of locals finding wreckage of an aircraft high in the Andes. Some of them probably came from unreliable sources and were likely to be influenced by the fact that BSAA offered a reward for anyone who could pinpoint the location of the wreckage. Although *Star Dust* is not the only aircraft to come to grief in that hostile region, rumours suggested that a local man was seen in the 1950s wearing an RAF pilot's wristwatch of the type worn by the crew. When the man was questioned, he said he had found some wreckage in one of the high Andean valleys on the Chile/Argentina border. It was believed at the time that it may have been the Lancastrian. Although this in itself proves nothing, the discovery and looting of aircraft wreckage by locals is not an unusual occurrence. In October 2002 an expedition was mounted to the Sahara in an attempt to find and recover some of the remains of a BOAC Handley Page Hermes which had crash-landed there in May 1952. When the location of the crash site was reached, it was discovered that local Bedouin tribesmen had found the wreckage some years earlier and having used it as a shelter for some time had then systematically broken it up and removed nearly all of it to re-use the scrap metal.

On 7 December 1955, several British newspapers, including *The Times* and the *Daily Telegraph*, carried the story of the discovery of the wreckage of *Star Dust* eight years after it disappeared. The news had been forwarded to them via a BOAC representative, Mr Reid, in Chile. The wreckage had apparently been discovered on the Chilean side of the border, but the person who claimed to have discovered it would not reveal the exact location in the hope that he could negotiate some sort of financial deal for the information. Further investigation by the AIB in Britain revealed that the Chilean authorities were not planning to mount an expedition to the rumoured crash site unless they received firm evidence of its existence. Indeed, since there was still no certainty that the wreckage was on the Chilean side of the border, they made it clear that even if its discovery was proved they would act only if it was on Chilean soil. The BOAC representative wrote to the Ministry of Transport and Civil Aviation in London asking them to make a formal request to Chile to mount an expedition to locate the wreckage as he was being put under pressure by relatives of the victims of the *Star Dust* accident, including the brother of Radio Officer Dennis Harmer. The Ministry declined, as they did not want to influence Chile into mounting an expensive expedition which Britain might subsequently have been asked to finance.

In January 1958 a German mountaineer named Kurt Hoyl claimed to have found the wreckage of the Lancastrian near San Gabriel, high in the Andes. In spite of requests from the Ministry of Transport and Civil Aviation for more information, these claims were never substantiated. Again, on 23 May 1960, *The Times* carried an article about the Chilean Search and Rescue Service having located aircraft wreckage near the peak of the Overo volcano, over 15,000ft above sea level while searching for an Argentinian transport aircraft lost on a flight from Buenos Aires to Panama. *Flight* magazine carried the same story on 3 June 1960, incorrectly referring to *Star Dust* as a Tudor and claiming it was lost on 9 September 1947. The Chilean team were asked by the British authorities if it was possible that the wreckage was that of *Star Dust*, but after examination of fragments, they concluded that it was not.

Nearly fifty-three years after *Star Dust* disappeared, in January 2000, two Argentinian climbers stumbled upon the wreckage of the Lancastrian over 15,000ft up on the slopes of Mount Tupungato, the second highest peak in the Andes. The wreckage was heavily fragmented, as would be expected after an impact with the side of a mountain, but sufficient evidence was discovered to prove beyond any doubt that this time the wreckage found was indeed that of *Star Dust*. Its position appeared to indicate a track at the moment of impact of between 210° and 240°. As well as parts of the Lancastrian, including an engine, a propeller and a wheel with a fully inflated tyre, human remains were found and recovered which were later matched to nine of the eleven people on board using DNA from surviving relatives. An Argentinian Army team was sent up the mountain in February 2000 on an eight-day expedition to recover as much as they could. The recovery and identification of most of the people on board enabled memorial services and funerals to take place, including a funeral on 8 July 2005 for Captain Reginald Cook.

After the discovery and retrieval of parts of the wreckage, Argentinian investigators concluded that the aircraft had encountered the high winds of the jetstream, leading the crew to believe their ground speed was far greater than it actually was due to the strong head wind. As this narrow band of winds can reach speeds of up to 150mph, it seems the crew thought they had already crossed the high mountain peaks and were safely on the western side of the mountains. They would therefore have been descending when the impact occurred. They may also have encountered a phenomenon known as a mountain wave, which occurs when air is disrupted by high mountains to cause swirling downdraughts or rotors which are sometimes sufficiently severe to cause the structural failure of aircraft. If we accept the approximate heading of the aircraft deduced from the wreckage, and its position on Tupungato, it is possible to estimate fairly accurately that *Star Dust* was around 35 miles further east than it should have been and had therefore encountered headwinds of around 100mph. The likelihood is that when the Lancastrian hit the side of the mountain, it triggered an avalanche which immediately covered the wreckage, making it impossible for those searching to find it. Over the years it would have gradually become embedded in a glacier which, after fifty years, had travelled far enough down the mountain for pieces of the wreckage to emerge once more as the ice started to melt.

Many reports have suggested the jetstream was an unknown phenomenon in 1947, despite reports from American B-29 pilots who had encountered unusually high speed winds at high altitudes towards the end of the Second World War. Evidence at the National Archives in Kew indicates that not only was it known about, but that Bennett himself had been pressing the British government for assistance with research into the phenomenon as early as 1945.

He had written a letter on 14 December 1945 to the Ministry of Civil Aviation asking whether two de Havilland Mosquito aircraft could be made available to him for the purposes of investigation into high altitude, high speed winds. In his letter he asked the Ministry to quote him a price for the use of the aircraft. Unfortunately a response was not forthcoming. Bennett wrote again on 9 April 1946 reiterating his request and stating that due to the Ministry's tardiness in replying, the situation was now more urgent. A subsequent internal Ministry memo revealed that there had been some misunderstanding over the use to which the Mosquitoes would be put. The memo claimed that BSAA intended to use them 'as relief aircraft for freight and mail for the service UK – Buenos Aires' and at the same time to collect meteorological data at high altitudes along the route. The Ministry subsequently produced a cost estimate internally for operating the Mosquitoes as freight and mail carriers which suggested the operation could be made profitable, however this estimate never reached BSAA.

On 23 June 1947 Bennett wrote another letter to the Ministry, this time addressed to Air Vice-Marshal Sir Conrad Collier headed 'Upper Air

Investigation'. In it he said he was still awaiting a reply to his letter of 9 April the previous year and he emphasised the purpose for which he intended the aircraft to be used, stating that as it would be useful information for the development of future jet transports (such as the de Havilland DH.106, later known as the Comet) he felt the Ministry would be supportive of his efforts. Indeed he closed the letter by suggesting that maybe two Gloster Meteor aircraft could be used instead of the Mosquitoes, thus gaining valuable experience in the operation of jet aircraft at high altitudes in addition to the research into high level winds. Bennett received a reply from Sir Conrad Collier on 21 July 1947 saying that the Ministry felt the Meteor offered no significant advantage over the Mosquito for the use which Bennett proposed and the greatly reduced range would be a distinct disadvantage compared with the de Havilland aircraft. This letter was acknowledged on 23 July by Eileen Gummer, Bennett's private secretary, stating that he would reply when he returned from a trip abroad.

Ten days later *Star Dust* was lost, presumably a victim of the weather phenomenon which Bennett had been pressing the government to help him investigate for the previous twenty months. The final line was drawn under Bennett's efforts to investigate the jetstream when he received a letter on 21 October 1947 from Wing Commander Davis at the Ministry saying that he did not feel justified in authorising any more expenditure on 'gust investigation' until 'a substantial amount of work has been completed by the BEA under their contract and we have had some reports on which to judge whether an extended area of investigation is necessary'. One can only assume that the work being carried out by BEA would not have been a great deal of use in predicting high altitude winds over the Andes, and was certainly too late to help the passengers and crew of *Star Dust*.

Chapter 10

The Tudor Fiasco

More often than not, aircraft accidents are avoidable. They may be prevented by better maintenance, improved training, thorough planning and many other factors which combine to make a 'safe' airline. In some cases, however, by sheer bad luck an accident becomes almost inevitable. Such was the case with Lancastrian G-AGWK *Star Trail* on the night of 4 September 1947. It was only the skill of the pilot which prevented a far more serious outcome.

Captain A.H. Woolcott was flying service number JW14 (which had originated in London) on the sector from Santa Maria in the Azores to Bermuda. This particular route was one of the most challenging in the BSAA timetable due to the sheer length of the flight, over 1,960 miles of ocean and the navigation challenges involved in finding a 22 mile-long island at the end of well over 12 hours of flying. On board with Captain Woolcott that night were four other crew and fifteen passengers, including the BSAA Commercial Manager Leonard Hough. The other crew members were First Officer W. Hancock, Second Officer M.J. Warner, Radio Officer G.C. Fearon and Stargirl C.A.F. 'Crystal' Bendall.

Details of this accident remain elusive even now, but it appears that the weather forecast given to the crew in the Azores did not prepare them for the atrocious weather conditions they faced when they reached Bermuda. After 12 hours flying, as they approached the islands they were informed by radio that a thunderstorm was raging and conditions were totally unsuitable for landing. The comparatively remote location of Bermuda meant that aircraft flying there from the Azores had to make a decision quite early in the flight on whether or not to commit to a landing on the island. Bermuda had no alternatives nearby. Captain Woolcott had no option but to circle near the islands awaiting an improvement in the weather. This he did, for an hour and a half, at the end of which his fuel situation was so critical he simply had to attempt to get his aircraft onto the ground before the tanks ran dry. Unfortunately there was no ILS (Instrument Landing System) to help him down in those days so he had to rely heavily on his flying skills and the only facility available to him, the radio range, to locate the runway in appalling visibility. He very nearly made it. On its final approach, the aircraft struck the top of the centre aerial of the radio range which damaged the undercarriage. It is said that the mast was on the extended centreline of the runway so his directional accuracy was extremely good, but judging the distance to the threshold (and therefore the correct altitude) was nearly impossible in the conditions. As the aircraft touched down on the rain soaked runway, the undercarriage collapsed and the Lancastrian skidded to a halt on its belly. All passengers and crew exited the stranded aircraft without difficulty and then had to wait nearly 20 minutes for a vehicle to arrive from the terminal, as the airfield was so flooded. In the circumstances the captain had done a fine job in bringing the aircraft down without any injuries.

It is a tribute to the fortitude and resolve of airline passengers in those pioneering days that having climbed out of a wrecked Lancastrian during the night, the following day they were all flown in an identical BSAA Lancastrian (*Star Light*) to their final destinations of Nassau and Kingston. For one passenger, the BSAA manager Leonard Hough, this was to be the first of two very similar experiences, as he was again a passenger on Lancastrian *Star Light* when it suffered a very similar fate on landing in Bermuda just two months later.

* * *

An unfortunate incident occurred on 23 October 1947 at Heathrow airport which was to write off another BSAA aircraft, the Avro Lancaster G-AGUL *Star Watch*. When they were not required for transporting freight, the company often used its Lancasters for crew training. Such was the case on the night of 23 October when a training flight was planned for two First Officers, Pete Worrall and John Smurthwaite. The Radio Officer was Mr Bunker and the man in command was Training Captain Frank Griffin. At the controls was John Smurthwaite, who flew B-24 Liberators in RAF Coastal Command during the war and who would go on to serve with distinction for many years as a VC10 captain with BOAC. As the aircraft landed, a swing quickly developed, which the pilot was unable to control. The swing turned into a ground loop and when the sideways forces on the main undercarriage became too much it snapped off and the aircraft skidded along on the underside of the fuselage. There was no fire and the four men on board climbed out, uninjured, without any difficulty, but the aircraft was deemed to be damaged beyond economic repair and was subsequently scrapped.

* * *

Avro Lancastrian III, G-AGWG *Star Light* was scheduled to fly twelve passengers from Bermuda to London (via the Azores) on the night of 12 November 1947. It had been flown in to Bermuda earlier in the day by Captain Gilbert M. Allcock, who had signed it off as fully serviceable. In command for the flight to the Azores that night was Captain Albert Charles Graham. The Lancastrian was the same one in which history had been made by Air Vice-Marshal Bennett and crew on 1 January the previous year when it became the first commercial airliner to depart from the newly opened Heathrow airport. Captain Graham was 35 years old and had served in the RAF for nearly eighteen years between 1928 and 1945. He joined BSAA on 7 January 1946 and was licensed to fly the Mosquito, Lancastrian, Proctor and York. He was an experienced pilot whose total flying hours (in both the RAF and BSAA) amounted to 3,608, of which 2,811 were as first pilot. He was accompanied on *Star Light* by First Officer William G. Stonehouse, Radio Officer William Arthur Gould and Stargirl Dora Barzilay. William Stonehouse held a pilot's 'B' class licence in addition to a First Class Navigator's licence. He joined BSAA on 3 March 1947 and had accrued a total of 1,756 hours flying time. Gould had joined the airline in September 1945 and had flown for a total of 910 hours, of which 491 were with BSAA. Dora Barzilay had 1,127 hours in her logbook since joining BSAA.

They took off from Kindley Field at 23.50 GMT on the first leg of the service to London, planning to make a refuelling stop at Santa Maria. After flying for 1 hour and 10 minutes, at a cruising height of around 9,000ft, Captain Graham noticed a rise in the coolant temperature of the starboard outer engine. This was accompanied shortly after by a rise in the oil temperature and drop in its pressure. About five minutes later flames appeared from the right hand side of the engine. As the First Officer closed the fuel supply to the engine and attempted to feather the propeller, the radio officer signalled to Bermuda that they would be returning on three engines. To the relief of the crew, as the engine shut down and the propeller slowed to a stop the flames also died down and the fire went out, without the need to use the fire extinguisher.

The captain gently turned the Lancastrian on to a reciprocal heading and around 2 hours 25 minutes later, at 03.30, they were once again flying at 2,000ft over Bermuda. All aircraft have a maximum landing weight which is generally significantly less than their take-off weight. In this case, *Star Light* had taken off from Bermuda at a gross weight of 64,100lb and in its flight out over the Atlantic and back had used approximately 5,000lb of fuel, which meant that at 59,000lb its weight was still 1,000lb over the recommended maximum landing weight. As a result, Captain Graham decided to fly away from the islands a short distance in order to jettison fuel. After transferring fuel from the number two tanks to the number one in each wing until they were full (it was only possible to jettison from the number one tanks), the aircraft was flown parallel to the north shore and the jettison flaps underneath each wing were opened. Although the fuel flowed freely from the tank in the port wing, the starboard tank seemed to drain very slowly, taking over 15 minutes before it was down to the desired 50 gallons on the gauges. By this time, a very strong smell of fuel was pervading the cabin, such that the crew opened windows at the side of the cockpit to try and introduce more fresh air. The fumes were so concentrated that the radio officer was warned not to operate the radios until they had dissipated, for fear of fire caused by an electrical spark.

They headed back to Kindley Field air base, arriving overhead at just before 04.00, where they received the weather information and their landing instructions for runway 01. Captain Graham reduced his height to 1,600ft as he flew the downwind leg of the circuit and as they received final landing clearance from the Bermuda Air Traffic Controller he lowered the undercarriage and selected 10° of flap. When the aircraft was on the base leg, the altitude was reduced to 1,000ft and the flaps were lowered to 15° before turning onto finals. The flaps were then progressively lowered to 35° with the speed steady at 130mph. When instructed to do so by the Captain, the First Officer increased the engine revs and centralised the rudder trim. In this condition the aircraft was fully controllable and the directional instability of flying on three engines was easily managed by diligent use of the rudder. However, as Captain Graham selected full flaps, to his alarm he found the aircraft became very difficult to control, dropping its starboard wing, yawing to the right and losing height and airspeed at a very high rate. He immediately opened up both inboard engines to full power and increased the throttle on the port outer as far as he could while trying to prevent the yawing to the right with full left rudder. At such a late stage of the approach with the aircraft directionally unstable, low and slow, an accident became inevitable. The Lancastrian hit the ground 250ft short of the runway threshold with such force that the undercarriage collapsed. The propellers then struck the ground and while still 50ft short of (and to the right of) the runway, the fuselage settled onto the ground and the aircraft skidded for 500ft before finally coming to rest. Miraculously, there was no fire, and the airport emergency vehicles were on the scene immediately to help get people out. The escape hatches were used and all the passengers and crew vacated the aircraft without difficulty. Of the sixteen on board, the only injury was to Captain Graham who suffered lacerations of the scalp and chin.

The Accidents Investigation Branch of the MCA carried out the investigation, the results of which were published just twelve days later. The investigation was led by Wing Commander Ware. He focused mainly on the engine failure, the fuel jettison procedure and the captain's judgement. On examination of the starboard outer engine, a hole was discovered near a joint in the cylinder block. It appeared that the joint had failed, allowing hot exhaust gases to gradually open up a larger hole until the water jacket around the cylinders was fractured and the coolant fluid was lost. The flames seen by the crew were the result of unburned fuel being ignited by the leak of hot gases, and the sudden rise in the coolant temperature noticed by the captain was the result of much of the glycol coolant escaping through the hole. It was noted that the actions of the crew in closing the fuel supply and shutting down the engine were correct and performed just in time to prevent a total engine seizure with the ensuing possibility of a serious oil fire. After this accident Rolls-Royce made a minor modification to the cylinder blocks of their Merlin engines which prevented any similar occurrences for other operators.

The question of problems with the fuel jettison procedure was examined carefully. It was clear that the fuel did not drain correctly from the starboard tank and examination of the starboard jettison flap revealed the reason why. Each fuel jettison flap is like a small trapdoor underneath the wing. It is hinged downwards and is opened by means of a hydraulic valve pulling on a strong cable which in turn pulls out a release pin on the door latch. In the case of Star Light, investigators found that the release pin had been secured with locking wire so it could not move. Further enquiries failed to reveal why this had been done or who had done it but the result was that when the crew attempted to jettison fuel, the slack in the cable allowed the fuel to start draining from the tank, and as it did so it slowly accumulated within the wing structure itself and then trickled out past the hinge in the door. This explained the length of time it took to drain the starboard tank and also was the reason for the overpowering petrol fumes which entered the cabin.

The investigation commented that the captain's technique on the final approach with the undercarriage down, 35° of flap lowered, airspeed higher than for a normal approach, landing lights on and the rudder trim set to neutral was absolutely correct for a three-engined landing. However, they felt that when he lowered full flaps he had misjudged the distance from the runway threshold and his height above the ground. The application of full flaps on a Lancastrian only increases drag with no gain in lift so at that point he made the aircraft very difficult to control with little chance of reaching the runway. It was felt that the best course of action would have been quickly to raise the flaps to a high lift setting and open up the throttles fully on the inner engines. Captain Graham believed that his judgement may have been impaired by the petrol fumes, so the investigator consulted the Bermuda government Senior Medical Officer who stated that a high concentration of fuel vapour can cause dizziness, tremors of the hands and arms and drowsiness, among other symptoms. Statements were taken from the other members of the crew. The Stargirl said that fortunately she had already warned the passengers not to smoke while the fuel was being jettisoned, which reduced the risk (although it still remained high) of a catastrophic explosion. She also stated that the fumes were very strong in the passenger cabin with all passengers being affected and she believed this was responsible for making the two small children on board 'more difficult to control'. Accordingly the accident report included the following statement:

> Undoubtedly, the concentration of petrol fumes was high and the pilot was at some degree of nervous tension under the abnormal circumstances. Since the pilot's experience is considerable, his record good, I feel that these petrol fumes might easily have affected his faculties at a time when very precise judgement is required. Unfortunately the amount of petrol vapour that he inhaled cannot now be determined and in a test it would be very difficult to prepare exactly the same conditions.

In summary, the investigation found that the cause of the accident was the captain lowering full flaps too soon on the three-engined approach, but they believed his judgement may have been impaired by the inhalation of petrol fumes. When witness statements were taken from the passengers they all remarked on the cool efficiency shown by the Stargirl after the accident, but one passenger, Richard Huffner, added, 'I admire the skill with which the pilot landed the disabled craft and I will be glad if you will convey my congratulations.' This additional sentiment was echoed by other passengers.

The accident to *Star Light* was yet another case of a number of small problems coming together to create a major one. If the cylinder joint in the engine had not failed, it would have been a normal flight. If the fuel jettison flap had not been wired shut, the dumping of fuel would have been normal and the captain would not have suffered the effects of fumes. In the civil aviation of the late forties, there was a very fine line between routine and disaster.

* * *

Despite the restrictions mentioned earlier on Britain's development of large transport aircraft during the war years, there is one area in which Britain wasted no time in taking the lead immediately after the war, and that is the pressurisation of airliners. *The Aeroplane* magazine in early 1946 described pressurisation as 'a very important aeronautical accessory which is bound to affect profoundly the future of aviation'. When Roy Chadwick and his design team at A.V. Roe started work on the Avro Tudor in 1943, they decided that in order for it to be a successful passenger transport, it had to be capable of flying at high altitudes above the worst of the weather yet still provide a comfortable environment for the passengers. It therefore had to have a fully pressurised passenger cabin and cockpit. The appeal to passengers of a cabin with reduced noise, less turbulence, a carefully controlled environment and oxygen masks only fitted for emergency use was clear for all to see. The Tudor I was designed primarily for use on the North Atlantic route which experienced severe weather in the winter months. Roy Chadwick realised that if the aircraft could be designed to cruise at up to 25,000ft it would be able to fly above the worst icing conditions and thus make the North Atlantic route much safer to operate.

The advice of medical experts was sought to determine the highest altitude which would still provide a comfortable environment for the human body on long flights. The designers realised that the pressure differential between sea-level and 25,000ft was nearly 9.5lb/sq in and to build a fuselage which was sufficiently strong to cope with this large differential would be, although possible, extremely inefficient in terms of structural weight. It was established that passengers and crew would be able to comfortably cope with long periods at altitudes equivalent to 8,000ft with no adverse effects, provided the change in pressure was gradual. This meant that a pressurised fuselage capable of flying at 25,000ft need only be strong enough to withstand a pressure differential of around 6lb/sq in, a far more realistic and achievable figure. The optimum rate at which the cabin pressure changed was determined for passenger comfort to be 300ft/min regardless of the actual climb or descent rate of the aircraft, and again medical advice was sought to determine the amount of fresh air needed for each person to be comfortable. This was established at 1.5lb/min/person, so the designers provided a cabin blower system which was easily capable of maintaining this flow of fresh air. The stressing and structural problems involved in designing a passenger cabin to meet all these criteria necessitated building and testing a number of static fuselages which could safely be subjected to a very large number of pressure cycles and the results observed.

When the Avro 688 Tudor I prototype (G-AGPF) first took to the air on 14 June 1945 piloted by Avro Chief Test Pilot Sidney A. 'Bill' Thorn and J.H. 'Jimmy' Orrell, it became Britain's first fully pressurised airliner, offering a level of passenger comfort far in excess of that provided by the Lancastrian and York. Unfortunately, this substantial change in airliner design brought with it a flaw in the Avro Tudor, namely the cabin heating system.

Many people with only a passing interest in the Tudor will have heard of the Janitrol manufactured Daniels heater and know of its reputation for poor reliability. The system worked as follows. Both heating and ventilation were combined in the same system. Fresh air was drawn into two filtered intakes (one on the underside of each wing leading edge) positioned outboard of the outer engines and well away from the effects of exhaust gases. Ducting then fed the air along the wing leading edge into a Marshall Type XV blower fitted to the gearbox on each outer engine. It then passed through two silencers and an air cooler before being fed into the fuselage under the cabin floor. There was a non-return valve at this point of the system so that if one of the blowers should fail, pressurised air would not be lost from the fuselage. The ducting fed the fresh air into the Janitrol heater, which was situated in the forward fuselage under the floor of the flight deck near the flight engineer's seat. It is incredible to imagine in these days of sophisticated air-conditioning systems that the heater in the Tudor was basically a paraffin burner with a naked flame and a heat exchanger. The heated air then passed along the fuselage under the passenger cabin and into outlets built into the arms of the seats and through louvres in the ceiling. There were also outlets positioned at the crew stations and in the toilets. Some of the cabin air was recirculated before being expelled through a valve at the rear of the cabin. There were controls on a special pressurisation panel at the flight engineer's station which controlled the flow of air through the system.

All the joints in the fuselage were sealed with a special compound to maintain pressure and the doors and windows were sealed with inflatable rubber tubing. As with any pressurised aircraft, there was a small amount of leakage, partly through unsealed rivets, but this was well within the parameters required for the system to maintain a safe and comfortable environment. The only modification which the Tudor fuselage required as a result of the extensive testing programme was the replacement of the cockpit windscreen.

The design of the system appeared to be sound on paper, but in service the Tudor's heater was a constant source of problems. One of the major flaws was that it could only be ignited on the ground, so that if the paraffin flame was extinguished in flight for any reason, as happened on too many occasions, the remainder of the flight had to be conducted in an unpleasantly cold cabin. There was also the inherent danger of having a naked flame under the floor of an aircraft. In this case the problem is more difficult to quantify as although it was a constant source of worry for engineers and crew alike, there are no recorded incidents of the heater causing a fire in flight. The question will always remain as to whether the cabin heater played any part in the losses of the Tudors *Star Tiger* and *Star Ariel*, but unless wreckage is miraculously found at some point in the future, it is a question which will, in all probability, never be conclusively answered.

Although the Tudor I had been designed to fulfil the need for an interim pressurised transport its initial configuration was for only twelve night or twenty-four day passengers. The Air Ministry specification 29/43 issued in March 1944 called for a 72,000lb all-up weight carrying a payload of 3,760lb for 4,000 miles at a cruising speed of 235mph at 25,000ft. An initial order for fourteen production aircraft, later increased to twenty, was placed by the Ministry of Supply on behalf of BOAC, although as events unfolded it would become increasingly obvious that BOAC wanted to buy American. Early flight tests revealed a directional instability and serious pre-stall buffeting. The instability was eventually cured by the fitment of a large, and many thought ungainly, fin and rudder and the pre-stall buffet resulted in extending the wing root fillets and inner engine nacelles and sealing the joint between the wing leading edge and fuselage. When flight trials were carried out up to a weight of 80,000lb a significant bounce was experienced on landing. The solution was to fit a shorter undercarriage. Calculations of still-air range produced an estimate of 3,600 miles as opposed to the requested 4,000 miles, therefore more efficient Rolls-Royce Merlin 621 engines were fitted to replace the earlier Merlin 600 units.

At around this time Avro seemed to suffer from an excessive amount of indecision by BOAC which delayed the programme considerably. Meetings between representatives of A.V. Roe's design department and BOAC always resulted in new or changed requirements, with the airline seemingly unable to make decisions which they did not change before the next meeting. The Tudor I was already running behind schedule due to the aerodynamic modifications mentioned earlier and this indecision by BOAC only added to the delays. The situation came to a head at the final design conference on 12 March 1946 when BOAC demanded 343 individual changes to the cabin layout and décor. On 21 January 1947 the flagship of the BOAC fleet (G-AGRF) was christened *Elizabeth of England* by Her Royal Highness Princess Elizabeth in a naming ceremony at Heathrow airport. Less than three months later BOAC decided the Tudor I was unsuitable for transatlantic operations and cancelled their order.

In the meantime BSAA had been awaiting the Tudor eagerly and saw it as an ideal replacement for their Yorks and Lancastrians. Its requirements were slightly different from BOAC as it saw no need for the flight engineer and realised the economic benefit of reducing the seat pitch slightly to fit in more passengers. Consequently four of the original Tudor I airframes were built to Tudor IV specification for BSAA. These were *Star Panther*, *Star Lion*, *Star Leopard* and *Star Tiger*. They had the flight engineer's station removed and were fitted with thirty-two passenger seats. The first of these, *Star Panther*, flew for the first time on 9 April 1947, just two days before BOAC cancelled its order. The early Tudor Is, G-AGRD and G-AGRE, were also due to be converted for use by BSAA as Tudor IVBs, the only difference being the retention of the flight engineer's position, thus reducing the passenger capacity to twenty-eight. Ultimately only one of them, G-AGRE *Star Ariel*, was used by the airline.

Being keen to fly the flag for British aviation and to promote the new airliner in South America as soon as possible, Bennett organised a route-proving and goodwill flight to Santiago, to depart from Heathrow on 29 September 1947. As the day of departure loomed closer it seemed clear the trip would have to be postponed. The Tudor IV which Bennett planned to take, *Star Lion* (G-AHNK), had not yet been delivered by A.V. Roe. Finally on 29 September *Star Lion* was given its maiden flight by Jimmy Orrell and Bennett flew up to Woodford in person to collect it. The aircraft paperwork was hastily put in order, and at 17.10 Bennett gave it a 40-minute test flight, after which a couple of minor problems had to be rectified. By the time Orrell and Bennett were ready to depart on the delivery flight to Heathrow it was getting dark. Cars were positioned along the runway and their headlights used to illuminate it sufficiently for the Tudor to take off. The aircraft arrived safely at Heathrow after an uneventful flight and departed the very next morning for South America. The departure was only 24 hours late and this was made up en route and by reducing the time spent in Rio. The crew for this important flight comprised Captain D.C.T. Bennett, First Officer R.C. Alabaster, Second Officer E.E. Rodley, Third Officer P.P. Kerrigan, First Radio Officer R.W. Chandler, Second Radio Officer P.A. Smoker, Engineering Officer R.E. Wilby, Stargirls C.M. Hepworth and B.J. Riley.

Mrs Bennett accompanied her husband on the trip, along with thirty-two passengers initially, of whom twenty-seven would go as far as South America. Fifteen hundred pounds of freight was also carried. The route chosen was London – Lisbon – Dakar – Natal – Rio de Janeiro – Montevideo – Buenos Aires – Santiago. While in Buenos Aires on 4 October, Bennett made a couple of sightseeing flights over the city for local journalists on which they were served champagne while being treated to spectacular views of Buenos Aires landmarks. These flights generated very favourable comments about the new Tudor and BSAA in the Argentinian newspapers. The Andes crossing was notable for the fact that it was flown at 25,000ft in pressurised comfort. Various other demonstration flights and receptions were organised and at the end of the trip *Star Lion* had flown 15,500 miles with the only problem being a faulty terminal on an electric starter, which was quickly replaced.

While the Tudor I was still in the early design stages, an initial specification was issued by the MCA for a variant which would have shorter range, but greater payload capacity. The specification stated a maximum range of 2,880 miles with a take-off run of not more than 1,200yds. The cabin was to be suitable for forty-one day passengers or twenty-two in the sleeper version. An initial order was placed by the Ministry of Supply on behalf of BOAC for thirty aircraft. BOAC and the Ministry had talks with both Qantas and South African Airways with a view to running parallel services from England to South Africa and England to New Zealand. The other airlines were in broad agreement with the plan and the Ministry duly increased the order from thirty to seventy-nine, with a proposal that an additional six should be built in Australia.

Thus, the Tudor II was born. It had a slightly larger diameter fuselage than the Tudor I (11ft as against 10), but was significantly longer at 105ft. BSAA also needed a larger capacity Tudor and because of their slightly different requirements for cabin layout, this variation was designated the Tudor V (the Tudor III was a variation on the Tudor I intended for VIP use).

The problems of indecision on cabin layout which so delayed the Tudor I were to repeat themselves on the Tudor II. In early 1945 it was intended by BOAC and the other Commonwealth operators that the cabin should comprise convertible day and night accommodation. By May 1945 BOAC decided that sleeping accommodation was not justified and it asked Avro to deliver the first twenty aircraft as a priority in a conventional seat 'day' version. By July 1945 the requirement had reverted to a convertible day/night version for which a mock-up was built by September. BOAC inspected the mock-up and called for a number of modifications. Avro resisted by pointing out that the changes would cause considerable delay. The response was that the delay was acceptable and that no further modifications would be required. This was not to be the case. Just one month after making this promise to Avro, BOAC asked for a change of colour scheme (resulting in a large order for new materials) and a modification to the dressing rooms in the cabin; then in December it asked for a new type of seat to be used, which was yet to be designed, developed and approved. Many at Avro were beginning to feel that BOAC was deliberately delaying delivery of the new Tudor. This would have two results. First, if it delayed for long enough it would be allowed its preferred choice of buying American aircraft as an 'interim' solution; and second, any delays would cause far fewer problems for BOAC than for BSAA with the latter's smaller fleet and more urgent need for the higher capacity aircraft.

The work which Avro carried out on the aircraft to meet the ever-changing requirements of BOAC was to prove too late for the other operators. In July 1946 Qantas decided not to proceed and by the autumn of that year South African Airways had also pulled out. As a result, the order was reduced from seventy-nine to fifty, of which six were earmarked for BSAA as Tudor Vs. In February 1947 BOAC made the astonishing statement that it now only required six of the sleeper version, resulting in Avro having to scrap a significant number of parts and materials procured specifically for that version. In a meeting in July 1947 BOAC announced it was not prepared to pay for the costs of the latest changes it had requested, as it had not yet formally accepted the Tudor II. This led to months of wrangling over costs and it was not until January 1948, when the Ministry of Supply assumed financial responsibility, that Avro was able to complete the first production aircraft incorporating all the changes requested by BOAC.

The prolonged Tudor troubles were serious enough, but in August 1947 a tragedy occurred which was to have far-reaching consequences not only for

Avro, but for British aviation as a whole. On 23 August the Tudor II prototype G-AGSU crashed after take-off from Woodford, killing Chief Test Pilot S.A. 'Bill' Thorn, and the brilliant designer Roy Chadwick who was on board for the test flight. The co-pilot, Squadron Leader D. J. B. Wilson, and the Radio Operator John Webster, also lost their lives. Two men survived the accident. Some maintenance had been carried out overnight which, unknown to the pilot, had involved dismantling the aileron circuit. It had been reassembled with the aileron controls reversed, and an accident was almost inevitable.

Following poor results from the tropical trials of the Tudor II in Nairobi, the order total was cut once more to just eighteen aircraft, including the six for BSAA, but none for BOAC which finally decided the Tudor no longer met its requirements. The government called for an enquiry into the whole Avro Tudor fiasco. It was chaired by Air Chief Marshal Sir Christopher L. Courtney and resulted in the publication of the Courtney Report at the end of June 1948. The report was most scathing of BOAC, primarily for its continual indecision and also for the unyielding position it took with regard to weight saving. The enquiry felt that had BOAC compromised on its grand ideas for the interior fittings to the Tudor II, the aircraft would not have been overweight and consequently performance would have been more competitive.

Unfortunately the entry into service of the Tudor V for BSAA came too late for it to carry passengers. It was just after the unexplained loss of Tudor IV *Star Tiger* and the Tudor Vs were converted immediately for use (in unpressurised form) on the Berlin Airlift, where they performed admirably.

In spite of the aircraft's lack of commercial success, Avro Tudor development continued for some time, culminating in the Tudor VIII which was powered by four Rolls-Royce Nene turbojets. This aircraft became the world's first four-jet powered airliner, making its first flight ten months before the de Havilland Comet took to the air, although it was only ever a prototype.

* * *

At the end of July 1947 a flight to Jamaica was arranged for tropical trials of the new Tudor IV (G-AHNJ). This aircraft had initially been named *Star Lion*, but for some reason its name was later changed to *Star Panther* and G-AHNK became *Star Lion*. In command was Don Bennett with James B. Linton as first officer. The Stargirl was Joan Thompson and there were a number of BSAA staff as passengers, including the company accountant. The route as originally planned was from London to Jamaica via the Azores, Antigua and Trinidad. The airline had not flown to Antigua before and the leg from Santa Maria to Beane Field in Antigua was marginal on fuel, being 2,750 miles. Eventually Antigua refused landing rights, so the flight plan to Jamaica was changed to route via Prestwick, Gander, Bermuda and Trinidad.

When the Tudor was some way out over the Atlantic on the leg from Prestwick to Gander, there were signs that something was seriously wrong with the fuel system. The gauges for the inboard fuel tanks were not dropping as they should have been, whereas fuel appeared to be feeding from the other tanks as normal. The fuel system on the Tudor consisted of four large tanks in each wing, numbered one to four from the wing root out to the tip, and a small distributor tank behind each of the engines which received fuel from the main tanks and fed it through a pump and pressure regulator to the engine. All four main tanks were gravity fed with the number four (outboard) tank feeding directly into the number three, and tanks one, two and three feeding into the small distributor tanks. There was one vital difference between tank number one and the others. It had a service cock installed, which enabled the fuel flow to the distributor tanks to be manually shut off. The implication of the number one tank gauges not dropping was that the 960 gallons of fuel contained in them was not reaching the distributor tanks and would not be accessible.

The crew made a quick calculation which led them to conclude that if the fuel in the inboard tanks was indeed unavailable, the remaining fuel in the auxiliary tanks (a total of 2,250 gallons when full) would only be sufficient to get them to a point over the ocean about 50° West, and then they would face the unpleasant prospect of ditching in the sea 250 miles from their destination. Fortunately, there were some technical staff on the flight, among them the Superintendent of Aircraft Development, an experienced engineer named Raymond E. Wilby. Bennett left the cockpit and went back into the passenger cabin for a discussion with him. The two men agreed that the only explanation for the strange fuel gauge readings was that the fuel cocks in each undercarriage bay had been unaccountably closed. They were, of course, inaccessible from the cabin. At some point in the ensuing discussion, one of the technical team suggested that they could cut through the cabin floor and the emptying number two tank into the wheel well below to turn on the service cocks. Such a plan would have made a perfect story line for one of the *Airport* movies so popular in the 1970s, but in the grim reality of an Avro Tudor running out of fuel over the Atlantic in the 1940s it was dismissed very swiftly.

The only fuel cock which could be operated from the cockpit was in a pipe below the cabin floor linking the tanks in each wing. Its purpose was to enable the relative quantity of fuel on either side of the aircraft to be balanced in the event of an engine failure. It was decided to feed all the engines from the fuel in the port wing tanks. If the engines cut out when the numbers two, three and four port side gauges showed empty, then it would prove that the fuel service cocks below the number one tanks were closed. After a while, the gauges on the port side read empty, and sure enough the engines started to cut. The feed was quickly switched to the starboard tanks, and the situation began to look very grim indeed.

Bennett radioed ahead to Gander to inform them of the emergency, and Gander started to alert the search and rescue authorities in preparation for the ditching. Meanwhile, the Stargirl was told to prepare the passengers for the possibility of evacuation from the aircraft in water. She is said to have reacted very coolly to this news, no doubt due to the fact that she had served behind enemy lines during the war and was used to dangerous situations. A rumour still circulates to this day that when Bennett felt a ditching was likely, he told her (with a smile on his face) that if the life rafts were too crowded she should leave the accountant behind!

All this time the aircraft flew on, and as the starboard gauges read empty the tension in the cockpit must have been immense. Still the aircraft flew on. In fact, much to the relief of all on board, it continued to fly on to a normal landing at Gander. As Bennett was stepping out of the Tudor, he called Ray Wilby to one side and asked him to personally inspect the service cocks in the wheel wells and report directly back to him. On doing so it was discovered that the port service cock was turned off and wire-locked. The starboard cock was open, but it was later found that the starboard inboard fuel gauge was stuck on full, even though the fuel level was going down. This was an odd coincidence, and one which served to reinforce Bennett's long-standing opinion that the airline was being sabotaged. A sobering thought is that had the flight plan not changed at the last minute to a refuelling stop in Gander rather than Antigua, the Tudor would definitely have finished in the ocean and who knows whether it may have been the first Tudor mystery, coming as it did a few months before the disappearance of *Star Tiger*.

* * *

The reactions of the crews who flew the Tudor were mixed. Gordon Store was not impressed. He thought it was built like a battleship, was noisy and he had no confidence in either its engines or in any of its systems. He was, however, a fan of American aircraft, believing the Americans to be fifty years ahead of the British in their engineering. He complained that the aircraft had many of its systems packed together under the floor and there were always problems with the cabin heaters. Captain Geoffrey Womersley, on the other hand, thought '. . . at that time it was the best civil airliner flying'.

For the cabin crews the experience of working in a Tudor galley was not one they enjoyed. It was in the rear and had a sliding door which saved space but had a tendency to slam shut with the movement of the aircraft. Many of the Stargirls ended flights with their hands bandaged after getting them caught in the galley door. The door was not the only hazard they had to contend with. The astrodome had a set of portable steps for the cockpit crew to stand on, but there was no illumination in this section and, if they forgot to put the steps away, the Stargirl would invariably crash into them, ladder her stockings and, if she was unlucky, cut her legs as well. Stargirl Priscilla Vinyals recalled one Tudor flight during which she banged her head, sustaining a nasty cut, crashed into the steps, grazing her legs and ruining her stockings and also had her fingers trapped in the sliding door. When the aircraft landed and the door was opened, the ground staff who met the flight took one look at her and asked if they should call an ambulance. Priscilla also remembered often feeling sick at the rear of the Tudor as it had a distinct yawing motion more usually associated with aircraft with swept wings. On one particularly bad flight she had to thrust a pile of paperwork into the hands of a nearby passenger so that she could dive into the lavatory to be sick.

* * *

In October 1947 BSAA took over all of BWIA's assets and, temporarily, the airline took the name of BSAA's subsidiary company, British International Air Lines (BIAL). It continued operating under this name while Vickers Vikings were ordered to replace its Lockheed Lodestars. In February 1948 BSAA's service between Port-of-Spain, Caracas and Kingston was transferred to BIAL and in June the company was relaunched as BWIA once again, with Kenneth Murray as its new General Manager. The following month the first of its Vikings arrived.

Soon after the relaunch BSAA pilot E.D. 'Wyn' Fieldson was sent to Wroughton in Wiltshire to pick up a Vickers Supermarine 309 Sea Otter, G-AJLU, which he ferried back to Langley. The aircraft was one of four Sea

Otters which BSAA purchased to use as feeder aircraft between the smaller Caribbean islands and they were brought to Langley for modifications to make them suitable for the needs of BWIA. The work was never completed and when the merger between BSAA and BOAC took place the aircraft were sold. While they were parked at Langley apprentices Richard Enser and Keith Johnstone used to sit in one of them to have their tea breaks.

In January 1949 BSAA also acquired the share capital of Bahamas Airways. Sadly, in the short time it had left, BSAA was not able fully to develop either of its Caribbean subsidiaries and when it was, itself, swallowed up a few months later both smaller companies became subsidiaries of BOAC. By 1951 BOAC had taken over the profitable routes of BWIA for itself, leading the *Trinidad Guardian* to comment in an article that February: 'We had a purely West Indian air service of which every West Indian could be proud, and in which every West Indian took pride. And now what? It becomes a half-baked adjunct to a company with headquarters 3,000 miles away.'

At the beginning of December 1947 BSAA moved its London headquarters to Starways House, King Street, St James, SW1, holding its first board meeting there on the 19th. The Grafton Street offices were kept to house the finance department of the growing company.

In the new year, 1948, the financial reports of the three state-owned airlines were published. On 21 January the results were put before the House of Lords and a lively debate ensued. Lord Swinton, the first Minister of Civil Aviation, began by saying:

> We now have the reports and accounts for the year ended March 31, 1947, of all three of the Government air corporations. Two of them present a very gloomy picture. I doubt whether any of your Lordships expected to see great profits, but I do not suppose any of your Lordships expected to see such enormous and formidable losses. The BOAC, whose accounts cover a full year, have lost no less than £8,000,000. The BEA, doing the European and the domestic services, whose accounts cover only eight months, have in that eight months lost over £2,000,000. British South American Airways, whose accounts were published last night, present an agreeable and striking contrast. Without taking credit for the profit of about £75,000 which was made in the first four months by the private enterprise company which was established to run those South American airways and which the Government Corporation took over (and I am glad to see that the

Corporation still has the same Chairman and Managing Director, and, to judge by the results, the same method of conducting business) BSAA in the last eight months has shown a profit of £32,000.

He went on to explain that BOAC had given a long report, detailing the reasons for the massive losses it had incurred. It cited the use of uneconomical aircraft, the fact that its maintenance bases were widely spread and the difficulties in organising the routes as the main reasons for its deficit. These excuses were swept aside by Lord Swinton. He pointed out that BSAA had operated the same aircraft types as BOAC and that BSAA also had difficulties with its maintenance facilities and declared that: 'They are all in the same boat. And the organisation over the route – in part the same route as the others – has certainly not been perfect on the South American or the Caribbean route.'

He might also have pointed out that while BOAC was complaining about the organisation of its routes and the difficulties it had encountered, BSAA had not even been allowed to do an initial survey flight to make plans for its routes and had had to begin operating and conduct survey flights at the same time. Furthermore, it had been BOAC which had been given the task of operating the first survey flight to South America, which was hardly an acceptable state of affairs for BSAA given that BOAC had, from the start, been trying to steal the routes from the smaller corporation.

When Lord Nathan stood up to speak after Swinton had finished, the way he spoke of BSAA and his excuses for BOAC were astonishing:

I may fairly ask your Lordships to look a little more closely at what has, in fact, been achieved. . . . BOAC's net route mileage in 1946–47 was 53,998 and 62,000 in August, 1947. BEA's route mileage by the latter date was already 17,000, after only one year's effective operation. BSAA's figure was 21,000. Remember, too, though it is often forgotten, that BOAC, as such, had had no previous peace-time experience; it was born only in 1940, when the war had already started.

Nathan's attempt to champion both BOAC and BEA, while being completely indifferent to BSAA's achievements, seems misleading and rather pathetic. However, as will be seen, he may have had personal reasons for being so dismissive.

Chapter 11

A Tiger Goes Missing

The disappearance of a BSAA aircraft on the night of 29/30 January 1948 gave Lord Nathan the excuse he was looking for to make more trouble for the airline. One of the most enduring mysteries in aviation is the fate of *Star Tiger*, the BSAA Avro Tudor IV G-AHNP, which disappeared without trace on a flight from the Azores to Bermuda. There is always an element of mystery surrounding the loss of an aircraft where no wreckage is ever found. This has unfortunately led to so much speculation as to the cause that some of the theories are rather far-fetched. It is tempting in these circumstances to suggest dramatic and unusual causes, when it is often established years later that the truth is rather more mundane.

We already know a number of facts about the final flight of *Star Tiger*. The last part of the flight was at night, and cloud cover would probably have prevented the navigator from taking an astral fix. The crew would have been tired after the long flight from the Azores. The Tudor's troublesome cabin heater was not working so the cabin would have been cold. The crew encountered much heavier than forecast headwinds en route. As they neared Bermuda, the winds had changed strength and direction significantly from those originally forecast. They had obtained one good radio bearing from Bermuda before silence reigned. They were heading for an island chain roughly 22 miles long and 4 miles wide.

We also know a good deal about the experience of the crew and the history of the aircraft itself. In command of *Star Tiger* was New Zealander Brian W. McMillan who was the captain of Lancastrian *Star Glow* when it was written off on take-off at Bathurst in 1946; however, the aircraft was being flown by the first officer on that occasion. Captain McMillan was an experienced and steady pilot who had flown 2,912 hours in the RAF and 1,673 hours in command of BSAA aircraft. The First Officer on this flight, Captain David Colby, had flown 1,690 hours in the RAF and 1,403 hours for BSAA, 1,066 of those in command. The Second Officer was Cyril Ellison, another experienced ex-RAF pilot. The Radio Officer was Bob Tuck, known as 'Tucky' to his friends and colleagues, who had served for fourteen years as a ship's radio officer and four years as senior radio officer at North Atlantic Control, Prestwick. Since then he had flown 1,787 hours as radio officer on BSAA aircraft. He was the comedian of the crew, who was often laughing and joking, but took his work very seriously. The two Stargirls were Lynn Clayton and Sheila Nicholls. Cyril Ellison and Lynn Clayton had also, like Brian McMillan, experienced an accident in a BSAA aircraft before *Star Tiger*. They were both in the Avro York *Star Speed* which crash-landed at Dakar nine months earlier, resulting in the death of six passengers.

Star Tiger itself was a nearly new aircraft which had made its maiden flight from the Avro factory at Woodford just two and a half months previously on 4 November 1947. Due to poor weather that day, its first flight was only 25 minutes long, but it made a full test flight the following day to check out various systems, at the end of which the aircraft landed at Heathrow airport to be handed over to its new owners. As the test flights had been satisfactory it was issued with a short-term Certificate of Airworthiness (valid for two months). On 6 November a local flight was made from Heathrow and remarkably, having taken to the air for the first time two days previously, at 23.00 that night *Star Tiger* left for a flight to Havana, Cuba. When the aircraft returned to Heathrow from Cuba on 12 November, it was employed continually on the route between London and the West Indies. It had received its full Certificate of Airworthiness on 2 December. At the time of its disappearance it had 576 hours in its logbooks, including eleven return journeys to the West Indies, and was one of only three Tudor IVs built to date, the others being G-AHNJ *Star Panther* and G-AHNK *Star Lion*. There were a couple of restrictions placed on the C of A issued to the three Tudor IVs. One was that the all-up weight should not exceed 80,000lb and the other related to a ban on flight in icing conditions. The Air Registration Board had asked for evidence of the efficiency of the Tudor IV de-icing equipment before lifting the ban, but by the end of January it had not been given any. This was not considered a problem by BSAA as the three Tudor IVs were at that time only flying routes on which there was no risk of airframe icing. They had agreed that as soon as suitable conditions could be found, they would carry out the necessary flights to test the equipment.

Although *Star Tiger* was only a couple of months old, the maintenance schedule for the Tudor stipulated a routine maintenance at or before every 600 hours flown. Coincidentally this milestone occurred just before the end of

January so the aircraft was subjected to a thorough maintenance check just before leaving London on the journey during which it disappeared.

The aircraft took off from London bound for Bermuda as flight number MW14 on 27 January 1948 with twenty-three passengers on board in addition to the six crew. One of the passengers who embarked in London was Air Marshal Sir Arthur Coningham, former leader of the Desert Air Force and commander of the Second Tactical Air Force during the invasion of Europe in 1944. His RAF career was coming to an end and he was busy making contacts which would allow him to embark on a second career in civilian life. He was looking forward to the challenge and to the prospect of spending more time at home with his wife and 13-year-old daughter. After a relatively uneventful flight, the Tudor landed at Lisbon later that day where it was scheduled for an overnight stop before proceeding to Santa Maria the following day. The troublesome cabin heater had failed on the way to Lisbon and this was worked on by BSAA engineers as soon as the aircraft landed. A component was changed, but the problem persisted. Also, the captain reported a problem with one of the Distant Reading Compasses (DRC). This problem was fixed but, as it turned out, only temporarily, as it failed again on the way to the Azores.

As the crew attempted to start the engines for the onward flight to the Azores the following day, the port inner engine failed to start. The problem was traced to a faulty priming pump, which was changed. In order to change the pump the fuel cock on the port side was closed. This was the same fuel cock which was found to be wired shut on the Tudor used in the tropical trials the previous July, with near disastrous consequences. The Station Engineer on this occasion is certain that he opened this fuel cock after the pump was changed and locked it in the open position ready for flight. There is no reason to doubt this as at no point did Captain McMillan send any signals indicating problems with fuel gauge readings. Two additional passengers boarded the aircraft at Lisbon, bringing the total to twenty-five, and the aircraft finally left Portugal bound for Santa Maria in the Azores at 11.45 on 28 January.

The schedule was for the aircraft to refuel at Santa Maria and then proceed directly to Bermuda. When Captain McMillan checked the en route weather on arrival at Santa Maria, he realised it was not favourable for the onward flight and announced that the aircraft would remain overnight, leaving for Bermuda the following afternoon. The passengers and crew were accommodated in an austere airport hotel, where they were served dinner, and many stayed up late for a drink and a chat at the hotel bar. After dinner Captain McMillan commented that he was feeling very tired and made his way to bed at around 21.00 (local time).

The decision made earlier to delay the flight had been a joint one. There was another BSAA aircraft on the tarmac at Santa Maria that night. The Lancastrian G-AGWL *Star Guide* had arrived earlier, flown by Captain Frank Griffin, and was awaiting an improvement in the weather. It was carrying no passengers on this occasion, but instead it carried freight which was to be transferred to *Star Tiger* when both aircraft were in Bermuda. Captain McMillan and Captain Griffin discussed the weather situation and had made the joint decision to await an improvement the next day. While relaxing in the hotel bar that night Frank Griffin bumped into an old acquaintance from his RAF Pathfinder days, a man named Tony Mulligan. He was travelling on *Star Tiger* to Bermuda with his wife and father. Griffin told him that he was taking the Lancastrian to Bermuda the following day and Mulligan asked if he and his wife and father could be transferred from the Tudor to fly with him. He was very keen to show his wife what flying in a Lancaster was like, and the Lancastrian was as close as she would get. Despite Mulligan's obvious enthusiasm, Griffin reluctantly had to refuse as the company's insurance would not have covered him for carrying passengers on this occasion.

When Thursday 29 January dawned, Brian McMillan, Frank Griffin and David Colby visited the Meteorological Section at Santa Maria to get the latest weather information. The news was good. The strong headwinds of the previous evening had abated somewhat and the conditions were generally more favourable (although by no means ideal) for the long flight to Bermuda. The three men discussed their flight plans and decided that, taking into account the cloud base and forecast winds at various altitudes, the optimum height for both aircraft to fly would be an unusually low 2,000ft. This would give the navigators the added benefit of calculating drift information by observing the surface of the sea in the early (daylight) part of the flight. The crews planned to depart from Santa Maria later in the day to enable accurate positional fixes by astro-navigation before the halfway point of the flight. The decision was also taken at this stage that Captain Griffin would fly his Lancastrian one hour ahead of the Tudor and could therefore pass updated weather information en route to McMillan's crew. The wind situation was not as critical for Captain Griffin as it was for Captain McMillan. The Lancastrian had a longer range than the Tudor, with an endurance of almost 19 hours as opposed to the Tudor's 16 hours. Brian McMillan knew that

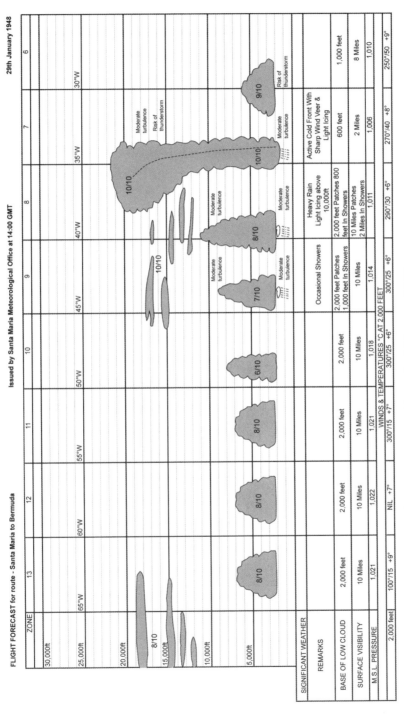

Weather forecast for *Star Tiger's* route from Santa Maria to Bermuda, 29 January 1948.

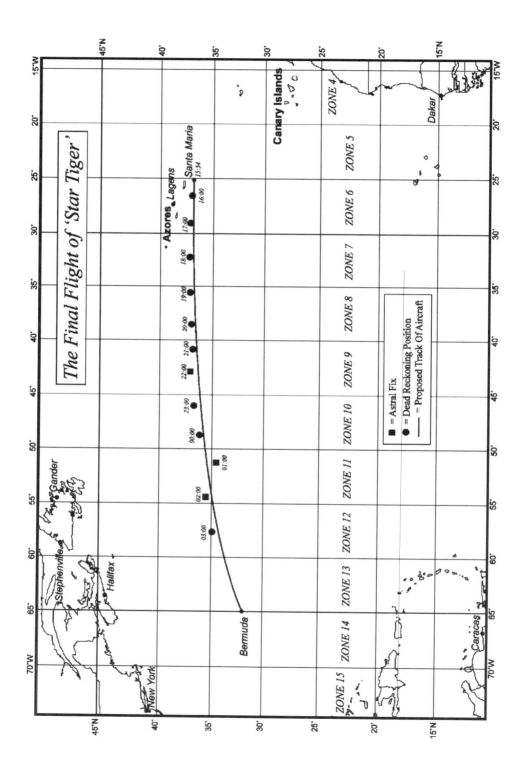

The Final Flight of 'Star Tiger'

FLIGHT PLAN

Tudor IV G-AHNP (*Star Tiger*) - Santa Maria to Bermuda   Date – 29 January 1948   (All times are GMT)

(Service MW.14)

From	To	Track	W/V	Comp. true	R.A.S.	Height	Air temp.	T.A.S.	G.S.	Dist. to go	Time	E.T.A.
Santa Maria	30°W	272	250/50	266	175	2000	+9	180	133	232	01:44	01:44
30°W	35°W	269	270/40	269	175	2000	+8	179	139	240	01:43	03:28
35°W	40°W	267	290/30	271	175	2000	+6	178	149	241	01:37	05:05
40°W	45°W	263	300/28	268	175	2000	+6	178	154	243	01:35	06:39
45°W	50°W	260	300/25	265	175	2000	+6	178	158	247	01:34	08:13
50°W	55°W	257	300/15	260	175	2000	+7	179	168	251	01:30	09:43
55°W	60°W	255	L. & V.	255	175	2000	+7	179	179	254	01:25	11:08
60°W	Bermuda	252	100/15	250	175	2000	+9	180	194	252	01:18	12:26

Flight Time	12 hrs 26 mins	E.T.D.	15:30
Endurance	16 hrs 0 mins	E.T.A.	03:56 (30/1)
Distance A. to B.	1,960 N. Miles	Fuel Carried	3,250 gallons
Still Air Range	2,860 N. Miles	Fuel Required	2,660 gallons

the 1,960 nautical miles between the Azores and Bermuda was the longest route the Tudor IV could safely operate, especially given the prospect of strong headwinds en route. There had already been two instances when, on the same route, *Star Tiger* had to divert to Gander through lack of fuel caused by stronger than forecast headwinds. Undoubtedly this was in the back of his mind when he later instructed the engineer in charge of refuelling to 'fill her up to the gills'. This meant a fuel load of 3,300 gallons, 150 gallons more than the amount entered on the load sheet. He would have known that this made the Tudor slightly overweight, but was experienced enough to know that the excess fuel would quickly be burned off after take-off and that it would give him an extra safety margin when approaching Bermuda. The amount of fuel entered on the flight plan was 3,250 gallons, which is assumed to be the actual quantity of 3,300 minus 50 gallons for engine starting, warm-up and taxiing.

There were two crucial points to be calculated in the flight from the Azores to Bermuda. The first was self-explanatory and was known as the 'point of no return', the point after which the aircraft would have insufficient fuel to make a safe return to Santa Maria. The second critical point was known as the 'point of no alternate'. At any time between the point of no return and the point of no alternate the aircraft would be able to divert to another airport if Bermuda became unavailable for any reason. Once the point of no alternate was passed, the aircraft was committed to a landing in Bermuda regardless, as it would have insufficient fuel to reach anywhere else. Thus it can be seen that the flight to Bermuda was effectively divided into three phases: during the first, the aircraft could return to the Azores; during the second, the aircraft could divert to, in *Star Tiger's* case, Stephenville in Newfoundland; during the third, the aircraft was committed to making a landing in Bermuda. The calculation of these points was extremely important to allow the captain to make a swift decision on what course of action to take if an emergency occurred en route. There was one more point which would normally appear on the prepared flight plan and this was the 'three-engine critical point'. This signifies the point on the route at which it would take equally as long to proceed to the destination as it would to turn back if the aircraft had to fly on three engines.

When a comparison is made between the flight plans filed for *Star Tiger* and *Star Guide*, there is a striking similarity, as would be expected for two aircraft flying the same route an hour apart. Both flight plans contained a common error which suggests that they were calculated by one of the captains and simply accepted without checking by the other. The point of no return for each aircraft was calculated based on returning to Santa Maria at the same altitude as the outbound route and arriving overhead the airport with the fuel exhausted. This is clearly not correct. However, the actual figure shown on the flight plan of *Star Tiger* was correct, whereas the corresponding figure for *Star Guide* was 80 nautical miles too far away from the Azores. Both flight plans stated the three-engine critical point as 815 nautical miles, whereas due to the headwinds forecast it should have been 1,072 nautical miles.

So it was that at 14.22 on 29 January Lancastrian *Star Guide* took off from Santa Maria with Frank Griffin at the controls, followed at 15.34 by *Star Tiger* flown by Brian McMillan. As the Tudor climbed quickly to its 2,000ft cruising altitude, the Lancastrian was already nearly 200 miles ahead. At 16.00 Navigator Cyril Ellison gave Bob Tuck the first position report, which he duly transmitted. They were at 37° 00' N, 26° 25' W, although this hourly report and the following five were all calculated by dead reckoning. At 16.11 they established communication with the Lancastrian ahead and ascertained that the winds they were experiencing were greater than forecast. In fact, Captain Griffin was flying into a 55-knot headwind and not the 30 to 40 knots forecast for longitudes between 25° and 35° W.

At 16.45 Captain Griffin's radio operator transmitted a message to Air Traffic Control in New York and BSAA in Bermuda asking for a landing forecast for Bermuda between 03.00 and 04.00 the next morning and a wind forecast for Zones 9 to 13 at 2,000ft, 6,000ft and 10,000ft. For ease of reference the route between the Azores and Bermuda was divided into zones of five degrees of longitude, numbered from 6 to 13 heading west. The request for wind information in Zones 9 to 13 covered longitudes from 40° to 65° W (Bermuda is approximately on longitude 65° W). When this information was not forthcoming another attempt was made, but still no wind information was given. Eventually the Lancastrian made contact directly with the United States Air Force at Kindley Field in Bermuda stating 'Landing forecast and upper winds urgently required'. This message met with an immediate response and by 18.05 the information had been passed to the aircraft. The news was not good. It forecast stronger headwinds than originally anticipated in all but Zone 13 (the very last part of the flight).

At 18.49 the Lancastrian passed a message to the Tudor informing it that the flight time had been recalculated to be 13 hours and 28 minutes. This was an hour longer than expected, which was not a major problem for the Lancastrian, but more of a concern for the Tudor with its shorter endurance, although it would still leave them enough fuel to be within safe limits at their destination. Cyril Ellison in *Star Tiger* had suspected they were facing stronger winds than anticipated, even though his position reports had all been based on dead reckoning. Indeed, it was not until 6 hours 26 minutes into the flight at 22.00, when they were nearly at the half-way point, that Ellison was able to get a clear enough view of the stars to get an astral fix for an accurate check on their position. This showed them to be at a point 36° 52' N, 43° 10' W, which was some way north of their proposed track. An hour or so later *Star Tiger* passed the point of no return and a return to the Azores was no longer an option.

As the Tudor flew on through the night the passengers would have been slightly warmer than on the leg from Lisbon to the Azores. Although the cabin heater was still not working, the outside temperature at 2,000ft was considerably higher than it had been on the earlier flight. One can only guess that they would have been buffeted around somewhat at such a low altitude and flying into such strong winds. The lucky ones would have managed to fall asleep after Lynn Clayton and Sheila Nicholls had cleared away the dishes from dinner, but as Sir Arthur Coningham is known to have taken an interest in the navigation of aircraft he travelled on, it is probable that he was sitting in his seat wondering exactly where they were. By midnight that was possibly a question running through Captain McMillan's mind, too. They had still only managed one star-sighting since leaving the Azores and that had put them north of where they intended to be. Hopefully his subtle course corrections since then had brought the Tudor back on track.

Earlier, at 20.43, both aircraft had received a message directly from the wireless station in Bermuda with a wind and landing forecast signed 'BSAA Bermuda'. This was of little use as the forecast was timed at 16.38. Just 8 minutes later, both crews received a similar forecast from Bermuda which was timed at 18.24. This was slightly more useful, but hardly an up-to-date forecast in the circumstances. No more meteorological information was received by either aircraft until at 02.00 the Lancastrian specifically asked for wind information in Zone 13 at 2,000ft. The reason for this specific request was that at 01.26 Frank Griffin's navigator had found enough clear sky to perform an astral fix which had told him they were considerably off course. Calculations showed them to be 68 miles north of their intended track. This could only be due to a dramatic change in the wind direction and speed. The reply they received from Bermuda was simply 'wait'. The request was repeated at 02.15 and then again at 02.33 before they finally received a reply at 02.42 informing them that the wind was 'S.S.W. at 20 knots'. This message was only sent directly to the Lancastrian but being such a large change from the previous forecast it would have been passed back to the Tudor straight away. Curiously the astral fix which Ellison obtained at 01.00 had shown *Star Tiger* to be considerably south of the proposed track, yet the 02.00 position report (again derived from an astral fix) understandably showed them to be too far to the north. By this time Captain McMillan had passed the point of no alternate and was committed to Bermuda. Armed with the new information gathered at 02.00, McMillan changed course once more slightly to the south and therefore straight into the headwind. He calculated that although the forecasts had not predicted winds of such severity, if they continued at their present rate they would be over Bermuda with one hour's fuel remaining in the tanks. This was a very slender margin, but barring a dramatic change in the weather at Bermuda it should have been enough.

At 03.00 cloud cover once again prevented an astral fix, but a dead-reckoning estimate of position put the Tudor slightly north of track but still on a good heading for Bermuda. By this time Frank Griffin in the Lancastrian was only about an hour from landing and he radioed back to Brian McMillan that he was switching over to voice communication with Bermuda Approach Control. He signed off with the words 'See you at breakfast'. His job in command of the aptly named *Star Guide* was nearly done. The Tudor was now on its own.

Bob Tuck in *Star Tiger* transmitted their 03.00 position report at 03.02 and at 03.04 he contacted Bermuda to obtain a radio bearing. This was usually obtained by the radio operator transmitting a continuous signal and the receiving station using a directional aerial to ascertain the direction from which the signal originated. With the Tudor still so far from Bermuda the signal was not sufficiently strong to obtain a bearing. The radio direction finding equipment had variable range, depending on weather conditions, but it would usually give a bearing up to about 150 miles out from Bermuda. At 03.00 *Star Tiger* would have been 380 miles away. Tuck tried again at 03.15 and this time the operator in Bermuda picked up the signal strongly enough to confirm a first-class bearing of 72°. In this case a first-class bearing meant it should be accurate to within two degrees. He transmitted this vital information to the aircraft and Bob Tuck acknowledged its receipt at exactly 03.17. This was the last anyone ever heard from *Star Tiger*.

At 03.15 the Tudor would have been approximately 2 hours and 15 minutes or around 340 miles from its destination. Frank Griffin later stated that as he got nearer to Bermuda the cloud thickened, but that even at 2,000ft he had been able to see the marine lights from 25 miles away. If we assume that McMillan had to use that single radio bearing from 340 miles out to find the islands, in order to take him within a 25-mile radius of Bermuda (to be able to see the lights), the bearing would have to be accurate to within 4.2°. If it was not, then *Star Tiger* would have flown right past Bermuda.

The radio procedures were not strictly adhered to by the ground station in Bermuda. It was stipulated that the radio station monitoring the progress of aircraft on this oceanic sector should not let more than 30 minutes pass without communication with the aircraft. The radio logs show that after receiving a message from *Star Tiger* at 22.10, the Cable and Wireless Radio Telegraphy Station in Bermuda did not make contact again until 55 minutes later at 23.05. Again, after a position report at 23.15 no further contact was made until 23.57. This may not be significant when one realises that at the crucial stage of the flight, i.e. the last communications with the aircraft, a period of only 33 minutes elapsed between the acknowledgement of the radio bearing by *Star Tiger* at 03.17 and a routine call from Bermuda at 03.50 which received no reply. Whatever had happened to the Tudor it was either something which prevented radio transmissions to Bermuda, or the aircraft was down in the ocean sometime between 03.17 and 03.50. When the operator received no reply at 03.50 he called Approach Control to ask if *Star Tiger* had contacted them. It had not. He tried to make contact with the aircraft again at 04.00. Still nothing. When he was unable to contact the aircraft by 04.40 he raised the alarm.

Stargirl Priscilla Vinyals was in Bermuda waiting to take out the next leg of *Star Tiger*'s flight to Havana. At 03.00 (local) she was awoken with the news that the aircraft was missing. She dressed quickly and joined the rest of the crew who were being briefed on the situation and who, instead of working on the Tudor, would now be searching for it. Together they went to the airport and boarded the Lancastrian that had been flown in earlier by Frank Griffin. Captain Jeff Rees took the controls but Frank Griffin, although tired after his long flight, insisted on going too.

They flew backwards and forwards over the area where they believed *Star Tiger* may have come down, each of them straining their eyes for a glimpse of something, however small, that would give them a clue as to what had happened. After 8 hours they had not seen a single thing that even hinted at *Star Tiger's* fate.

Tired and upset they returned to Kindley Field. British South American Airways was a relatively small airline and the crews all knew each other. *Star Tiger* had now been missing for so many hours that they all knew that, barring a miracle, they were unlikely to see their workmates ever again.

Arriving at the White Horse Tavern, they went to the restaurant for their first meal of the day. Knowing where they had been and what they had been doing, Arthur, the proprietor, was not his usual jovial self. He took them to a table, sat them down and brought them drinks. Having eaten their dinner and talked endlessly about what could have happened to their friends, the members of the makeshift search party were beginning to get a little bit rowdy. Arthur was happy to let them get on with it, appreciating how upset they all were. After a few more drinks had been consumed one of them decided to demonstrate his skill with a trick which involved a raw egg and a glass. The trick went wrong and the egg went flying across the restaurant, just missing the ear of another diner, and smashed against the wall. Not knowing the reason for their behaviour, the man was outraged and complained loudly to Arthur but, instead of receiving the expected apology, Arthur told him that if he did not like it he could leave and promptly turned him and the rest of his party out of the restaurant.

At the news of the disappearance of the Tudor, a massive search operation had sprung into action. By 07.16 (03.16 local) a Boeing B-17 equipped with a radar scanner was airborne. In total thirty other aircraft took part in the search, most flying as low as 200ft above the waves. Three ships were also involved. It was only called off at nightfall on Tuesday 3 February after 104 flights had been made, totalling 882 hours in the air. The search was coordinated by the USAF at Kindley Field and every possible sighting of something on the surface of the water was investigated. Even on 1 February when the weather was appalling and made landing at Bermuda hazardous, seven aircraft continued to search. Later, the enquiry praised the USAF highly for its supreme efforts and courage in mounting such a search in difficult conditions. It is tragic that all their efforts were in vain as not one single item connected with *Star Tiger* was found.

Many have speculated that as there was no distress message received from the aircraft, whatever brought it down must have been something violent and sudden. This is not necessarily the case. A complete radio failure at a crucial part of the flight could have produced the same result. There were question marks over the safety of the cabin heater in the Tudor and it has been said that this could have exploded with catastrophic results. We know that the heater on this particular aircraft had been giving problems since the aircraft left London and it is almost certain that it was not operating on the final flight. It is therefore unlikely that, as some have suggested, fuel was continually being pumped into a non-functioning heater which was then ignited by a spark, causing an explosion. Controlled tests were carried out on a Tudor heating system by BSAA staff in the spring of 1948 during which they deliberately shut off the heater, but continued to pump fuel into it. It did not explode.

The loss of *Star Tiger* attracted a great deal of public attention and resulted in the first report of a Court Investigation to be published since the R.101 airship disaster in 1930. Indeed the Court of Enquiry itself was extremely thorough and called a great many expert witnesses to help ascertain the most likely cause of the accident. Lord Macmillan was appointed by Lord Nathan to preside over the enquiry. The court sat for 11 days in public and met in private on four occasions, one of which was a visit to London airport on 4 May 1948 to inspect a similar Tudor IV, including a short flight in the aircraft. This examination of *Star Lion* by MCA experts in London showed that the maintenance of the aircraft had been carried out by BSAA engineering staff carefully and correctly. The only anomaly they discovered was that the pressure of gas in the operating bottles for the emergency dinghies was slightly lower than required for reliable operation.

An examination of the position reports from both *Star Guide* and *Star Tiger* showed some anomalies. The planned altitude for both was 2,000ft, but there would inevitably have been variations in the actual height above the sea. The navigation log for the Lancastrian showed variations in height ranging from 2,150ft down to 1,500ft. These log entries stopped at 19.50, but the meteorological log was maintained throughout the flight. The height recorded in this log was 2,000ft every single hour, even when the navigation log showed a different figure. All the hourly position reports from *Star Tiger* gave its height as 20,000ft. This is almost certainly an error by the radio officer, but it indicates that the position reports were unlikely to give a true representation of the height of the aircraft above the water and it means that we cannot therefore be certain of the exact height of *Star Tiger* at the time of its last transmission. Also, the forecast issued at 14.00 for Zone 13 gave the QNH pressure as 1021 millibars, whereas the actual QNH was found to be 1016. Assuming the altimeters were set to 1021 millibars this would only account for an inaccuracy in the indicated altitude of around 150ft. Not a significant error, even at 2,000ft.

The responsibilities of the BSAA Station Manager in Bermuda, Wing Commander Ralph, were discussed in depth at the enquiry and his handling of the transmission of accurate weather information was criticised. Coming in for particular scrutiny were the delays in transmission of the weather forecasts specifically requested by *Star Guide* and the fact that the crucial weather report at 02.42 had only been addressed to the Lancastrian. This highlighted an anomaly, in that the station manager claimed at 02.42 he was engaged in obtaining further weather information specifically for *Star Tiger*, yet there is no record of this taking place and the forecast issued to the aircraft of winds 'S.S.W. 20 knots', using the points of the compass, was not in a format usually issued by the Meteorological Office.

The investigation also looked into BSAA maintenance standards and in particular the qualifications of engineers who had maintained *Star Tiger*. This resulted in a disturbing discovery. It was found that while all the engineers involved in the maintenance of the aircraft were suitably licensed and qualified, the standard of one of the engineers stationed in Santa Maria was found to be seriously lacking. Further enquiries revealed that the engineer in question had previously been employed by BOAC as an engineering inspector and his care and skill in the certification of the safety of aircraft had been found unsatisfactory. However, when he left BOAC for another airline, still in the same engineering role, BOAC gave him a glowing reference which seemed completely at odds with the information on his personal file. When questioned, BOAC was unable to offer a satisfactory explanation. The result was that when the engineer later applied to work for BSAA the company was told that he had received excellent testimonials from BOAC and it went ahead and employed him on 22 November 1947 as Station Engineer at Santa Maria. The corporation then received numerous complaints from commanders of aircraft passing through the Azores regarding his poor standard of work, and BSAA wrote a letter to Santa Maria dated 28 January 1948 recalling him to London. Before the letter arrived, he inspected and certified as safe the engines of *Star Tiger* prior to the aircraft's final take-off. There is no evidence to suggest that this last action was improper, or that he acted incompetently in any way on this occasion, but it does raise the question of why BOAC gave misleading references.

When the Report of the Court Investigation was published, advance copies were sent to various key people, including the Chairman of BSAA, John Booth, and the newly appointed Chairman of BOAC, Sir Harold Hartley, who was away at the time on a tour of South Africa. The covering letter from George Lindgren at the Ministry of Civil Aviation warned Sir Harold that the report contained a criticism of BOAC and felt he would appreciate being aware of it before the press got hold of the story. When Sir Harold returned from South Africa, he wrote to Lindgren saying that he had already investigated the circumstances and that there was 'conflicting evidence as to the engineer's competence on the file'. In a later correspondence from J.O. Blair-Cunynghame at BOAC it was stated that the engineer's work had deteriorated when he was posted to Dorval, but until that time his work and conduct were very good. He had resigned from BOAC shortly after being recalled from his posting in Dorval, Montreal, being faced with demotion, and sought employment with the Argentinian airline FAMA, but eventually joined BSAA instead. John Booth was not happy with the BOAC explanation and wrote to Sir Harold Hartley to request that his personnel officers take more care with the accuracy of employee references in future as he believed that BSAA had been misled.

When the results of the official enquiry and other independent investigations were published, they proposed many possibilities to explain the loss of *Star Tiger*. These included: radio failure, total electrical failure, constructional defect, meteorological hazard, errors of altimetry, incapacitation of crew, mechanical failure of engines, fuel fire, engine fire, shedding of a propeller, loss of control, auto-pilot malfunction, loss of engine power, deployment of dinghy and loss of freight door.

While all these were examined in detail, there was absolutely no evidence to promote any of them from possibility to probability.

After the accident, BSAA issued prudent instructions to its captains stating that the Santa Maria to Bermuda sector should not, in future, be flown below 4,000ft and that the autopilot should not be used at altitudes of 2,000ft or below. A number of other recommendations were made regarding fuel reserves, radio procedures, crew fatigue and weather reporting. All these changes undoubtedly improved the safety of future flights to Bermuda, but they were too late to help the thirty-one people aboard *Star Tiger*.

At the end of the enquiry on 21 August 1948, Lord Macmillan published his conclusion:

In closing this Report it may truly be said that no more baffling problem has ever been presented for investigation. In the complete absence of any reliable evidence as to either the nature or the cause of the disaster to *Star Tiger* the Court has not been able to do more than suggest possibilities, none of which reaches the level even of probability.

He ended with:

What happened in this case will never be known and the fate of *Star Tiger* must remain an unsolved mystery.

It is hard to disagree with that.

Chapter 12

Lord Nathan Deals a Crushing Blow

The two weeks following the loss of *Star Tiger* brought about a frenzy of activity; not all of it concerned the crash.

On Monday 2 February the Parliamentary Secretary was given notice of a question which would be asked in the House of Commons that afternoon by Air Commodore Harvey, MP for Macclesfield and chairman of Westminster Airways. Harvey wanted to know if the Minister would be making a statement about the missing aircraft and also if the Tudor IVs were to be grounded.

Lord Nathan telephoned Don Bennett to tell him that since the question of the crash was being discussed in the House later that day, he hoped that he could tell the members that BSAA was suspending its service the following day. Bennett was flabbergasted. In his opinion there was no reason to ground the aircraft and he said that both he and BSAA had confidence in the Tudor. He found it hard to understand why the aircraft should be withdrawn from service when there was not a scrap of evidence that the crash had been directly caused by something that was wrong with it and he pointed out to the Minister that a suspension of services would involve a serious commercial loss.

Later that afternoon Nathan had a meeting with the deputy chairman of BSAA, Sir John Stephenson. Sir John asked what Nathan proposed to do and was told that failure of the aircraft could not be eliminated and so it was likely that the ARB would recommend that the Tudor IV should not only be taken off its regular service the following day, but that it should also be transferred to another route altogether. The logic of his statement was not immediately apparent and Sir John told him that the Tudor IV had already made forty-eight successful flights on this same route.

One wonders why the Minister thought that it would be safer to take the aircraft off the route if in fact the crash had been caused by 'failure of the aircraft'. The position of the Azores and of Bermuda made the recovery of aircraft parts from the crash very unlikely since both places were tiny dots of land in the vastness of the Atlantic Ocean. However, it would seem reasonable to investigate the aircraft type to ascertain if any problems existed. By simply removing it to another route would merely make it easier to collect the pieces should it be discovered that the type was not airworthy and another crash occurred.

Following the afternoon session in the House of Commons and a meeting with officials of the ARB, Nathan again telephoned Bennett that evening and told him that after seeking advice from the ARB, he intended to ground the Tudor IV. Bennett wanted to know if the C of A had been withdrawn as it seemed to him that that would be the only way to legally ground the aircraft. Curiously Nathan said that it had not been as there was no positive evidence as to the cause of the crash, which would justify the withdrawal. He merely felt that, as the ARB had advised that it would be prudent to ground the aircraft while investigations were underway, he had to take its advice. He accepted full responsibility for the decision which Bennett described as a 'shocking blow to civil aviation'. Nathan said that he understood Bennett's reaction, but thought that he was exaggerating when he said that he believed it would take years to overcome the effect on British civil aviation. Bennett advised him to check the foreign newspapers the day after his decision was announced and see what they thought. When he again said that the Tudor still had its C of A, Nathan replied that there was a question about whether or not the aircraft had been through sufficient trials. Sensing defeat Bennett replied that it was for Nathan to make the decision and that he would, of course, carry out the Minister's wishes. He immediately called Sir John Stephenson to give him the bad news.

The White Paper of December 1945 had expressly decreed that all three corporations would be required to use British aircraft for their operations. Of the two long-haul companies BSAA was the only one to have abided by the order and now, in doing so, was being forced to suffer. The Minister's statement about the insufficient trials must beg the question as to why BSAA was allowed to use the Tudor IV in the first place if he truly believed what he was saying.

Sir John Stephenson telephoned Lord Nathan immediately after receiving the call from Bennett. Nathan told him that he had had no alternative but to ground the Tudor. Sir John replied that BSAA might as well close down and that he thought the board might all resign following the Minister's action. Nathan could not see why that might happen and cited cases of other aircraft types that had been grounded following accidents. Sir John acknowledged that it had happened, but pointed out that this had been done for a specific fault and that there was no proof that there were any faults on the Tudor.

Lord Nathan was not about to change his mind and Sir John was becoming increasingly annoyed so said that he had better leave it there and hung up.

On 4 February Don Bennett wrote to the Minister acknowledging his telephoned instructions that the Tudor IV was to be grounded. Lord Nathan also received a number of telegrams from the concerned chairman of A.V. Roe, Lord Dobson. He was even buttonholed by Lord Rendell in the House of Lords with the suggestion that Tudors should be scrapped altogether. One wonders what would have happened to civil aviation if the Americans had panicked in such a way every time one of their aircraft had crashed. There certainly would not have been any DC-3 Dakotas left. During the time that BSAA was flying, crashes of DC-3s worldwide caused more than 980 deaths and yet they still fly today.

The British public woke up to a headline in the *Daily Express* on 5 February which said:

'I contest Lord Nathan's grounding of Tudor IV'
by Air Vice-Marshal D.C.T. Bennett, Chief Executive of British South American Airways Corporation, whose Tudor IV airliners have been grounded by order of the Ministry of Civil Aviation (in an exclusive interview with Basil Cardew)

There are two outstanding forces at work in civil aviation today. In the first category are those who are openly anti-British in aviation. In the second those who entered it either for selfish interests or for other reasons – but are totally ignorant of aviation.

These two categories are far more influential than the professionals and those who have given their lives to it.

At the end of the war we were in a weak position in civil aviation in purely physical assets. But we were more than generously blessed with people with the 'know how'.

Unfortunately civil aviation at once became a political football and has been kicked about this dirty arena ever since.

Many criticise the results of the nationalised airways over their first year's operation. I cannot help but agree in many respects with this criticism. But had more natural laws of enterprise and results been permitted, this unhealthy situation would never have occurred.

Surely it is clear that if there is to be a State-owned policy then the best chance of its succeeding would be to permit as much freedom within the structure as possible.

The complete opposite has, in fact, been the case. Interference with management has now reached such a degree that it has become increasingly difficult for an airline executive to be held responsible for the results he achieves.

Take Tudor IV

For example, if there were any faults in the Tudor IV – and I do not for one minute consider that there are – then I would point out that the ultimate responsibility lies in the fact that the executives concerned have not been able to obtain their requirements.

The fault here has been the procedure laid down by the Government in the ordering of aircraft for the operators. The operator is not allowed to go direct to the aircraft constructor, but must go through Ministry channels. The ordering of aircraft is a vital factor in the management of an airline, yet it has remained outside the control of the corporation boards.

The present case concerns the Tudor IV. This airliner, after being handed over to the airline has in fact been thoroughly tested in every conceivable way.

As far as has been humanly possible every investigation and precaution has been carried out with it. Very special and abnormal inspections have been instituted to ensure the highest degree of safety. Training of crews handling the Tudor IV has been meticulously executed and the crews have been checked.

That we should have lost a Tudor IV in spite of all this is as unbelievable as the circumstances of the accident themselves.

But it was with the deepest possible regret that I heard from Lord Nathan, the Minister of Civil Aviation, on Tuesday night that he found it necessary to interfere with what I took to be a matter for my own decision namely, whether an aircraft which is fully certified as airworthy should be withdrawn from service without any evidence.

I add at once that I would be the first to withdraw a plane from service given even the faintest grounds of expectation for improved safety.

But on the advice of all the authorities concerned, including the Accidents Investigation Branch of the Ministry of Civil Aviation and the Air Registration Board, I have been unable to find the slightest grounds for any suspicion of that in the Tudor IV. None whatever.

My confidence

I very deeply regret, therefore, that I should have been ordered to withdraw the Tudor IV from service, thereby inferring a lack of confidence in this type of airliner.

All those interested in civil aviation can be assured that I have no lack of confidence whatever in the Tudor IV nor in the ability of British aviation in general to achieve the success which British temperament and ability are bound to win if given their freedom.

From the moment that the article appeared in the newspaper the attitude of Lord Nathan towards BSAA altered. When he had spoken to both Bennett and Stephenson he had expressed sympathy for their plight and had said that he regretted the action he had to take. On the afternoon of 5 February at a meeting with Sir John and various officials of the MCA his tone changed. He might have been expected to condemn the piece in the *Daily Express* and, later on in the meeting, he did just that. However, he began with an attack on BSAA itself. The record of the meeting at The National Archives in Kew is designated, not as a minute but as a 'Note of the salient points of a meeting between the Minister and the Deputy Chairman of BSAA'. It leads one to speculate that, had the record been a minute, perhaps it might have been significantly different. Given the content of the 'note' it seems extremely unfair to BSAA (and to history) that it was not properly minuted.

Lord Nathan began by giving an account of BSAA as it appeared to him. He spoke of letters that had been sent to him about the three airline corporations and said that although some were praising their services the majority were letters of complaint. He found it to be important that although the letters about BOAC and BEA criticised the traffic management of both of the companies, those about BSAA complained about operational standards. If he were to be believed, then things must have changed drastically from two years before when passengers were full of praise for BSAA's operational standards. The 'note' says:

By way of example, he quoted from a letter he had received the previous evening and from a letter of last December from a distinguished and reliable person in Civil Aviation, who had expressed his views on the basis of knowledge gained on the route to South America and of his experiences on a flight in the Tudor IV on returning to the UK.

The names of the people who had written to Nathan were obviously not regarded as being 'salient points' as they do not appear in the note.

It is in the nature of human beings to complain and it would be very surprising if BOAC and BEA had not received complaints about its operations. Only a month before the meeting in question, a Vickers 610 Viking belonging to BEA had crashed at Ruislip while making an approach into Northolt airport on a scheduled domestic flight. In the time since the Civil Aviation Act of January 1946 setting up the three state corporations had been passed, there had been several other accidents to aircraft, belonging not only to BSAA, but to BOAC and to BEA as well. It is inconceivable that these incidents had not elicited a single complaint about operational standards.

Having made his detrimental remarks about BSAA, Lord Nathan then went on to speak about the article in the *Daily Express*. He said that this was not the first time that Bennett had overstepped the mark and had gone to the press with complaints about the government, its policies and the MCA. He reminded those present that:

At a meeting with the Chairmen [of the three corporations] in February, 1947 [he] explained that highly paid executives of Government Corporations could obviously not dissociate themselves from their obligation loyally to carry out the policy laid down for them. Moreover, it was implied that any contribution by a highly paid executive to the press carried with it the approval of the Board.

Sir John Stephenson acknowledged that the article had created problems for him and the other members of the board as they had had no idea that Bennett had given the interview to the *Daily Express*. He agreed that it was 'gravely improper', but said that he wanted to wait until the return of the Chairman, who had been away in Bermuda but was due back on the following Saturday, before discussing what steps could be taken to repair the situation. Lord Nathan said he wanted to see both Booth and Stephenson on 9 February, after Booth's return.

Sir John, in the meantime, asked if he could see a copy of the letter sent to the Minister from the ARB about the recommendation to ground the Tudor. He had been told of the contents by a reporter who, it was alleged, had seen the letter before the Minister had received it and he wanted to satisfy himself that what he had been told was, in fact, true. Nathan said that he was unable to show it to him and that he had given the same reply to Sir Roy Dobson at A.V. Roe when he had made the same request. His reason for the refusal was that:

> . . . any disclosure either by [him] or by the ARB of contents of communications between them would be destructive of the confidence which must necessarily exist in their relations. . . . At the same time [he] stated that if a letter were brought to his notice purporting to be a copy of the communication to him, and the two documents did not tally, he would feel bound to say so. . . . He, as Minister, fully accepted the responsibility for his decisions and did not wish to divest himself of that responsibility. The ARB were his advisers and he was free to accept, or reject, their advice.

Sir John said that he had been told the letter stated that nothing had been brought to the attention of the ARB that would demand the withdrawal of the C of A and that any decision was a matter for the Minister's judgement. Lord Nathan simply said that it was not correct. It does seem rather odd that Nathan was unwilling to discuss with the deputy chairman of an airline which had just lost an aircraft what the ARB had actually said about it when he himself had claimed responsibility for the decision. If the ARB *had* recommended, as he had said they had in his previous conversations with both Bennett and Stephenson, that the Tudor should be grounded, how could he be breaking their confidence by showing that statement in writing? His reluctance to confirm the ARB's recommendation to either BSAA, as operator of the aircraft, or to A.V. Roe as manufacturer, seems to be open to misconstruction and leaves one wondering if, in fact, the ARB did recommend grounding the Tudor at all. It seems more likely that Nathan made the decision himself but, unwilling to be seen to have done it, blamed the ARB instead. This, of course, also throws up doubts as to his reason for grounding the aircraft. His motives may have been entirely proper, but the manner in which he implemented the decision will, for ever, cast doubts on them.

In 1949, following the loss of *Star Ariel*, a factually incorrect article appeared in the *Daily Graphic* about the suitability of Tudors for passenger flights and referred to the *Star Tiger* enquiry. It was contested by Air Commodore Vernon Brown of the Accident Investigation Branch who said:

> Whatever may have been the criticisms at that time, the fact remains that the Air Registration Board had recommended a Certificate of Airworthiness to the

Star Tiger and, despite the reservation about the flight testing of the de-icing installation in icing conditions, considered the issue of a Certificate was justified.

Nowhere was there a single word indicating that the ARB had recommended that the Tudor be grounded.

The morning after the *Daily Express* article, Don Bennett requested a meeting with Lord Nathan, whose private secretary contacted Sir John Stephenson to canvass his opinion. Stephenson said that he would prefer any meeting to wait until after he had had a chance to speak to John Booth who would be arriving back in Britain the following day. The private secretary concurred with this decision and pointed out that it was not normal practice for the minister to 'communicate direct with Chief Executives'. He was obviously either unaware of, or had forgotten, the telephone calls made by Lord Nathan to Don Bennett on 2 February, only four days before; perhaps 'normal practice' was dependent upon who was initiating the communication.

Because his request for a meeting had been denied, Bennett then wrote a letter to the minister which said:

My dear Minister,
I have just run into a difficulty concerning our TUDOR problem on which I would like to enlist your support.
   Obviously the most likely cause of the loss of STAR TIGER is sabotage. After preliminary discussions with members of MI5 we felt that there was a very good case for investigating possible criminal aspects of the loss of this British aircraft. MI5 were apparently themselves anxious to help but have since been informed that it is not within their terms of reference. They did, however, on my behalf, contact CID to request their assistance in this matter. I am now informed by MI5 that CID have refused to co-operate.
   I wondered whether there was anything which you might do to help.
Yours sincerely,
D.C.T. BENNETT

In his biography of Don Bennett, *Master Airman*, author Alan Bramson says of the loss of the Tudor:

He [Don Bennett] will tell you that in the case of *Star Tiger* . . . a known war-registered saboteur was seen standing nearby shortly before it left Santa

Maria in the Azores for Bermuda on its last flight, that with the aid of Air Commodore Pointer (head of MI5 who knew the names of those involved) he was getting uncomfortably close to the truth in his enquiries when Prime Minister Attlee gave instruction for the matter to be dropped because of the effect such findings might have on international relations.

On 9 February Lord Nathan met with John Booth and Sir John Stephenson. The meeting was also attended by the Parliamentary Secretary, Permanent Secretary and Deputy Secretary to the Ministry of Civil Aviation. The record of the meeting was made by Lord Nathan's staff again as 'notes' not minutes and, as such, it may be unwise to regard it as the definitive version of what happened that day.

Booth is said to have told the Minister that he would resign from his position as chairman as he could no longer work with 'a Chief Executive who displayed so little loyalty to the Board and to the Minister'. He said that the newspaper article was the climax to 'a series of disagreements and acts of disloyalty' and the board had decided that it could no longer work with Bennett. They had asked for his resignation which he had refused and so they only had two courses of action – they could resign themselves or the Minister could terminate Bennett's position on the board. Lord Nathan then said that Bennett would have to go and advised Booth to take legal advice about the grounds for his termination of employment as he did not want an action to be brought for wrongful dismissal. Booth said that they had already considered the terms and wanted to give him a generous settlement which would include one year's salary. Nathan thought that this was too much and that three months' would be perfectly adequate as it was not usual to make a payment at all in the case of dismissal for misconduct. He thought that dismissal was definitely justified as the newspaper article showed that his conduct was incompatible with the post of chief executive. The note of the meeting says:

Both Mr Booth and Sir John Stephenson concurred and stated that this was precisely their view. Later, in a reply to an enquiry, Mr Booth indicated that the basis, but not necessarily the precise terms of the Board's conclusion, was that they could no longer work with AVM Bennett as Chief Executive. The Board had lost confidence in him, and in view of the large number of matters on which differences of opinion exist, and have existed for some time past, they had decided to dispense with his services.

There was then further discussion about terms and it was agreed that six months' salary would be sufficient as Bennett's appointment to the board would have expired the following July anyway. Nathan would have been pleased if Bennett could have been persuaded to resign 'in order to obviate the implications of a generous payment on dismissal' but was told that this was very unlikely as 'he would regard it as tantamount to an admission of having failed in the discharge of his duties'. The note goes on to say:

> In the ensuing discussion, Mr Booth explained, more specifically, that for some considerable time past he had had serious anxieties about AVM Bennett's disloyalty to the Board. He had either failed to implement decisions of the Board or had circumvented them in an evasive manner. Sir John Stephenson interposed to say that there had been many examples, with unfailing regularity. Mr Booth added that quite apart from the *Daily Express* incident, it had been his full intention to have a 'show down' in any event. The *Daily Express* article was the climax, and signified disloyalty to the Minister and to the whole set up for which AVM Bennett is working.
>
> The Minister enquired whether AVM Bennett was to be regarded as a safe operator. He did not, of course, mean a pilot.
>
> Mr Booth replied that AVM Bennett had always had a plausible answer to any doubts expressed by the Board or by the Chairman of any particular project. But, summed up Mr Booth, his record condemns him.

Nathan then disclosed the contents of the letter that Bennett had written to him regarding his theory of sabotage. Their reaction was said to have been 'a tacit agreement that this was an indication of lack of perspective'. It might also be construed as being a lack of confidentiality on the part of Nathan in disclosing the contents of one letter to the board of BSAA while refusing to do the same for another; that of the ARB letter. It would surely have been incumbent on any Minister of Civil Aviation to treat a claim of sabotage as being serious, whether or not he himself believed that the theory had any value. His oft-quoted claim of taking responsibility might have backfired on him if Bennett had not been prevented from pursuing his investigations.

Lord Nathan went swiftly on to ask what the board of BSAA intended to do about replacing Bennett. Booth said that he would like to split the position between two managers – one on the commercial side and one on the operational and technical sides. Nathan, it was said, felt that he might be able to help the board in its search for new managers and suggested three names for them to consider – Ashley of Skyways, McIntyre of Scottish Aviation and Brancker of BOAC. In view of the fact that his qualifications for the job of minister were said to have been that he had received a few pointers from an enthusiastic amateur pilot, it is a wonder that he felt competent to suggest anyone. But considering the ultimate choice to replace Bennett, perhaps he did not make this particular suggestion at all. Booth was said to have replied that the board had already considered the question themselves and favoured D. Handover, formerly of BEA and BOAC, who was now working with Swedish Airlines, and Air Vice-Marshal Herbert Brackley. A discussion ensued after which Booth was reported as saying that perhaps a combination of Brackley and Brancker might work.

The following day Lord Nathan wrote a letter to Prime Minister Clement Attlee telling him that the board of BSAA was, that day, giving notice to Air Vice-Marshal Bennett and that a statement would be given to the press as soon as Bennett had received the letter terminating his employment. He told Attlee that it had not been necessary for him to comment or take any action about the article in the *Daily Express* which had prompted the decision to sack Bennett. He had received a visit from Sir John Stephenson, deputy chairman of BSAA who:

> . . . came to tell me that this interview had created a difficult situation for him and his colleagues and had brought to a climax a situation which had been developing for some little time, and that he was proposing to give to Mr Booth on his return home on the following day certain advice which, though it was not put into terms, I was able to surmise.

While not actually lying, Nathan, was certainly bending the truth. It is difficult to know why he did this, but a brief re-examination of the sequence of events might lead one to believe that perhaps he was at pains to distance himself from the decision to sack Bennett because he had, in fact, instigated it.

Bennett had long been a thorn in the side of Nathan, who had become Minister of Civil Aviation in October 1946, only months after BSAA had begun its operations. Nathan did not like the Australian's plain speaking and impatience with bureaucracy and expected unquestioning loyalty from him. It seems that the chief executives of the other corporations were happy to toe the line, but Bennett believed in free speech and exercised his right to act on that belief.

On 2 February 1948, three days after the crash of *Star Tiger*, Nathan had, in the absence of John Booth, telephoned Sir John Stephenson to talk about the accident. When, the following day, he decided to ground the Tudor he called not Stephenson, but Bennett, to give him the news. This seems to have been a strange decision when one bears in mind the claim of his private secretary that it was not normal practice for the Minister to 'communicate direct with Chief Executives'. Knowing Bennett's temperament and his belief in the superiority of British aircraft, he would surely have expected Bennett to be angry at the decision. It was left to Bennett to inform Stephenson, which he did. This elicited a call from the deputy chairman to Nathan. Stephenson was also furious, declaring that BSAA might as well close down and that the board might all resign because 'people were entitled to know about these decisions'.

It seems that an argument ensued with the Minister trying to justify why he had made the decision and Stephenson claiming, as had Bennett, that the Tudor had done all the tests and had proved to be a sound aeroplane.

The *Daily Express* article appeared on 5 February and later that day Nathan met with Stephenson and began his attack on BSAA. Sir John mentioned that:

> ... he felt that the Board had been insufficiently consulted or kept informed on important matters, among other things, he cited the lack of knowledge amongst members of the Board of matters discussed at the periodical meetings of the Minister with the Chairmen.

At this point there was no mention by him of any problems with Bennett and his way of working and it was only when the Minister brought up the subject of the newspaper article that he is said to have admitted that he thought it was 'gravely improper' and that it had created an extremely difficult situation for the board. When Nathan enquired what steps the board intended to take about it Stephenson had expressed the wish to talk to Booth on his return before voicing any opinion. Then Nathan said that he wanted to see them both on the following Monday.

It was at this meeting that Nathan declared that the newspaper article showed that Bennett's conduct was incompatible with the post of chief executive, to which Booth and Stephenson were quoted as saying that this was precisely their view. Then Booth also said that neither he nor the board could work with AVM Bennett as Chief Executive, the board had lost confidence in him, and in view of the large number of matters on which differences of opinion exist, and had existed for some time past, they had decided to dispense with his services.

One wonders, if the Minister was indeed a truly impartial observer, why he did not censure Booth or Stephenson. He had spoken to them many times in the past and there had been a lot of contact between them since the *Star Tiger* crash and yet it seems that he had not questioned their ability to serve on the board of a state-owned airline when they had not brought to his attention their concerns about the way Bennett undertook his duties as Chief Executive, if in fact they really did have these concerns. Would it not have shown inefficiency on their part to have ignored what they claimed were the 'large number of matters on which differences of opinion exist'? If Bennett's conduct was as bad as they were now reported as saying it was, why had they not sought to dismiss him well before he had the chance to give the interview to the *Daily Express?* Perhaps because they were saying what someone wanted to hear rather than what had actually happened.

If Lord Nathan had contacted Sir John Stephenson and told him he had decided to ground the Tudors it would have been Sir John who would have passed the decision on to Bennett. Bennett would have had no cause to give the interview in which he made claims of interference if his own deputy chairman had told him to ground the aircraft. In calling Bennett directly, Nathan had forced a response from him, which he got in Bennett's letter to him acknowledging his instructions. But it had left him angry and frustrated and in a perfect state of mind to grant the interview to the newspaper.

The speed with which Nathan passed on the names to be considered as replacements for Bennett would suggest that the subject of his removal had been on his mind before the article ever appeared. Although Booth is said to have told him that the board had two people in mind as replacements for Bennett, at the end of the discussion 'Mr Booth appeared to think that a combination of Brancker and Brackley, assuming they could work together, might be satisfactory'. But if this were true he was agreeing with one of the Minister's suggestions without having had the opportunity to consult the board.

The record that exists of this meeting is described as a 'note of a meeting' rather than the minutes, and also bears the title 'Extract relating to Air Vice-Marshal Bennett'. Had they been minutes the account may have been a little more objective. According to the note it appears that Stephenson had completely forgotten his anger at the grounding of the Tudor and, despite having views that coincided entirely with Bennett's on 3 February, by the 9th he was actively stabbing him in the back.

Perhaps it had been the intention of His Majesty's Government to get rid of Bennett from the start. He had been appointed by the board of BLAA when it was a privately owned company, but even then had not received a vote of confidence from the government, possibly because of the fact that it, via the Air Ministry and Ambassador Leche, had been pushing for Lowell Yerex to become the chief executive.

Government papers are usually classified secret for a period of thirty years. In some particularly sensitive cases this can be extended. The folder containing all the material relating to the dismissal of Don Bennett as chief executive of BSAA was collected together on 12 February 1948, marked confidential and was closed until 2024. It is only due to recent Government legislation that it, along with other closed documents, has been released early. It does seem to be rather extreme to close a handful of documents and letters to the public for over seventy-five years when their subject matter was, on the surface, unimportant in terms of national security and it makes one wonder exactly who wanted to keep the details of those few days in February 1948 so secret.

Examination of a document written by John Booth on 28 January 1948 sheds some light on who was most likely to have had his name protected by the closure of the file. Booth called this document 'MEMORANDUM on the CONCEPTION and DEVELOPMENT of BSAA' and it was written two days before the loss of *Star Tiger*, the event which had started the furore culminating in the dismissal of Don Bennett ten days later. The document, which seems to have been written to coincide with the release of BSAA's first annual report, is a record of John Booth's experience in starting the airline, the backing he received from the shipping companies and the successes he, and the airline, had enjoyed up to that point. He mentioned mistakes, but also said that the airline's organisation was 'fundamentally different in set-up and outlook from that of the other two Corporations', a fact that he regarded as being positive. He cited the losses made by the other corporations saying, 'It is possible that if BSAA had been modelled to the same pattern as BOAC and BEA, our loss would have been proportionately smaller than theirs, but it would have approached, if not exceeded, seven figures.' This does not sound like the opinion of a man who had, for some time, harboured concerns about the way his company was being run and who felt that he could no longer work with the man who was running it. In fact, the part of the report which seems to settle the matter of Booth's thoughts about Bennett conclusively, says:

> After what I now consider a lucky escape, when we were toying with the idea of bringing in Lowell Yerex as the driving force, I made contact with Air Vice-Marshal Bennett through Captain Lamplugh of British Aviation Insurance Company, and it did not take me long to make up my mind that here was the man for the job. My judgement was backed by the representatives of the companies who were putting up the great bulk of the money. . .

Nowhere in the entire document does it state that he now felt differently about Bennett, nor is there a record of any negative thoughts regarding the Chief Executive from any one of those representatives who put up the funds for the airline or from any member of the board of BSAA. It is strange that this should be so if, in fact, Lord Nathan's version of events is to be believed. It rather suggests that the Minister had again overruled the board of BSAA. In the meeting with Sir John Stephenson on 5 February he had said that 'highly paid executives of Government Corporations could obviously not dissociate themselves from their *obligation loyally to carry out the policy laid down for them*' [authors' italics]. His policy seems to have been to get rid of Bennett.

A week after Bennett's departure from BSAA, Air Vice-Marshal Sir Conrad Collier, Director General of Technical Services at the Air Ministry, resigned. Asked by a newspaper reporter if his resignation had anything to do with disagreements with senior officials at the MCA regarding the nationalised airlines he said, 'You will have to fathom that out for yourself. I am not resigning because of my health.'

Following the letter terminating his services with the company he had worked so hard to set up, a statement made on Don Bennett's behalf was issued to the Press Association on 10 February 1948. It merely said: 'AVM Bennett has been forced to discontinue his appointment with BSAA because of an interview he gave last week to a newspaper correspondent'.

BSAA issued its own statement at 3.30 p.m. the following afternoon:

> In view of inaccurate statements made by the BBC and the Press, the Board of BSAA Corporation wish it to be known that they terminated the appointment of their Chief Executive owing to a difference of opinion on matters of policy resulting in his forfeiting the confidence of the board.

It is denied that the decision of the Board was in any way influenced by the Ministry of Civil Aviation.

Allegations that there have been resignations from the Staff, or that any general increases in pay have been promised, or even contemplated, are unfounded and are denied.

The suggestion that the Chief Executive's appointment was terminated because he exercised the right of freedom of speech is not in accordance with facts.

All members of the Board, including the late Chief Executive, have a collective responsibility for public statements on matters of general policy in relation to the Board's business. In making a public statement at variances with the views of the Board as a whole, the late Chief Executive was placing himself in a position which was incompatible with the relationship which must exist between the Board, which is responsible for policy, and the Chief Executive, who is responsible for carrying it out.

Despite Nathan's reluctance to compensate Bennett for the loss of his job and the subsequent discussions about the amount the board of BSAA wanted to give him (which Nathan wanted to be no more than three months' salary), he actually received one year's salary, described in the letter terminating his position as '. . . compensation for loss of office'.

On 11 February, the day after receiving his dismissal letter, Bennett gave another interview to the press, this time to Air Commodore L.G.S. Payne, air correspondent of the *Daily Telegraph*. Under the headline 'Airways Chief Made to Resign by Board' Bennett gave a much fuller statement than that made on his behalf the day before. He said:

A small team of professionals in British civil aviation two years ago started to create an airways system of vital importance to Britain.

As the leader of that team I have been proud of the extensive development and the results achieved over most difficult routes and in spite of all kinds of obstructions. We have used only British aircraft and we have taken the initiative on all the trunk routes we have followed.

In spite of difficulties we have, through a determination on the part of all concerned, managed to achieve success financially, which must be heartening to the British taxpayer.

Last week in view of current misinformation on certain affairs of this corporation, I granted an interview to a newspaper correspondent at which I expressed views concerning the obvious ills of British civil aviation in general and concerning recent interference with management by the Minister of Civil Aviation (Lord Nathan).

It is because of this newspaper article that I have been forced to discontinue my appointment. I feel that I should make it clear that I have been forced to take this course for exercising what I consider to be a right, namely the freedom of speech.

The article continued by reporting what Bennett had had to say when he addressed the Oxford University Cosmos Society, the previous evening: 'I warn you, never be successful: you will suffer enormously. Today, I have had the proudest honour of my life conferred on me. I have been sacked for having spoken my own mind.'

A Ministry of Civil Aviation spokesman was at pains to point out that Bennett had been dismissed by the board of BSAA and that the decision had nothing to do with Lord Nathan. John Booth also made a statement in which he said:

I fully support what Air Vice-Marshal Bennett says about the good work done by him and his team. There are no hard feelings about that.

It is simply that there is a fundamental difference of opinion between him and the Board, and that there comes a stage when those differences are such as to make it impossible to carry on working.

The same day that the *Daily Telegraph* article appeared, Lord Swinton, Minister of Civil Aviation when BLAA was formed, asked Lord Nathan for a statement in the House of Lords on the dismissal of Bennett. He also wanted to know whether or not Nathan had interfered in the grounding of the Tudor. Nathan responded by telling Swinton that it had always been his policy to avoid interference with the freedom of management, but that in the case of the grounding of the Tudor he felt that he could not ignore any possible cause of the accident to *Star Tiger* for the sake of the travelling public. He concluded his answer by saying: 'I am authorised by the Chairman of BSAA to state that his Board (with the exception of Air Vice-Marshal Bennett) unanimously approve the action taken by me and, further, he has informed me that had I not taken such action they would have done so.'

Bearing in mind the argument that had taken place when Nathan said he wanted the Tudor to be grounded, one wonders what Sir John Stephenson would have told Lord Swinton had he been asked directly for his personal opinion.

Meanwhile, business had to continue and John Booth sent out a letter to all BSAA's overseas managers telling them of the termination of Air Vice-Marshal Bennett's services. He asked them to give him the same level of loyalty that they had to Bennett and paid tribute to the former chief executive, saying:

> First, I would like to make clear that the Board and I are fully appreciative of the magnificent job the Air Vice-Marshal has done for British Civil Aviation, and for BSAA in organising and establishing this Corporation. He has worked extremely long hours with the greatest enthusiasm, and with unique knowledge of flying operations, and as a result has produced an organisation which in many respects is without rival throughout the world.

On 14 February, in accordance with the provisions of the Civil Aviation Act of 1946, Lord Nathan declared Air Vice-Marshal Bennett's position on the board of BSAA vacant. On 6 March the vacancy was offered to Herbert Brackley of BOAC; he accepted the post of chief executive four days later.

Herbert George Brackley, or 'Brackles' as he was known to family and friends, was born in Islington on 4 October 1894, the second of seven children. The family soon moved to Kent where Brackley was educated at Sevenoaks School. At the age of 18 he found himself a job with the news agency Reuters and began his lifelong passion for aviation during the First World War when he joined the Royal Naval Air Service in 1915. Later in the war he commanded a bomber squadron based in France and made seventy bombing raids.

In 1919, with the war over, Brackley went to Newfoundland with a new Handley Page aircraft to try to make the first direct crossing of the Atlantic Ocean. He was beaten in his attempt by John Alcock and Arthur Whitten Brown and, rather than be a disappointing second in the race, he instead flew from Newfoundland to New York, becoming the first man to do so. He made more record-breaking flights within the United States and the following year joined the Handley Page Transport Company which was beginning commercial flights between London and Paris. He remained in his post for only one year. In 1921 he was invited to join the British Air Mission to Japan and spent three years helping with the organisation and training of the Japanese Naval Air Service before returning to Britain to become superintendent of operations in the newly formed Imperial Airways.

His career with Imperial Airways was to last for fifteen years during which time he made many survey flights including those to establish long-distance routes using flying boats. The appointment with Imperial Airways ended because of the start of the Second World War when, at 45, Brackley joined the Royal Air Force. He served in both Coastal and Transport Commands and became an air commodore in 1943. At the end of the war he was appointed special assistant to the chairman of BOAC.

Brackley was approached on 2 March 1948 and was asked what his reaction would be if he were to be offered the post of chief executive of BSAA. He discussed it with his wife, Frida, and with others, including Lord Nathan.

Before he became involved in aviation Nathan had been a solicitor. One of his clients was Sir Robert Mond, chemist, industrialist and archaeologist, and son of Alfred Mond, 1st Baron Melchett, who had been one of the founding fathers and chairman of Imperial Chemical Industries (ICI). Nathan had become a very close friend of Mond, whose daughter Frida was Herbert Brackley's wife and, indeed, it was Mond, then chairman of the Liberal election campaign organisation, who gave Nathan significant help when he sought adoption as a parliamentary candidate. He was elected as a Liberal MP in 1929 and although he changed his allegiance to the Labour Party four years later, he and Mond remained firm friends.

Brackley had been hoping for a directorship in BOAC, but it had not materialised and he felt that perhaps the position in BSAA would give him the chance to use his many organisational skills to their full advantage. He was offered the position by John Booth on 6 March and accepted it four days later at a BSAA board meeting. Booth welcomed Brackley to the company and was pleased to tell him that the Ministry of Civil Aviation approved his appointment. As a friend of the family the Minister would hardly have done otherwise.

Nathan himself was also on the move. At the end of May he wrote to Clement Attlee telling him that he wished to resign, as his partner, Herbert Oppenheimer, was getting old and could no longer cope with the work at their law firm without Nathan being there to help. It seemed to be a very flimsy excuse for leaving such high office. Nathan's private secretary made a point of writing to his former boss saying:

> Rather to my surprise I have not heard one single person express any disbelief in the official and (unusual combination) true reason for your resignation. . . . I have not recently had much to do with the Corporations

or charter firms etc., but insofar as I have I have not heard anyone in those circles repeating any of the rumours we both expected.

Nathan left the MCA and returned to his law practice to assist his aged partner. It is difficult to see just how much help he gave when one also learns that he sat on eleven charitable committees, was master of two worshipful companies and a member of no less than nine Freemasonry lodges, becoming worshipful master of three and finally Grand Warden of the United Grand Lodge of England. After this he served on several medical committees, on some as vice-chairman or chairman. One wonders where he ever found the time to even see Herbert Oppenheimer, much less relieve his burden at the law practice.

Nathan's position at the MCA was taken by Lord Pakenham who, in 1961, became the 7th Earl of Longford, under which name he was well known as the champion of murderer Myra Hindley.

* * *

Herbert Brackley, meanwhile, began work as chief executive of BSAA. Although an extremely able man with extensive experience in aviation, he was very different from Don Bennett and would run the airline in much the same way that BOAC was managed. Where Bennett had been impatient with the pedantic, slow-moving civil servants with whom he had to deal, Brackley took them in his stride and played along with the 'old boy' ways of doing things. He seemed to favour doing business at social occasions and his wife recalled that his first month with BSAA was a constant round of engagements. These included a BSAA dance at Caxton Hall and, curiously, a cocktail party at the Dorchester which was hosted by Brackley and, according to Mrs Brackley was 'the only time in my husband's career he had ever been helped with a grant for entertainment'. The curious fact was that although he was being helped financially by BSAA to throw a party, it was not to introduce him to the staff or even to introduce the staff to him; it was for former members of Imperial Airways, not only those in BSAA, but in BOAC and BEA as well, and was described by his wife as being 'a very happy informal reunion when so many old friends, who had really done the spade work in the past, met for the first time and were remembered'. It sounded like a self-indulgence, since it was a meeting of people who already knew each other, rather than a useful way of spending taxpayers' money, and one cannot help but wonder if the name of

former Imperial Airways pilot Air Vice-Marshal Donald Bennett was on the
guest list.

Brackley obviously felt that, in being offered the post of chief executive of
BSAA, he was being asked to change the entire ethos of the airline rather
than just replace Bennett and thought of it as 'the tremendous task ahead in
the reorganisation of BSAA'.

Since he was new to the company it seems reasonable to assume that
he had not taken this decision alone and had, in fact, been told to make
sweeping changes. It is hard to understand why this should have been. John
Booth's glowing tribute to Bennett, despite his dismissal, would suggest that
if he and the board were at odds with the former chief executive at all it was
only over his own personal methods of working rather than with the overall
organisation and progress of the airline.

Brackley, an avid supporter of the flying boat, planned big changes for the
airline and in September decided to do a tour of inspection of BSAA facilities
in Lisbon and West Africa. He noted that the purpose of his journey was
'to assess the importance of transferring our base from Dakar to Bathurst
following many complaints from passengers and crew of the conditions under
which we operate at Dakar; to inspect Yundum airfield at Bathurst, the Rest
House in Fajara and the flying boat base at Half Die, Bathurst'.

He left for his tour of inspection on 20 October but did not travel on his own
airline. Instead he took a BOAC flight to Tripoli, then went on to Kano and
then Lagos in Nigeria, where he lunched with the governor at Government
House before flying on to Accra in Ghana where he stayed overnight. The
following day he went on to Freetown, Sierra Leone, via Abidjan in the Ivory
Coast and Monrovia in Liberia, before finally reaching a destination that had
actually been on the BSAA route – Bathurst, capital of The Gambia. Here
Brackley stayed with the Governor, Sir Andrew Wright. About his visit there
he said:

I made a close examination of runways, the buildings and working
of International Radio at Yundum and inspected Fajara Rest House
and flying boat base at Half Die. The 5 year old laterite runways had
consolidated but the pierced steel planking, with normal maintenance,
will take the full weight of Tudor or equivalent aircraft for a number of
years. I recommend adding 200 yards of PSP to down wind leg. Ample
PSP is available at Bathurst.

In all four Colonies I had a most cordial reception and was grateful to
the Governor for the arrangements made to discuss possibilities of BSAA
operating along their coasts.

All expressed keen regret that BSAA had forsaken Bathurst for Dakar and
expressed the hope that we would soon return.

. . . Returning via Casablanca and Lisbon I inspected the new flying boat
base under construction at Lisbon. It is ideally situated near the Airport and
designed to take large flying boats of the Saunders Roe 45 class; it should
be ready by the time we may wish to make use of it.

Brackley left Lisbon on a BSAA aircraft, the first he had taken on this trip,
and arrived in London exhausted, having spent the previous night at an
embassy ball.

In November it had been arranged that the still relatively new chief
executive would make a trip to South America. His wife described it as one
'with many State visits to pay and much disciplinary action to take behind
the scenes'. The trip began on 10 November when Brackley left London in fog
for Lisbon, then on to Dakar, Natal, Recife and Rio de Janeiro where he stayed
in the Copacabana Palace Hotel. All along the way there were meetings with
both government officials and those of BSAA's handling companies. By the
time he reached Rio he was tired but not too tired to write a letter to his son,
David, in which he complained about the workmanship of the York, saying
that it vibrated so badly that cutlery kept bouncing off the tables when the
meals were being served. He finished the letter by saying that it was proving
to be a hectic trip and that he hoped he would find time the next morning for
a swim before starting the day's meetings.

The next morning Brackley did make time for his swim. It was to be his last.
Ignoring the red flags and the warnings not to swim at Copacabana Beach
that day, he was caught in a strong current and, under the unseeing eyes
of the statue of Christ the Redeemer high in the hills overlooking the bay,
he drowned sometime before 9 a.m. The alarm was raised when the BSAA
manager at Rio, Wing Commander W.J.R. Shepherd, went to the hotel to fetch
him for his morning meetings.

His body was brought back to his stunned family and friends in England
in BSAA York G-AHFC, *Star Dew*. At every transit stop flowers had been
taken on board and when the aircraft arrived at London airport on the
afternoon of Sunday 21 November, only eleven days after Brackley had left

for South America, their perfume, as the doors were opened, was said to be overpowering. On Friday 26 November the chief executive's body was again placed in an aircraft and flown to his home at Langham in Norfolk for burial. The aircraft had been arranged by John Booth and was another BSAA York G-AHFD, *Star Mist*. Booth said of Brackley in a tribute in *The Times*:

> The British South American Airways Corporation has suffered a cruel loss in the untimely death of its chief executive. It was not only that he was a fine airman, one of the outstanding pioneers of our great overseas air routes, and also an air officer who rendered great service to his country in two wars, but he had gifts of character and personality that won him esteem of a kind that few men are able to command. After long and immensely valuable services to civil aviation, he came to British South American Airways to undertake a task for which he was admirably equipped and in which he had already added to his great reputation.

For the second time in less than a year BSAA had lost its chief executive. This time he would not be replaced.

Chapter 13

A Magnificent Achievement in Berlin

At the end of the Second World War Germany was divided among the victorious Allies. Each country – Britain, America, the Soviet Union and France – was given a slice of the land and a sector of the capital, Berlin, over which it had control. The Soviets wanted to keep Germany weak to ensure that the Soviet Union would not be attacked again. The Western Allies' policy was to put Germany back on its feet so that the mistakes made at the end of the First World War would not be repeated and the country would be allowed to prosper. Britain and America had formed this policy before the end of 1944 when France was included, and so the latter had no influence on the decision.

After three years of growing tension between the Western Allies and the Soviet Union, after the end of the war, all road and rail links between Berlin and the West were closed by the Soviets on 25 June 1948. Their objective was to force the Allies out of Berlin and to take over the capital as a prelude to assuming control, ultimately, of the entire country.

The decision by the Western Allies to supply the beleaguered West Berliners with food and fuel led to an airlift lasting for eleven months. It was not without danger: the Soviets, while not directly shooting down any Allied aircraft, employed harassing techniques which sometimes led to crashes or to diversions into their own territory where they were able to confiscate precious cargoes. Eventually the Soviet leader, Stalin, realised that the Allies' will could not be broken and he capitulated. The airlift came to an end and the Allied sectors of Germany and Berlin remained free of Soviet control.

When the airlift began it was operated by military aircraft, but it soon became clear that civilian airlines would have to help deliver supplies to Berlin and in the late summer of 1948 they began arriving to join the airlift. The American companies made more than 250 flights, 12 of these being operated by Pan American and TWA.

The first British company to reach Berlin was Sir Alan Cobham's company, Flight Refuelling, with whom BSAA had cooperated on the in-flight refuelling trials. Its aircraft had been operating since July, bringing in desperately needed fuel oil and, with the other British airlines on the airlift, it operated under the control of the BEA manager for Germany, Edwin Whitfield.

* * *

The grounding of the Tudors by Lord Nathan following the loss of *Star Tiger* was reviewed shortly after Don Bennett left BSAA and three months later the flying ban was lifted.

By September 1948 BSAA had joined the airlift using two Tudor I freighter aircraft, G-AGRH and G-AGRJ. Both aircraft were owned by the Ministry of Civil Aviation but had been leased to BOAC. Since BOAC did not want anything to do with the Tudor they lent the aeroplanes to BSAA. G-AGRH was to have been used by BSAA anyway and would have been given the name *Star Ceres*. It gave great service and when the airlift was over the aircraft was stored before being sold in 1953. It ended its days in 1959 when it hit Mount Suphan Dag in Turkey, en route from Ankara to Bahrain, having strayed into the mountains from its proper course. The other Tudor, G-AGRJ, named *Star Celia*, was finally scrapped at Southend in August 1956.

During the course of the airlift these two Tudor Is made 114 and 117 flights respectively, carrying between them over 2,300 tons of supplies. They were joined by the two Tudors belonging to Airflight, the company set up by Bennett after he left BSAA and on 7 January 1949 by three Tudor Vs of BSAA. Five should have been delivered, but two were delayed and did not arrive in Germany until 2 and 14 February. All nine Tudors performed well throughout the entire time they were on the airlift although, as will be seen later, the two belonging to Bennett were involved in some incidents which made his earlier claim of sabotage seem much less fanciful than Lord Nathan and the board of BSAA had supposed.

* * *

Having previously flown Lancastrians for Silver City Airways and then worked for a small airline at Croydon flying Dragon Rapides, pilot Roy Day decided that he wanted to work for a big airline again. Seeing an advertisement for BSAA he applied in August 1948 and was accepted. He had done his initial training with the airline and had been told that he would be flying down to

Santiago, the Chilean capital, but when BSAA joined the airlift, instead of exotic South America Roy found himself flying to Berlin.

A team of three complete air crews, ground crews and an assortment of aircraft spares left London for the former Luftwaffe base of Wunsdorf in the British zone of West Germany. They were housed in the sergeants' mess and began their duties flying twelve hours on and twenty-four hours off. They flew from Wunsdorf to Gatow in the British zone of Berlin and usually made three round trips a day. At the beginning they used the two Tudor Is which Roy disliked. He found the Tudor I to be '. . . not a very pleasant aircraft to fly, its short fuselage making it difficult to control on take-off'. Because the aircraft had been originally destined for BOAC the cockpit layout was to its design and included a flight engineer's panel. BSAA carried three suitably qualified pilots (captain, first and second officers) rather than a pilot, navigator and flight engineer, and since he was the most junior crew member at the time Roy, as second officer, sat in the flight engineer's seat which, for some unknown reason, faced backwards. The engineer's panel had also been changed around and everything seemed to be back to front. He thoroughly disliked it and was sure that he was not the only pilot to find it disorientating. When at the beginning of 1949 he was transferred onto the Tudor V he felt much more at home and found it a better aircraft all round. It had a longer fuselage and was consequently easier to take-off and more stable in flight.

There were mixed cargoes at first which the crews supplemented with their own offerings such as cocoa, bought in Britain and traded for typically German items like steins.

After a short while the crews were moved from the airfield to the Hotel Hannover in Bad Nenndorf, a few miles away, and were brought to the airfield each day by a shuttle bus. Bad Nenndorf was a spa town with pleasant gardens and a *Kurhaus* used by people who came to take the waters, but the ground and air crews hardly had a chance to notice their pleasant environment. When they were not working long hours they were sleeping, and then periodically would return to Britain so that more major maintenance to the aircraft could be carried out at Langley. These trips back home gave them the chance to reward themselves for all their hard work. The radio officer's seat in the Tudor had an enclosed space beneath it with a seat lid held in place by a bolt. By removing the bolt with a spanner the seat lid could be removed and a bottle or two, bought from the mess at Wunsdorf, could be hidden. When the aircraft arrived back in Langley the ground engineer was kept out of the cockpit long enough for one of the crew to unbolt the seat cover, remove the bottles and bolt it all back together. Then the engineer who had been waiting patiently would be given a bottle for himself and the crew would take theirs home.

It soon became clear that the needs of the 2.5 million inhabitants of West Berlin were vast. The meagre reserves that had been built up after the war were soon depleted and had to be replaced urgently. They were short of everything – food, clothing, coal, fuel oil, newsprint (to keep the population informed about what was happening) and medical supplies. To play its part in helping to supply some of these things, BSAA took on many extra pilots to cope with the number of flights that they had to do each day. Roy described the way it all worked: 'The entire operation was one of split second timing. Aircraft flew out of eight different airfields and landed at the rate of one every 3 minutes (5 minutes in bad weather) at three Berlin airfields. . . . Any aircraft drifting outside the corridor would be pounced on by MiGs and forced to land in East Germany.'

This precision operation was controlled by the use of MF radio beacons at each end of the corridors and Eureka beacons at the airfields, which picked up impulses from the Rebecca sets carried on board the aircraft and enabled the controllers to guide them safely into the airport. Gatow, the Berlin airport used by British civil airlines and the RAF, had been a Luftwaffe night-fighter station during the war and was a well-equipped airfield. During the airlift it was run by the RAF under the command of Group Captain B. Yarde and handled 480 landings every 24 hours. While the aircraft flew in and out every few minutes, work was going on to extend and repair the runways using debris from bombed buildings in Berlin as hard core. The manual labour on the airfield was undertaken by the Berliners themselves, with women working alongside the men.

Engineer A. Morley, who was based at Langley, went to Berlin as part of BSAA's team and described his experience of the airlift:

I went to Wunsdorf near Hanover in January 1949. There were eight of us backing up the line engineers already there under Mr Parry [Bill Parry – senior engineer]. We worked 12-hour shifts six days a week. We had five Tudors to look after and although there was no snow in England, out there it was six inches deep and much colder. The aircraft had been stripped out and four tanks had been fitted inside each to carry eight tons of fuel. This was loaded by the Army from bowsers. The aircraft themselves were fuelled by Germans working with us. Tudors were the faster aircraft so left after the RAF Yorks and arrived at Gatow first. They were away for about 3 hours.

Night flying was the hardest part. Whereas today's airports are well lit, apart from runway and hangar lights ours was pitch black. The taxiways were metal tank tracks.

We were billeted in a small hotel at Bad Nenndorf and the aircrew were in one nearby, 10 or so miles from Wunsdorf. We had no difficulty with the language as they were well versed in English.

We worked a fortnight of days and a week of nights. We were transported to the airport by coach.

The RAF were at one end of the drome, by flying control, and we were at a remote part, using a large hangar, half of which was used by Air Vice-Marshal Bennett who, with his two aircraft, was also on the lift.

When the airlift first started, petrol and diesel oil was brought in by the Americans in big drums. It was a dangerous and labour intensive way to transport it, as each drum had to be securely tied down in the C-47s and C-54s that they were using. If a drum came loose in flight it could have been disastrous and was not the most efficient means of carrying liquid fuel anyway as the drums did not fit the shape of the aircraft. When the Flight Refuelling aircraft began flying in July 1948 the Americans were relieved to be able to hand over the transportation of oil to them. BSAA's Tudor Vs also took on the role of tankers when they came to Berlin in January 1949, carrying 2,300 gallons of petrol or 2,100 gallons of fuel oil on each flight.

Jack Eade, who had joined BSAA in December 1946 and worked at Langley, recollected that:

. . . fuel tanks were fitted into the aircraft in cradles made locally by the BSAA fitters. They were fitted on the left hand side of the fuselage. The tanks were connected together by hoses which were fed down the fuselage to a connector near the rear door. This was so that the fuel could be pumped in and out of the tanks quickly in Germany to shorten the turnaround time.

Eventually the handling of the fuel was made even more efficient when some spare piping was discovered that had been used during the war for PLUTO (Pipe Line Under The Ocean) to supply fuel for the Allied armies after D-Day. It was quickly laid underground from Gatow to the shores of Lake

Havel, enabling fuel to be pumped directly from the tanker aircraft through the pipeline and into the tanker barges that were moored at the lake for onward distribution throughout Berlin.

It was difficult to produce appetising food with the lack of choice available to Berliners, but they did have the advantage of once more being able to drink real coffee rather than the substitute that they had been used to for so long. It was found to be more economical and efficient to carry in the coffee beans than waste fuel in the manufacture of the ersatz variety. Times were very hard but it was little luxuries like coffee and chocolate that ensured the Berliners' morale remained high, and the former enemies worked amicably together in their common cause.

Although working round the clock, the efficiency targets that BSAA had set itself were not being achieved and in December 1948 Air Commodore Fletcher, the General Service Manager, arrived in Wunsdorf to find out how the situation could be improved. He set up new operations rosters and by the end of January the figures had greatly improved with the airline flying 3.65 flights per aircraft each day. Edwin Whitfield, manager of the airlift, reported that 'BSAA in January produced the best effort on the Civil Air Lift'. By March the airline had carried more than one million gallons of fuel into Berlin.

Despite their constant use there were very few incidents involving BSAA Tudors. One was hit while in the hangar and put out of action for a week while repairs were undertaken and there was also an accident involving Tudor G-AKCD piloted by 28-year-old Captain William Jeffrey Rees on 3 March 1949. The aircraft arrived at Gatow from Wunsdorf in the early afternoon. The weather was fine with good visibility, but with a surface wind gusting to 20 knots. They landed in a cross-wind and touched down about 200 yards along runway 26. When the brakes were first applied to keep the aircraft straight they appeared to be working, but towards the end of the runway they did not slow the aircraft at all and Jeff Rees had to ground loop to port in an attempt to avoid a 3ft high earth bank at the end of the runway. He nearly succeeded but when at right angles to the bank, the starboard wheel hit the obstruction, the aircraft swung around and came to a stop with the tail wheel on the bank. The aircraft was not badly damaged and no one, either on board or on the ground, was hurt.

Later that month John Booth received a letter from Lord Pakenham, Minister of Civil Aviation, congratulating him on the performance of BSAA on the airlift. He told him that he had received a report, from which he sent an extract and which:

... makes it clear that BSAA are doing extremely well; in fact they produced the best civil performance of the month.

[The report said:]

'This company put up an excellent show in January in spite of the handicap of having a Tudor out of commission from the 16th to the 24th after it had been damaged by a bowser in the hangar. Considerable credit for this improvement must go to Mr Bailey, the BSAA representative sent to replace Mr Morris, as he tackled his job with energy and enthusiasm.

The regularity of this company's efforts over the 24 hours of each day was very creditable indeed and they also achieved a serviceability factor of 86%.'

Lord Pakenham added his own comment, saying:

The daily average of 3.65 sorties per serviceable aircraft during this month was a splendid effort and reflects the greatest credit on all concerned. I should like to congratulate you and the staff of BSAA engaged on the Airlift in Germany on the Corporation's fine performance during the first month of this year.

In total BSAA's seven aircraft flew 2,562 operations taking 6,972.43 hours and carrying 22,125.2 tons of supplies, 19,812.8 tons of which were fuel. By comparison BOAC made 81 trips in 223.7 hours and carried 294 tons. The entire airlift operation brought in 146,980.2 tons of supplies; a massive 15.05 per cent being carried by BSAA, although for some inexplicable reason most accounts barely mention the airline, and it has been given very little credit for its efforts.

* * *

When the airlift began, Don Bennett contacted A.V. Roe and bought two Tudors from it for his new company, Airflight. He got together a number of pilots and engineers and joined the other civil airlines who were bringing supplies to Berlin, on 3 September 1948. Airflight's aircraft, a Tudor II and a Tudor V, were also fitted with tanks for the transportation of oil. Although strictly no longer part of the BSAA story it is perhaps worthwhile noting two incidents that occurred involving Bennett's company.

The first happened on a damp, foggy day at Wunsdorf when flights were being delayed due to the weather. Bennett had gone to speak to a forecaster while his co-pilot, Ken Hagyard, was already on board the Tudor working on the flight plan. While the aircraft was parked, for safety reasons external elevator locks, marked by long red tapes, were in place on the port side of the aircraft. These had to be removed before take-off. Bennett left the met office when it became clear that a slight break in the weather could allow a take-off and sprinted across to the aircraft glancing, as he ran, towards the port side to satisfy himself that the elevator locks had been removed. As he climbed into his seat he asked, 'Everything OK?' He was answered in the affirmative and so told Hagyard to start the engines at once. Hagyard did as he was asked, climbing into his own seat as Bennett taxied out. They hurtled down the runway but as the aircraft reached its take-off speed and Bennett tried to ease it into the air he realised that something was horribly wrong; the elevator locks were still fitted and if he did not act immediately the aircraft would crash. With a full fuel payload, plus the operating fuel for the Tudor, he knew that it would be the end for all of them and for many of the German labourers on the airfield as well, if that were to happen. Since it was not possible to get the aircraft off the ground in the conventional manner and the runway was rapidly vanishing beneath the wheels, he quickly turned the small wheel in the cockpit that controlled the elevator trim tabs and in doing so forced the tail down which lifted the nose and the heavily laden Tudor heaved itself into the air. From the cockpit window Bennett and Hagyard caught sight of workers flinging themselves to the ground as the aircraft skimmed over their trucks and just missed hitting the approach lights beyond the runway.

Having successfully handled his first problem, Bennett then had to land the aircraft again as soon as possible. He made three approaches, each one too far off course. There was no chance of making a forced landing elsewhere as the cargo was too volatile to survive the ensuing crash and, in any case, the visibility was too bad to find a field or other clearing. On his fourth attempt Bennett managed to line the aircraft up and somehow got it onto the ground. It hit with a tremendous thump and raced down towards the end of the runway once more, until finally the tail wheel sank to the ground and the brakes could be applied.

Bennett was sure that when he had glanced at the locks before boarding the aircraft they had been removed. He was also convinced that when climbing into his seat he had pushed the control column forward to check its movement and that it was functioning perfectly. But, in spite of this, the locks were still in place.

Soon after this amazing display of airmanship a tragic event occurred. At that time Bennett had been the only one of Airflight's pilots to be qualified to fly the Tudor at night, but this was about to change when pilot Clement Wilbur Utting obtained his qualification too. On his first night flight out of Berlin on 8 December he was walking across the tarmac at Gatow when a truck came speeding towards him, hit him and then disappeared into the darkness without stopping. Clem Utting died where he fell on the cold, dark airfield.

An investigation was held, but curiously, in view of the meticulous organisation of the operation at Gatow, no one could identify either the driver or his truck. There was a strong suspicion that it had been a deliberate attempt to kill Don Bennett since until that night he was known to be the only Airflight pilot to fly at night. Both Aubrey Dare, who left BSAA soon after Bennett and went to work for him at Airflight, and his friend Frank Price of BSAA were convinced that Clem Utting had been a victim of mistaken identity. They both think that he was murdered and that the perpetrators were 'Commies' who wanted Bennett out of the way because of his efforts on the airlift and also because of his Pathfinder operations over Germany during the war.

In view of the circumstances of Clem Utting's death, Bennett may have been correct when he said that he had checked both the elevator locks and the control column on the earlier flight and found them to be ready. Perhaps the locks had been replaced after he boarded the aircraft as he was about to leave. Bennett accepted that, as captain, he was responsible for what had happened and did not seek to blame anyone but himself. The flight itself proved two things: he was an outstanding pilot and the Tudor was, even in a situation such as this, a very forgiving aeroplane. Sadly, it would not be enough for its detractors.

A.V. Roe sent a team to Berlin to study the contribution made by its aircraft to the airlift. In its subsequent report there is a rather poignant little comment:

As we waited for the return of the Airflight crew, the two Avro Tudor Is operated by British South American Airways, were being emptied of their 20,600lb loads. It was inevitable, standing there in the heart of Germany surrounded by Manchester-built aircraft, that we should feel a glow of pride and satisfaction. Here were the aircraft which had been turned down before they had been given a chance to prove their capabilities in service.

Chapter 14

The Disappearance of *Star Ariel*

The year 1949 started in the worst possible fashion for BSAA, with an accident which was to bear more than a passing similarity to the loss of the Air France Concorde in Paris in July 2000.

On Saturday 5 January 1949, Avro York G-AHEX *Star Venture* (flight BA221) took off from runway 12 of Parnamirim airport at Natal, bound for Rio de Janeiro. In command was Captain Albert Charles Graham. The other members of the crew were First Officer William C. Robertson, Second Officer Kingsley Mountney, Radio Officer/Navigator Arthur Milner and Stargirls Jean A. Mortleman and former model Margaret M. Owens. Margaret Owens only found herself on the flight after she had volunteered to take the place of a colleague who was ill.

Captain Graham had already been involved in an accident in his BSAA career: in November 1947 he was in command of Lancastrian *Star Light* which crashed short of the runway at Kindley Field, Bermuda (fortunately without casualties), when returning to the airfield after an engine failure. His total flying hours by January 1949 amounted to 4,333, of which 3,251 were as first pilot. The First Officer was 36 years old, had served in the RAF from 1940 to 1946 and joined BSAA on 20 May 1947. His logbooks showed a total of 2,560 hours as first pilot.

In addition to the six crew on board there were nine passengers: Mr M.R. Studart, Brazilian (Route Inspector); Mr T.B. Miani, British; Miss J.V. Cousillas, Spanish; Mrs E.R. Langrehr, German; Mr R. Kinnaird, British (King's Messenger); Mrs M.C. Mosqueira, Spanish; Dr Anne Gibson, British; Mr J. Christofanini, Chilean; and Mrs Christofanini, Italian.

At the time of the accident the weather was ideal for flying. Visibility was unlimited, there were very few clouds and the wind was calm. At 03.42 GMT (23.42 local) the York started its take-off roll. As it reached a point two-thirds of the way along the runway the crew on the flight deck felt a severe shuddering from the starboard side. Because the aircraft had almost reached flying speed it was considered too late to abort the take-off so the pilot chose to proceed. As they left the ground the shuddering abruptly stopped and the behaviour of the aircraft seemed normal. It would become apparent later that although the captain had only felt the aircraft shudder, several other members of the crew had heard a loud bang as they were speeding along the runway. The undercarriage was retracted successfully and a scan of the instruments revealed nothing amiss. The captain stated later that he believed the shuddering to be due to a burst tyre, although the radio officer (who was one of the crew members who had heard the bang) had previously experienced a burst tyre on take-off and remembered the noise being much louder on that occasion. As the aircraft was flying normally the captain felt there was no immediate cause for concern and decided that he would wait until dawn, when he could make an assessment of the nature of the damage to the tyre by lowering the undercarriage and looking through a window on the starboard side.

Captain Graham was clearly still concerned by the potential damage because as soon as they reached the cruising altitude of 10,500ft (and knowing that most of the passengers were by then asleep) he told Second Officer Mountney to take the left-hand seat and lower the undercarriage so that he could go back into the forward passenger cabin and shine a torch onto the starboard wheel to determine the nature of the problem. The only passenger in that part of the aircraft was Mr Studart, the Route Inspector, and he was asleep while the captain made his inspection. As he shone the torch through the window he saw that the tyre had not burst, but there was a great deal of oil covering the wheel. He went back to the cockpit and told the other members of the crew what he had seen. He felt that instead of a burst tyre, the oleo leg or shock absorber had ruptured, causing the oil leak. The other crew members agreed with this assumption, as it fitted well with the noise and shuddering on take-off. The captain still intended to make a better inspection at first light and instructed the radio officer to contact Rio de Janeiro to inform them of the problem and ask for a BSAA engineer to be present in the Control Tower to make a visual inspection when they arrived. He also spoke to the two Stargirls and told them the landing at Rio might be rather bumpy, but there was no cause for alarm. He asked that when they were next serving coffee to the Route Inspector, they should ask him if he would move to a seat in the rear cabin as he would be safer there if the undercarriage should fail on landing.

The flight proceeded normally for a while, but when the aircraft had been airborne for approximately 3½ hours Captain Graham noticed the number three engine (starboard inner) oil pressure gauge fluctuating. He later likened the effect to that which he had seen many times before when instruments were failing. The reading finally settled at a very low 20 to 30lb/sq in. The Second Officer was still sitting in the left-hand seat at the time, so the two men checked the other engine instruments and noted the oil and water temperatures were both stable at 55° and 62° respectively, which is normal. This further reinforced the feeling that it was a spurious reading on the oil pressure gauge. The Captain once again went back into the cabin and looked out of the window at the engine, but it looked normal. When he returned to the cockpit the oil pressure had fallen again slightly, the oil temperature had also fallen, but the coolant temperature was up to 82°.

Shortly afterwards, at 07.40 GMT, things started to go dramatically wrong. The starboard inner engine began to make, to quote Captain Graham, 'a tremendous noise'. A glance at the engine rpm showed it to be nearly 4,000 (the normal speed would be around 2,400). The Second Officer closed the fuel feed to the engine and at the same time raised the nose to reduce the speed of the aircraft to 120 knots in order to try to slow down the runaway propeller. The Captain pressed the appropriate button to feather the propeller blades, but nothing happened and the button jammed in. He managed to release it and tried again, but to no avail. The engine seemed to be completely out of control. The crew knew that if the speed of the propeller was not reduced quickly, there was a very real danger that it could become detached from the engine, with potentially disastrous consequences.

First Officer Robertson (who was navigating) told Captain Graham that the nearest airfield was Caravelas, less than ten minutes flying time away, and passed the course to the Second Officer. When they reached the vicinity of the airfield they were flying at around 8,000ft, but the damaged engine was still turning at over 3,000rpm. Captain Graham was hoping against hope that the engine would hold out for long enough for them to get down safely. The Radio Officer contacted Rio de Janeiro to inform them of the situation and then made contact with Caravelas tower.

The Captain decided to take over the left-hand seat from the Second Officer to make the approach to Caravelas, but just as they were changing seats the first officer glanced out of his side window and called out that the starboard inner engine had burst into flames. The Captain shouted to him to press the fire extinguisher button, but later believed he may even have reached across to do so himself as an instinctive reaction. Whichever man did so, it had no effect on the fire. Within seconds the wing itself was engulfed in flames which were streaming back almost as far as the tail of the York. One can only imagine what must have been going through the minds of the passengers on the starboard side of the cabin when they looked out and saw a plume of flames streaming back over 20ft from the wing.

The First Officer then left his seat and went to the rear passenger cabin to assist in strapping the passengers in ready for a forced landing. After making sure the passengers were secure he strapped himself into a spare seat on the port side. The second officer attempted to lower the undercarriage, but only one wheel came down so he raised it again. Shortly after this, something happened to make the starboard wing stall. Maybe the heat from the fire had twisted or distorted the wing in some way, or maybe it was caused by buckling of the wing skin, but suddenly the starboard wing dropped and the aircraft plunged into a spiral dive. As the ground rushed towards them, the two pilots between them managed to wrestle the aircraft level over some flat ground a short distance from the airfield. They fought to keep the wings level as the speed reduced, hoping to stall the aircraft onto the ground which by now was only a few feet below. As the aircraft touched down, the Captain saw to his horror that although they were sliding across flat ground, ahead of them was a wood. He tried desperately to turn the aircraft left to avoid the trees but it would not turn. When changing seats, he had not had time to fasten his straps, so he raised his right leg on to the windscreen support to brace himself against the impact, all the while pushing as hard as he could on the left rudder pedal to try to get the careering aircraft to turn away from the trees.

The impact with the trees was inevitable. Miraculously the nose of the aircraft did not hit any tree trunks head-on and when the crashing and splintering died down and the aircraft came to a halt the men in the cockpit managed to clamber out through the smashed windows. They raced around the burning starboard wing, clambering over broken tree branches as they did so. There was a roaring noise which was a mixture of the fire burning furiously and one of the port engines, minus its propeller, which was somehow still running. The Captain tried to shout to those inside but found he could not as he was choking on the smoke. The First Officer had managed to smash a passenger window on the port side of the cabin, after realising the Stargirls were unable to open the twisted emergency exit, and clamber through. It was through this window that the Captain and First Officer helped the passengers escape. They pulled them and the Stargirls onto the ground and told them to run as far from the burning aircraft as they could, as they believed the remaining fuel on board would soon explode.

Captain Graham remembered First Officer Robertson shouting to the German lady passenger Mrs Langrehr 'Don't bother about your ******* handbag, it's your life you have to worry about', but she insisted on clutching her bag as they struggled to pull her to safety through the window. Mr Kinnaird, the King's Messenger, could not fit through the window at first, but managed to remove his coat and squeeze through. As they pulled one of the passengers through, he told them that he was the last person inside the aircraft, so they hurried to a safe distance from the burning wreckage. It was only then that they did a head count and realised that three of the passengers were still missing, but by that time it was too late to go back and try to save them as the aircraft fuselage was burning fiercely.

Mountney and Milner went for help while the Stargirls and one of the passengers attended to the injured captain who had assisted with the evacuation of the passengers while in considerable pain from a broken leg. Help arrived after 10 to 15 minutes in the form of officers of the Brazilian Air Force, and the crew and surviving passengers were driven back to the safety of the airfield where they received attention for their injuries. Mrs Langrehr had suffered two broken ribs, presumably as she was pulled through the window clutching her bag. In Captain Graham's witness statement, he praised First Officer William Robertson very highly for his actions in rescuing passengers and crew from the burning aircraft, many of whom, he said, owed their lives to him.

The statements from the two Stargirls give an interesting insight into the accident from the point of view of what was going on in the passenger cabin while the rest of the crew were trying to control the aircraft. It also demonstrates their bravery and coolness under extreme pressure. It was normal practice for the two Stargirls to take it in turns to have a short sleep on a night flight such as this, leaving the other to attend to the needs of the passengers. On this occasion Jean Mortleman slept first with Margaret Owens waking her at around 03.30 local time so she could try to get some sleep herself. Margaret had only just dozed off when she awoke to the noise of the starboard inner engine overspeeding. She immediately looked out of the window and saw more flames than usual coming from the engine exhausts. It was quite normal to see a glow of flame from the exhausts of Rolls-Royce Merlin engines at night, but she realised these flames were not normal, especially as they were quite visible in the early dawn light. She got up and walked to the rear of the cabin to ask her colleague what was happening. As she did so the wing rapidly caught fire and flames spread the length of the fuselage. She started to smell burning in the cabin, so grabbed a fire extinguisher, secured the box containing drinks from the bar and tried to release the emergency exit in preparation for a swift evacuation from the cabin when they were on the ground. She was unable to release the door, but in any case at that point the first officer entered the cabin and shouted his warning that they should prepare for an emergency landing. She sat down on the floor next to one of the women passengers who was very distraught and held her to try to calm her down. All the time she was telling the passengers that they should keep calm and not to worry, showing remarkable coolness under the circumstances. The rest of her account is best told in her own words:

We then hit the ground. Finding that I was still alive I managed with considerable difficulty to cross the wreckage to the pantry, wrenched a door from the stove, the oven door, and pulled out and twisted a hinge from it with which I managed to open the door of the freight compartment but all the freight had fallen to the far (outer) side of the compartment.

I returned to the cabin and tried to open the emergency exit but could not do so.

I heard the First Officer say 'Break a window to save your life'. He was on the starboard side and I tried to break the window on the port side, [but] as I had lost my shoes I could not do this barefooted. I gave up the attempt when I heard the sound of breaking glass.

I then saw that the First Officer had managed to break a window and the passengers were getting out with the help of the Captain, the First Officer and Dr Gibson (one of the passengers). We got out quickly and made for the wood nearby.

A minute after we left the aircraft it became a furnace. We did our best to make the passengers comfortable and rendered first aid to those who needed it. Two Brazilian Air Force officers arrived with a Jeep and took the First Officer, Dr Gibson and three other passengers. We remained with the Captain and the German lady until a stretcher arrived for this lady. The Jeep returned and took the Captain, the King's Messenger, the other air hostess and myself to the Caravelas Air Base. Jean (the other hostess) and I gave such first aid treatment as was possible under the circumstances until the doctor arrived, which was at about 9 a.m.

When Jean Mortleman heard the noise of the overspeeding engine she was in the pantry with the door closed. She decided to make her way to the cockpit to try and find out what was wrong. On the way, she glanced out of one of the windows and noticed a small flame rising from the starboard inner engine. On reaching the cockpit she realised the crew were fully occupied so went back to attend to the passengers. At that moment the wing caught fire so she took a fire extinguisher and tried to help Margaret Owens, who was struggling with the emergency exit door. She took a small axe from the cabin wall and then heard the First Officer shout his warning so sat down on the floor near to the pantry to prepare for the crash landing. In her own words:

Shortly before we crashed the aircraft levelled out and then we hit the ground. We were all thrown forward, falling over each other and all the seats were dislodged and fell over. When the aircraft stopped I found that I was surrounded with wreckage and my legs were caught in the steel bottom part of a seat. The others were picking themselves up and after a while I managed to free myself and got up, observing that the seats and other objects had piled up on the main exit door and on the first seats. There was no exit that way and some flames entered the starboard side of the aircraft. It was very dark and difficult to see clearly.

All the passengers were up and moving about in a purposeless way. I said 'We must find a way out quickly', and tried the emergency exit which was completely jammed.

I ran to the pantry to try the only other exit and found the other air hostess there trying to move the door to the tail. We managed to move it at least 1 inch but this door was also jammed. I succeeded in getting my head into the compartment and saw a mountain of freight piled up against the exit door so that even if we had managed to open the door we would not have been able to move the freight and our efforts would, therefore, have been in vain.

Suddenly the navigator [Robertson] appeared. He had been buried under the wreckage in the fore part and had only just managed to free himself. We confirmed that all the exits were blocked. At this time dense clouds of smoke were pouring in from the forward part (all this was happening in the limited space of the rear cabin). We were therefore cut off from the forward part of the aircraft.

We felt that at any moment there might be an explosion, the engines were spluttering the whole time and the fire was increasing.

The Navigator asked that the windows should be broken. We hesitated to break them with our feet and I hunted for the fire extinguisher but failed to find it. I tried to pick up a seat but was so weakened by the fumes that I could not find the strength to do so.

Suddenly the navigator succeeded in breaking the glass (the windows had double glass) with his feet and continued beating it until he had cleared all the glass. He managed to get out and the other air hostess followed him. I was behind all the others and we were waiting for the King's Messenger to get out. I ran to push him through but failed as he made no efforts to help himself. I pulled him in again to take off his coat, and then became so desperate that I decided, being nearest to the window, to get out myself. I knew that, being the slimmest, I could manage it. The Captain and the navigator pulled me out. As soon as the Captain managed to get out of the aircraft he came to help people to get out. When the last person had been helped out we got as far away as possible, fearing an explosion. When we discovered that three passengers were missing it was too late to go back as the flames covered the whole aircraft.

We all sat down in a clearing. I administered first aid to the Captain who appeared to have a leg broken and had a cut on his forehead and several other cuts and serious knocks. I also attended to a German lady who complained of a pain in the side. The navigator could not stand up as he had an ugly cut on his foot and the second and radio officers had to go in search of help.

Everyone was, naturally, suffering from shock. Soon after, a rescue party arrived and we were all taken to the air base of the distant airport, some km. from the town of Caravelas, where we waited for the doctor who was coming from Salvador.

When the survivors reached the airport at Caravelas it became clear that the three passengers unaccounted for were Mr T. B. Miani, Miss J. V. Cousillas and Route Inspector Mr M. R. Studart. They were thought to have either been overcome by the smoke and flames immediately after the accident or to have been knocked unconscious in the initial impact and were unable to scramble to safety.

The Brazilian Air Ministry immediately commissioned an enquiry into the accident. One of the first pieces of evidence they received came from the York's departure airport. The day after the accident they received a radio message from the Natal Air Base to say that an examination of runway 12 resulted in the discovery of several large and heavy pieces of tyre rubber and some pieces of metal tube thought to have come from *Star Venture*. The material was subsequently sent to the Air Ministry which forwarded it (via another BSAA aircraft) to London for a detailed laboratory examination. The examination revealed that the tyre was a remould which was only slightly worn. Indeed it was established that since the remould work it had only carried out approximately fifteen landings. Closer examination revealed a crater in the rubber of around one inch in diameter which was thought to have been the origin of the tyre's disintegration. The engineers judged the remould work to have been of a good standard as the tread seemed to have adhered well to the carcass, but they were of the opinion that the sudden failure was due to high pressure air leaking between the tread and the tyre wall, causing large portions of the tread to be blown off. The combination of high pressure and the centrifugal forces on the tyre as it spun at take-off speed meant that the pieces of rubber hurtled into the engine nacelle with considerable force. There were several aluminium marks on the damaged pieces of tread which corresponded to the undercarriage bracing struts which had clearly been struck by large pieces of the damaged tyre.

When the results of the Brazilian enquiry were published, the investigation team had, unsurprisingly, concluded that the accident was as a result of a major fire on board the aircraft in flight, leading to a loss of control. The cause of the fire was found to be due to a number of contributory factors, as follows:

Undercarriage bracing struts and brake pipes had been severed by large chunks of rubber flying up from the damaged tyre on take-off.
The amount of oil coating the starboard tailplane and fin showed that a considerable quantity of oil in the tank immediately behind the number three engine had leaked out in flight from the severed pipes.
When the number three engine was stripped down it was found to have been completely lacking in oil, resulting in the failure of the propeller pitch system and the crankshaft bearings, followed by a catastrophic break-up of the engine. This in turn led to the oil coating the number three engine nacelle catching fire.

When the BSAA Assistant Station Officer in Rio de Janeiro, Heleno Bortkievicz, received the news that *Star Venture* had gone down in flames near Caravelas, he made arrangements to travel to the crash site in a Douglas C-47 which the Brazilian authorities had placed at the disposal of BSAA. After overflying the wreckage in order to take aerial photographs, the C-47 landed at Caravelas at 12.30. He went straight to the air base headquarters to introduce himself as the BSAA representative to the surviving passengers and crew before joining a party of doctors and Brazilian Air Force officials (and Captain Earnshaw, who had just arrived in another York, *Star Gleam*), who were given the unenviable task of trying to remove the bodies of the three victims from the wreckage. When they arrived at the scene they found the aircraft still smouldering, which made the task of recovering the bodies even more unpleasant. On returning to Caravelas, arrangements were made for Captain Earnshaw to fly the passengers and crew of *Star Venture* on to their original destination of Rio de Janeiro. Over the next few days, Bortkievicz returned to the wreckage of *Star Venture* several times and managed to recover three kilos of gold and a quantity of platinum from the bullion box carried on the aircraft as well as some items of jewellery and a Colt 45 pistol which he presumed had belonged to the Route Inspector. He also managed to establish that all the diplomatic and air mail, as well as all the other freight and baggage, had been completely destroyed by fire.

In addition to the Brazilian enquiry, a formal investigation was carried out by Wing Commander R. Warren of the Ministry of Civil Aviation and J. Watson, a BSAA station engineer in Brazil. They arrived at the scene of the accident a few days later and their initial conclusions mirrored those of the Brazilian investigators. They were able to prove conclusively that the undercarriage and tyre parts found on the runway at Natal were from the crashed York and they also noted the oil still dribbling down the starboard side of the fuselage near the tailplane, proving the existence of a massive oil leak while the aircraft was still in flight.

There was one final question which had not been answered. How could the oil pressure in the number three engine stay so low for so long while the temperature remained normal and the engine continued to run? The answer came from Rolls-Royce itself. When the oil lines were severed and the oil from that engine started to drain away, air would have entered the system and gradually aerated the oil. If the oil was full of air bubbles, the pressure would drop, but the quantity would still be sufficient for the temperature to remain normal. This discovery led to a BSAA engineering department committee examining the possibility of modifying all its remaining Yorks to be fitted with oil quantity gauges to give pilots valuable information in the event that anything similar should happen again. Not only was this carried out, but guards were also fitted to all BSAA York undercarriages to prevent damage to vital oil lines from pieces of tyre rubber.

Like the Concorde accident fifty years later, a simple tyre failure had started a chain of events which would lead to the loss of an aircraft and the lives of passengers. Captain Graham's actions in bringing the aircraft down for a crash-landing before the wing completely failed undoubtedly saved the lives of the majority of the passengers and crew, however, as is often the case in aircraft accidents, somebody is held responsible after the findings of the enquiry are published. In this case Captain Graham was strongly criticised in the BSAA Air Safety Committee report and deemed to be negligent for not returning to Natal immediately after he realised the aircraft was damaged. He was also sent a letter of commendation by BSAA for his actions after the accident in helping to save the lives of passengers and crew! He left BSAA shortly afterwards.

* * *

Sometimes it is possible to see a slightly humorous side to these serious occurrences. One such incident occurred with Avro York G-AHEX *Star Venture* on 12 November 1948 on its way to Dakar, just two months before it was destroyed at Caravelas in Brazil. The aircraft was commanded by Captain Maurice Aries, an ex-accountant and Navigation Captain, who ran the Navigation Department at Heathrow in 1948. He was a popular pilot and well liked by the crews who flew with him. Stargirl Priscilla Vinyals (later to marry Captain Fieldson) was in the galley when Captain Aries came back to get a drink, leaving the First Officer at the controls. Priscilla looked over his shoulder into the cockpit, and said to him 'What's the big red light for?' He spun round quickly and said 'Christ, there's an engine on fire', and rushed back into the cockpit!

Captain Aries' original report on the incident was kindly supplied to the authors by his son Michael, also an airline captain. It highlights the calmness and efficiency of the crew. As Captain Aries hurried back into the cockpit, the first officer had already noticed the problem with the port outer engine and disengaged the autopilot. With the First Officer and Captain working in close cooperation, they shut off the fuel to the number one engine, pressed the feathering button, cut the ignition, activated the fire extinguisher and then changed the fuel feeds, including switching on the fuel booster pumps, so the other three engines were feeding from the port tanks. All these actions were carried out in less than 45 seconds. They were trying to reduce the fuel in the port tanks as quickly as possible as they feared the port wing might catch fire behind the engine. A minute or so after the propeller was feathered the fire started dying down and three or four minutes later it was out completely.

In the meantime one of the Stargirls entered the cockpit asking if there was anything specific Captain Aries wanted her to do, and offered to bring tea for the crew. She was asked to help the passengers into their lifejackets, as a precaution, and the First Officer went to the back of the aircraft to check that the dinghy and other emergency equipment was ready for use if necessary. After five uneventful hours, the aircraft reached Dakar safely, thanks to the professionalism of its crew.

* * *

At 12.42 GMT on 17 January 1949, Avro Tudor IVB, G-AGRE *Star Ariel* took off from Kindley Field, Bermuda, on a direct flight to Kingston, Jamaica, with a crew of seven and thirteen passengers on board. It was never seen again.

The circumstances leading up to its final flight were slightly unusual. It had left London on 13 January on a flight to Gander, Bermuda, Nassau and Kingston as flight number BA511/022. Having completed the outbound route, it had taken off from Kingston on 16 January for the return flight to London. It made the scheduled stop in Nassau, and arrived back in Bermuda at 01.23 on 17 January. A routine maintenance check was carried out at this stage with no unusual mechanical problems being reported by the crew.

Meanwhile, another BSAA Tudor, G-AHNK *Star Lion*, had been assigned the London to Santiago flight BA401/118 routing via Keflavik, Stephenville, Bermuda, Kingston, Barranquilla and Lima. However, an engine had failed while approaching Bermuda and the onward flight had been cancelled. This aircraft's load and crew (with the addition of a flight engineer, a requirement of the Tudor IVB) were transferred to *Star Ariel* to complete the BA401/118 to Santiago. It was in this configuration that *Star Ariel* left Bermuda on 17 January bound for Kingston, an estimated 5 hours 25 minutes flying time away.

The aircraft had been manufactured by A.V. Roe as a Tudor Mk I, making its first flight on 20 June 1946. The Rolls-Royce Merlin engines had then been uprated before it was delivered to the BOAC Development Flight at Hurn in September 1946. After BOAC carried out 80 hours of handling tests, it was returned in February 1947 to the manufacturer for modifications to the airframe. In 1948 it was dismantled and rebuilt as a Tudor IVB with Merlin 621 engines. After undergoing a test flight in October 1948, it was delivered to BSAA as *Star Ariel* on 14 November 1948. After only 159 hours flying time since the conversion to Tudor IVB, the engines were again uprated to 1,760hp Merlin 623s. These engines gave increased power for take-off and climb, and permitted a higher all-up weight of 82,000lb. By 17 January 1949, *Star Ariel* was on only its fifth scheduled service for BSAA and had completed only 340 hours flying, during which time no major faults or failures had occurred.

In command of *Star Ariel* that morning was 30-year-old New Zealander John Clutha McPhee. John McPhee had learned to fly in the Royal New Zealand Air Force in 1941 and moved to England to fly B-24 Liberator bombers. Immediately after the war he joined BOAC but was not happy and in February 1947 he moved to BSAA where he felt his prospects were better. Since joining the company he had amassed 300 hours experience in command of the Avro Tudor. His total experience in command of BSAA aircraft of all types was 1,967 hours. Captain McPhee's First Officer was 27-year-old F. Dauncey, who had been with the company since September 1947 and had 303 hours Tudor experience out of a total of 1,071 hours time on BSAA aircraft. The other members of the crew of *Star Ariel* were Second Officer V.D.J. Shapley, Radio Officer Gordon C. Rettie, Flight Engineer J. Goodwin, Stargirl Judith B. Moxon and Steward R.W. Coleman. With the exception of the captain, all of the flight deck crew on *Star Ariel* had served with the RAF.

A flight plan was filed by Captain McPhee in Bermuda, showing a cruising altitude to Kingston of 18,000ft. He had initially given his ETA as 17.25hrs, but this was later changed to 18.10hrs. The weather conditions were almost perfect for the flight. Visibility below cloud was given as 4 to 8 miles, and above cloud was unlimited. Indeed there was no cloud at all above 10,000ft for the whole route. The freezing level at the time was 14,000ft, but there was no possibility of engine or airframe icing and the winds at 18,000ft were only 36 knots, approximately from the north.

All the radio messages transmitted from the Tudor after take-off from Bermuda were perfectly routine with no hint of any problems. At 13.32 the aircraft reported on the Kindley Airway frequency of 4220 kc/s (used to control aircraft in the Bermuda Control Zone) that they were 150 nautical miles south-west of Bermuda at 18,000ft, and changing to the Cable

FLIGHT PLAN

Tudor IVB G-AGRE (*Star Ariel*) – Bermuda to Kingston (Service BA401/118) Date – 17 January 1949

(All times are GMT)

From	To	Track	W/V	Comp. true	R.A.S.	Height	Air temp.	T.A.S.	G.S.	Dist. to go	Time	E.T.A.
Kindley Field	216° Kindley Field	216	330/24	224	140	10000 up	-1	164	171	85	00:30	
216° Kindley Field	30°N	216	330/28	223	155	18000	-14	208	217	88	00:24	00:54
30°N	25°N	216	300/20	221	155	18000	-12	209	206	370	01:48	02:42
25°N	20°N	216	300/14	220	155	18000	-11	209	207	371	01:48	04:30
20°N	036°W Morant Point	216	300/12	219	155	18000	-8	210	208	86	00:25	
036°W Morant Point	Morant Point	216	140/10	213	175	10000 down	+8	209	206	68	00:20	05:15
Morant Point	Palisadoes	273	140/10	271	175	2000	+20	183	190	33	00:10	

Flight Time	5 hrs 25 mins
Endurance	10 hrs 0 mins
Distance A. to B.	1,101 N. miles
Still Air Range	2,040 N. miles

E.T.D.	12:00
E.T.A.	17:25
Fuel carried	2,500 gallons
Fuel required	2,213 gallons

and Wireless Bermuda frequency of 6563 kc/s. At 13.35 a message was transmitted on 6563 kc/s to Oceanic Air Traffic Control New York, BSAA Kindley Field and Kingston, giving service number, time of departure, ETA Kingston and the ETA of 13.37 for 30° N (the boundary of New York Oceanic Control). The message stated that they were flying in good visibility and ended with 'Will you accept control?' Seven minutes later at 13.42, an hour after take-off, Gordon Rettie transmitted a message: 'I was over 30° N at 13.37. I am changing frequency to MRX Kingston (freq 6523 kc/s).' This message was acknowledged. It was the last anyone heard from *Star Ariel*.

Ironically, although this message was transmitted at 13.42, it was not collected by BSAA in Kingston until 15.15, almost certainly after the fate of the aircraft, its passengers and crew had been sealed. To compound the problem even further, the aircraft had effectively signed off from Bermuda Control, but Kingston was unaware of this, which meant it was not until over 4 hours later at 17.52 that BSAA Kingston contacted Air Traffic Control in Bermuda to say that the aircraft had not been in contact with Jamaica since leaving Bermuda.

This led to a string of messages passing between BSAA and the various control centres asking for news of the aircraft, of which there was none. This exchange culminated in a message from BSAA Operations in Bermuda at 19.05 ordering a search to be initiated by BSAA Tudor G-AHNJ *Star Panther*, which had landed at Nassau at 17.43 en route from Kingston to Bermuda.

At 21.08 a message was sent from New York Air Sea Rescue to USAF Bermuda planning an all-out search. A time of 7 hours and 26 minutes had therefore elapsed between *Star Ariel* transmitting its final message and the start of a thorough search for the aircraft. No one will ever know whether this long delay was significant in preventing the searching aircraft from finding any trace of the Tudor, but one of the areas on which the accident report focused was the operational procedure for handing off aircraft from one control zone to another and the subsequent actions which should be taken if the aircraft does not report in within a given timeframe.

It is hard to imagine how a relatively new airliner could be lost in such conditions without leaving some shred of evidence as to its ultimate fate. The crew was very experienced, indeed the captain had previously flown the same route four times each way. The aircraft was relatively new and had been carefully maintained. The weather could hardly have been better, with excellent visibility, no icing and moderate winds. The subsequent air and sea search was on a huge scale, involving between seventy and eighty flights per day, and lasted for six days before being called off. Nothing at all was found which could have come from *Star Ariel*.

The aircraft carried safety equipment in case of ditching in the sea, in addition to the standard provision of lifebelts for all passengers and crew. This consisted of three circular shaped dinghies, each of which could seat up to eighteen people. Each dinghy contained distress and sailing aids, and an emergency pack with a container of sealed provisions and first aid equipment. The aircraft was fitted with a device which electrically activated the dinghy inflation and deployment system if the aircraft struck water. A manual backup system was fitted to enable two of the three dinghies to be deployed and inflated if the automatic system failed to do so. One of the three dinghies contained a radio transmitter which was set to transmit on 500 kc/s, the international marine distress frequency. This radio would have had a range of up to 20 miles with a mast, 50 to 75 miles using a kite aerial, but less than a mile without either.

It is worth considering the navigation and communication aspects of the flight in order to appreciate the problems facing airline crews flying long trans-oceanic routes fifty years ago. In 1949 there were no mandatory internationally agreed procedures for civilian airliners to report their position on this particular route. This was because three years earlier in 1946, at the Caribbean Regional Air Navigation Meeting, no airline had expressed an intention to operate a route between Bermuda and Kingston. There was also no mention in the search-and-rescue procedures applicable at the time of any specific time interval which should elapse before the appropriate air traffic control authority should initiate search and rescue for an overdue aircraft. The responsibility for determining that an aircraft was overdue, and thereby initiating search-and-rescue procedures, was placed on the operating airline. The local control areas for both Kindley Field, Bermuda and Palisadoes aerodrome in Kingston were circles of 150 nautical miles radius centred on those airfields. The normal procedure used by BSAA was that aircraft on southbound flights should maintain contact with New York Oceanic Control until they reached 30° N. BSAA also recommended that contact should be made between the aircraft and control stations at least every 30 minutes, or 15 minutes on trans-oceanic sectors. Control centres should then alert rescue services if there had been no contact with an aircraft for more than 30 minutes. Transfer of BSAA operational control from departure station to arrival station would normally occur at approximately the mid-point of the route, by means of calls from the aircraft to both stations in turn requesting that they accept and relinquish control. Complications arise when messages from the aircraft have to be passed from one station to another before reaching their required destination. This inevitably introduces a significant delay which, in the case of *Star Ariel*, could have been critical. If there had been a major mechanical problem which meant the Tudor was unable to maintain height, it is reasonable to assume there would have been enough time for the radio officer to transmit a mayday message as the aircraft descended from its 18,000ft cruising altitude towards the sea. This raises the possibility of three options. Either there was a failure of all three radio transmitters fitted to the aircraft (possibly a total electrical failure), or the crew became incapacitated in some way and were unable to transmit a message, or the loss of *Star Ariel* was virtually instantaneous.

It is curious that although there is a great deal of documentary evidence held in many large files at The National Archives concerning the exhaustive investigations following the loss of *Star Tiger*, there is virtually nothing related to the loss of *Star Ariel*. There are, however, a couple of interesting documents which may have some relevance. The first takes the form of a letter dated 6 April 1949 from the Air Registration Board, addressed to Mr Woodhouse at the Inspection Department of BSAA Langley, recommending that the Tudor tailplane attachment bolts should be replaced after just 300 hours of use with a modified (presumably stronger) type of bolt. The letter stated that the new specification bolt should be inspected after 100 hours to ensure it was still at the correct torque, and thereafter it should be inspected at 300-hour intervals, but assuming these requirements were carried out it was cleared for indefinite life. It is not known what prompted this modification.

The second letter is from a Mr Powell at the Air Registration Board in Corsham, Wiltshire, to a colleague at the Board in London and it discusses potentially serious problems with the aviation fuel supply at Nassau. He refers to the results of examinations of four Merlin engines by Rolls-Royce technicians and their findings that all four engines seized as a result of a type of gum which they found present in the fuel. He mentions that he told Mr Woodhouse at BSAA that the concentration of gum found in the fuel supply at Nassau was sufficient to cause all four engines of an aircraft to fail in flight. He then went on to question whether there was a possibility that some of this fuel found its way into the tanks of *Star Ariel*. Mr Powell's letter is acknowledged with a reply, assuring him that the matter had been brought to the attention of the Chief Inspector (Engines) at the Air Registration Board, but there is no further evidence of the outcome.

Perhaps an indication of why there are very few publicly available documents lies in a section of the accident report headed 'Sabotage'. It states that very careful consideration was given to the question of sabotage, adding that 'it is not expedient to give in a report of this kind details of the scope of the enquiries that were made'. The report went on to say that no evidence had been found to suggest sabotage, but of course very little evidence of any kind was found as there was no wreckage to examine.

There are several possible scenarios which could explain the loss of the aircraft. If an explosive device had detonated on board *Star Ariel* there would have been no warning and no time for a radio message to be transmitted. It is likely that the extensive aerial search which took place along the planned route would have resulted in a sighting of at least some small fragments of wreckage. If an aircraft explodes at altitude the wreckage is scattered over a vast area. (When the Pan Am Boeing 747 *Clipper Maid of the Seas* exploded over Lockerbie in 1988, some small pieces of debris were found nearly 80 miles away from the point where the bulk of the wreckage fell.)

The possibility of a catastrophic structural failure cannot be completely ruled out. In 1949, the ability to predict clear air turbulence was not as reliable as today and weather radar was primitive. The official accident report contains a curious statement regarding the likely weather conditions which the aircraft would have encountered. It states: 'a low pressure system was centred about 28° N 53° W and an anti-cyclone about 32° N 14° W. The aircraft track lay about halfway between these co-ordinates.' This is a puzzling statement as 32° N 14° W is a point just south-east of the island of Madeira and nowhere near the track of *Star Ariel*. In spite of this anomaly, there is little evidence to suggest weather was an issue. Most of the route was flown in anti-cyclonic conditions and the report refers to the 09.00 upper wind forecast from Bermuda radar which predicted some wind shear between 14,000ft and 18,000ft, but by 15.00 they predicted little, if any. It was stated therefore that 'the chance of any marked clear air turbulence of a frictional nature was almost nil'. Although it is considered extremely unlikely, given these weather reports, it is remotely possible that while cruising at 18,000ft *Star Ariel* encountered turbulence which subjected it to sudden structural loads beyond its design capability, resulting in the aircraft breaking up. While the wreckage would be unlikely to be scattered over such a wide area as if a bomb had exploded on board, it is nevertheless still surprising that no trace of wreckage or fuel floating on the surface of the water was ever spotted by the search aircraft.

Another possibility involves incapacitation of the crew. The Avro Tudor was Britain's first fully pressurised airliner, designed to compete with the American airliners of the day such as the Douglas DC-4 and Lockheed Constellation. Being pressurised, it offered levels of passenger comfort far superior to the Avro Yorks and Lancastrians in widespread use at the time. A portable oxygen supply was provided for each member of the crew in case of a failure of the aircraft systems. This would rely on them being able to activate their emergency oxygen before the onset of hypoxia (a condition caused by a reduction in the supply of oxygen to the brain). If there had been a gradual failure of the pressurisation system, it is possible (although unlikely at an altitude of only 18,000ft) that the crew could have been suffering from the effects of hypoxia without realising, and before they were able to utilise their emergency oxygen supply. If this were the case, it would have been possible for the autopilot to be accidentally disengaged and the aircraft to descend steadily into the Atlantic with all on board unconscious, or even for it to fly on under the control of the autopilot until the fuel ran out, which would have placed it 1,000 miles beyond its destination in the sea south of Panama. In the latter case it would not be so surprising that the search aircraft found no trace of the Tudor, as they would have been searching in completely the wrong area.

As with any unexplained loss of an aircraft, there are a multitude of different scenarios which could explain the loss, some of which are extremely unlikely but nevertheless remotely possible. Having studied all the possibilities carefully, the most likely cause would appear to be related to the cabin heater. BOAC took a surprisingly keen interest in the outcome of the *Star Ariel* enquiry and went to some lengths to formulate its own opinions on the cause of its loss. In an internal memo sent to the BOAC Chief Executive Whitney Straight on 11 March 1949, H.S. Crabtree (former manager of the BOAC Croydon Engineering Base) described a series of tests which had been carried out at Farnborough on a rig to simulate the ventilation and heating system of the Tudor IV. The tests were designed to confirm a theory that leaking hydraulic fluid had come into contact with the Daniels heater, causing a fierce fire or explosion. During the first test, when finely atomised hydraulic fluid was sprayed through the ventilation ducting via the re-circulating fan on to the Daniels heater, it produced a cloud of dense fumes from the ducting. The engineers reasoned that if this occurred in an aircraft in flight, the crew would undoubtedly carry out the fire drill, which would involve shutting off the fuel supply to the heater and switching off the fan. As soon as these actions were carried out on the

Farnborough rig, the heater burst into flames and burned very fiercely. This is because the fan had been keeping the temperature around the heater down to a few degrees below the flash point of the hydraulic fluid vapour (around 430°C). As soon as the fan was switched off the temperature of the heater rose and the vapour ignited. It was felt that the resultant fire would have caused fumes sufficiently toxic to have suffocated the occupants of the aircraft in a very short time and would probably have burned with such ferocity that the aircraft could not have remained airborne for more than a few seconds anyway. The memo then went on to criticise both the manufacturing standards of A.V. Roe and the maintenance standards of BSAA, and to bring into question the skills and practices of the BSAA engineering personnel. It was not unusual for BOAC to openly criticise the BSAA engineering department in this way and to claim their own staff and methods were superior. It is ironic therefore that within months of this memo being written, most of those BSAA engineers had become BOAC engineers anyway.

The theory of leaking hydraulic fluid causing a catastrophic in-flight fire or explosion is one which was suggested to the authors by an ex-BSAA engineer Richard Beddoes. He told us that the hydraulically actuated Sperry A3 autopilot on the Tudor was notorious for leaking fluid. There was a reservoir in the nose of the aircraft behind the instrument panel which was very prone to leaks and needed to be topped up regularly. He reasoned that the fluid had to go somewhere and always felt it must have accumulated under the fuselage floor. When the aircraft was on the ground, the fluid would drain back and collect in the tail, but when it was airborne in level flight it would travel forward and remain in the vicinity of the cabin heater. It would then be easy for the vapour to build in density, especially in the cold air at altitude, until it was ignited by the heater.

It is unlikely that we will ever know what fate befell *Star Ariel* and its occupants that day. Some of the questions surrounding the disappearance of the BSAA Lancastrian *Star Dust* were answered fifty years later, but unfortunately the ocean does not give up its secrets so readily.

What is known is that the loss of *Star Ariel* was almost certainly the single event which spelled the beginning of the end for BSAA. In the absence of evidence as to the cause of the accident, the government stepped in to ground the Avro Tudor for passenger use once more, making it almost impossible for BSAA to continue operating at a profit with the aircraft remaining at its disposal.

Chapter 15

'I think I'll have a spot of lunch!'

Nine days before the disappearance of *Star Ariel* the board of BSAA had decided that the posts of chief executive and chairman would be combined. John Booth remained as chairman and now took on the extra duty of chief executive, while Bernard Porter became Administrative General Manager and Gordon Store, Technical General Manager.

Then came the loss of *Star Ariel*. Three days later a meeting was held at the MCA to discuss what should be done about the Avro Tudor. BSAA Chairman, John Booth, said that he and the board wanted another investigation to be made, similar to that carried out after *Star Tiger*'s disappearance. Their concern was that 'unless a reason for the two accidents could be found, they felt that the responsibility they would carry in operating the aircraft would be too great, so that until an explanation could be discovered they did not feel justified in continuing to fly the aircraft'.

Booth admitted that their concern was not shared by BSAA's pilots who were quite prepared to fly the company's Tudors in any tests necessary to ascertain if the accident had been due to any technical fault.

Mr S. Scott-Hall from the Ministry of Supply welcomed the tests, but wanted reassurance that the aircraft's C of A would not be withdrawn if no technical defects were found. Mr R.E. Hardingham of the ARB was happy to give this reassurance.

Lord Pakenham then asked Lord Brabazon of Tara if he would chair a coordinating committee whose remit would be 'to inquire into the design and construction of the Tudor 4 aircraft in relation to safety and airworthiness, and into any other relevant matters'.

During the course of the enquiry, which lasted for only a month, Lord Brabazon received a visit from a Lady Powerscourt who lived in Bermuda but who was, conveniently, in Britain that month. She wanted to tell him about an incident that had occurred on a BSAA flight two years before on which she had been a passenger. The main part of her complaint was that after having taken off from the Azores for Bermuda the aircraft flew through a storm, there was a flash and an explosion but it continued safely to Bermuda. After landing in Bermuda Lady Powerscourt spoke to a BOAC representative who, she said, acted for BSAA, and who told her that it was the radio transmitter fusing and that they had had to complete the flight with no radio at all. The aircraft then went on to Kingston, again, according to the BOAC representative, with no radio. Lady Powerscourt wrote a letter of complaint to Lord Knollys [then Chairman of BOAC], but received no reply.

Lord Brabazon sent these details to Air Commodore Vernon Brown, Chief Inspector of Accidents, asking for his opinion and telling him that Lady Powerscourt was an experienced traveller, having flown over 50,000 miles. He wrote back, saying:

As to the explosion and flash in the severe storm that was encountered, it is so typical of a lightning strike or static discharge that I should hardly hesitate to say that is what happened. The fusing of a radio transmitter, if the radio operator had not had time to earth the set, or the loss of a trailing aerial is quite a common occurrence on such occasions. There are hundreds of records of lightning strikes and although a few of them may have been associated with an accident, I can say truthfully that there are very few cases where the strike itself has proved catastrophic.

But the statement that the aircraft went on from Bermuda to Kingston without any form of radio at all is very hard to believe. In fact, with great respect to Lady Powerscourt, I really cannot believe it. It may be that that particular set was not replaced, but even in 1947 everything was duplicated and it is common practice in civil aviation to carry a spare set which can be rigged up within a few minutes.

Lady Powerscourt's letter raises questions that cannot be explained. When she arrived in Bermuda why did she speak to BOAC about what had happened? According to the BSAA annual report of 1949, the arrangement for a joint handling unit with BOAC in Bermuda was discussed during that financial period which began on 1 April 1948, fourteen months *after* the time that Lady Powerscourt said BOAC was acting for BSAA. Why did she write to BOAC's chairman to complain about a BSAA flight, rather than to BSAA itself, a fact commented upon by Vernon Brown? Having received no reply to her letter why did she wait for two years before doing anything about it and then only choose to act in the very month that Lord Brabazon was conducting his enquiry? Why did the BOAC staff member in Bermuda make such an outrageous claim about the radio? Quite apart from any regulation that might have been broken by not having a serviceable radio on board an aircraft, it is inconceivable that the pilot would have risked his own life by making the onward flight to Kingston, which is entirely over water, without having any facilities with which to communicate with the ground.

It may be that Lady Powerscourt's letter was genuine, but something about it does not make sense.

* * *

BSAA had expected to have nineteen Tudors flying on its routes by the summer of 1949 but with the Tudors I and IV withdrawn from service and the Tudor V flying as a freighter on the Berlin Airlift, the airline only had its Yorks to fall back on. Because the York was not suitable to fly across the North Atlantic, the Caribbean services had to be cancelled immediately with the majority of passengers being transferred to BOAC and a few to Trans Canada Airlines. Services between Buenos Aires and Santiago across the Andes were also cancelled.

Hoping that the grounding of the Tudors would soon be lifted the airline planned to continue operating to the Caribbean via Lisbon, Dakar, Natal, Georgetown and Trinidad. It made two trial flights over the route and found it satisfactory as a temporary measure. In addition to these changes the airline also requested permission to make a refuelling stop in Belem if necessary and to trans-ship cargo at Natal. On 4 February BSAA announced that it had reduced the east coast service from four to three flights per week and two Yorks were ferried to Nassau to keep the west coast service to Santiago running until a better solution could be found.

Three weeks later Lord Pakenham decided to ground the Tudor permanently. He based his decision on the fact that Lord Brabazon's enquiry had failed to identify 'one single fault, the elimination of which would restore confidence in the safety of the type. Accordingly I have reached the conclusion that there can be no question of putting the Tudor IVa [sic] back into passenger service.'

The decision was not made public until a debate in the House of Commons on 1 March. The grounding of the Tudor was slipped into the middle of a discussion about the annual reports of the three airlines and was therefore not given much attention. The focus was on the continuing losses, and the excessive overstaffing of both BOAC and BEA. Ivor Thomas, MP for Keighley who, at the beginning of 1946, announced to the House that BSAA would be the chosen airline for the South American routes, praised BSAA's efficiency by saying that 'the average member of the staff of BOAC turned out 3,105 capacity-ton-miles in the course of the year. In BEA the figure was 2,819 and in BSAA 10,758'. Lichfield's MP, Cecil Poole, was so uninterested in BSAA's efforts to run an efficient, thrifty operation that he merely commented 'So what?'

BOAC and BEA had eventually realised that they were excessively overstaffed. It was disclosed that the former had already sacked 5,000 employees and the latter 800 in an effort to reduce costs and there would be more to come.

That afternoon a meeting of the Cabinet Committee on Socialisation of Industries met at 11 Downing Street to discuss 'the serious position in which BSAA found themselves as a result of the unsatisfactory performance of the Tudor IV aircraft'. One of the points discussed was that there might be a case for reorganising the three corporations into one serving North and South America, one for the Middle and Far East and a third for Europe and inland services. It was decided that 'in practice, it was out of the question at this stage to disrupt BOAC in the way which this scheme would require'. Again everything centred around BOAC.

The next day the Prime Minister was informed that Pakenham had decided that BSAA and BOAC should be amalgamated. The note from the Privy Council Office stated curiously that 'the arrangements made in the Civil Aviation Act, 1946 were experimental in character and there has always been a case for the fusion of the two organisations operating long-distance airlines. Fairly substantial savings in staff and other overheads could be effected.'

* * *

While the staff of BSAA were blissfully unaware of the bombshell that was about to hit them, another incident occurred. Avro York G-AHFE *Star Vista* was damaged on take-off from Lima on 13 March 1949 while operating flight number 402/121 to Barranquilla. In command was Captain John Wright and the First Officer was P. Falconer.

As the aircraft was powering down runway 16 it reached 60 knots and started to swing to port more than would normally be expected. The swift application of right rudder failed to prevent the aircraft from leaving the hard surface and the crew found themselves at 80 knots on the grassland to the left of the runway. The Captain realised that they were racing towards a large irrigation ditch and an old Peruvian wall. He had to make a split-second decision and decided that to try and stop could result in a catastrophic collision with the wall; he therefore pulled the override on the throttles to give as much power as possible to achieve flying speed. As the ditch and wall loomed closer he pulled back on the control column and very nearly made it. Unfortunately the port main wheel clipped the top of the wall.

With the engines still at full power the aircraft was difficult to control and Captain Wright later said that he believed the starboard wing was giving more lift than the port, possibly because of a fault with the flaps. When they were safely flying, the power was reduced, the aircraft became more controllable and at 1,500ft Captain Wright carried out some checks. He discovered that he did indeed have an asymmetric flap condition with 20° on the starboard side and as little as 5° on the port. The undercarriage indicator showed that it was unlocked, however a visual inspection revealed the worrying fact that the starboard wheel was trailing and the port wheel was missing. It had been torn from the aircraft when they clipped the wall. The starboard wheel was immediately retracted. The flying controls were carefully checked and (with the exception of the flaps) were found to be working normally, although the port inner engine had to be shut down and the propeller feathered.

The Captain decided to leave the airfield circuit and hold 20 miles away on the coast for a few hours at 1,500ft to burn off fuel (there was no fuel dump facility on the York). The story goes that the controller in the tower, who had witnessed the take-off problems, contacted the aircraft and with a great deal of concern asked the Captain what he intended to do, to which he replied 'I think I'll have a spot of lunch!'

After about 4 hours of flying up and down the beach at 1,500ft Captain Wright flew back to the airfield and rejoined the circuit, where he made several passes down the runway to assess the conditions and the surrounding area. By this time, word of the plight of the British airliner had spread around the city and a large crowd had gathered at the airfield to witness the landing attempt. Eventually the crew were given clearance to land and Captain Wright made a very smooth belly landing with the aircraft coming to rest after about 200 to 300yds, just off the runway. The fire service made sure there was no danger of fire and the crew and passengers calmly vacated the aircraft. Captain Wright praised his crew for the professional manner in which they had carried out their duties and the way in which they instilled calm in the passengers. John Wright himself was hailed as a hero in the city of Lima for bringing the aircraft down safely and was awarded a medal by the mayor.

* * *

On 15 March the merger, which also named John Booth, and Whitney Straight of BOAC, as joint deputies under the BOAC Chairman, was announced in the Commons. It brought forth questions about the choice of having three corporations and some MPs seemed shocked that this policy had now been abandoned.

Oliver Stanley, MP for Bristol West, was confused and, addressing George Lindgren, Parliamentary Secretary to the MCA, said: 'The existence of the three Corporations was stressed by the Government as being most important because it was said that it was only by having three Corporations that there could be proper competition. What has happened to that viewpoint ?'

Lindgren asserted that if Stanley were to look at the Second Reading Debate of 6 May 1946 he would find that the Lord President of the Council had said that there was no virtue in having three corporations and that the number could be changed if it was found to be too many.

Stanley persisted: 'Are we then to understand that although it may be possible to reduce the number from three to two, it would not be right to reduce from three to one?'

Lindgren replied: 'Not at the present time. The two types of operation are totally different.'

George Ward, MP for Worcester, enquired: 'Does not the Parliamentary Secretary agree that the ability of BOAC suddenly to take on responsibility for the South American route with its existing flight of aircraft in addition to its own commitments indicate that BOAC has previously been over-established in aircraft and therefore in man-power?'

Lindgren replied emphatically 'No, Sir, that inference cannot be drawn.'

It is amazing that a government, whose policy it had been for the three corporations to use British aeroplanes, not only changed its mind to allow BOAC to buy American aircraft, it also abandoned British aircraft manufacturers at the first sign of any trouble and penalised the only one of the two long-haul carriers to abide by its wishes, by effectively shutting it down.

The government's remarkable deference to BOAC at that time is hard to understand as is the desire of BOAC to put BSAA out of business. Of the three corporations BOAC was the one to lose the most money and be the least efficient but in the Minister's eyes, if not in those of some MPs, it could do no wrong. It seems to have been overlooked that its Chief Executive, Whitney Straight, although British by naturalisation, had been born in America, of American parents. His cousin was Cornelius Vanderbilt Whitney, who had backed Juan Trippe when he founded the Aviation Corporation of America, and who had become president of the company himself. It will be remembered that the Aviation Corporation of America was the parent company of Pan American Airways, already shown as having been a ruthless rival on the South American routes. Was PAA using family connections to try to get BOAC to help it remove its main competitor in South America?

George Lindgren's answers to MPs' questions and his assertion that provision had been made at the second reading of the 1946 Civil Aviation Bill to change the number of corporations, should the need arise, would suggest that perhaps it had never been the government's intention for BSAA to operate for any longer than the time it took to get the company onto a sound footing. Once that had been done the routes would be handed over to BOAC.

In common with most airlines of that era BSAA had experienced problems, not least of which were the two unexplained disappearances of *Star Tiger* and *Star Ariel*, but it had established routes to South and Central America and to the Caribbean. It had acquired two other airlines, BWIA and Bahamas Airways, to supplement its routes and provide valuable feeder services in the Caribbean and, despite inevitable financial deficit, it had been run in a much more cost-effective way than either BOAC or BEA. Its reward for all its hard work was to be taken over by the very company that had sought its demise from before it had even made its first flight; the company which had consistently made huge losses and which, it had openly been admitted, was grossly overstaffed.

It was a great pity for BSAA, when it had worked so hard to be the government's choice of carrier to operate the South American routes, that it had not been told what was really required. It would appear that while BSAA wanted to be the best it could be, all the government wanted was a company that would not embarrass the other two corporations with its enthusiasm, innovation and sheer hard work, and that would do what it was told and not dare to be different.

* * *

Following the announcement of the merger, BSAA staff organised a protest meeting to be held at Caxton Hall on 21 March. They still hoped that the government could be persuaded to change its mind and allow the airline to continue operating. It was a forlorn hope. Meanwhile life, and work, went on.

* * *

In November the previous year BSAA had lost its entire stock of spare parts from its stores in Keflavik, Iceland, in a fierce fire. It may not have been an accident; on 8 April 1949, history repeated itself when the stock of spares worth £10,000 which was held in Santiago was also destroyed by fire. It seemed that even though the airline was going to disappear shortly it was still having its customary bad luck and odd incidents.

On 20 April 1949, Roger C. de Wilde (a 39-year-old BSAA communications pilot) flew the airline's Avro 19 (Anson) G-AIKM *Star Visitant* from London to Speke airport in Liverpool with the intention of flying south to Hatfield the following day with two passengers, James W. Kenny, BSAA Technical Development Controller, and his brother. With de Wilde was experienced BSAA Radio Operator S.P. Chapman. The aircraft had 120 gallons of fuel on board when it left London and was not refuelled at Speke before leaving for the return flight. The Anson took off early and the flight south was uneventful until they were in the vicinity of Hatfield above cloud, where the weather was deemed to be too bad to let down and land. The decision was made to divert to Luton where it was planned to let down through the cloud using the Luton radio beacon. As they broke cloud 500ft over Luton Aerodrome the pilot entered the circuit and lowered the undercarriage at around 400ft. As he did so the starboard engine suddenly stopped. Despite opening the throttle fully on the port engine, he realised that the aircraft was too low to make a single-engined landing on the airfield from that position with their current descent rate, so promptly raised the undercarriage again to make a forced landing in a field.

The aircraft clipped the tops of some trees before crash landing in a ploughed field 200yds further on. It slid for 40yds before spinning round through 180° and coming to rest on its belly on the top of a small hill. The port engine broke away from its mountings in the impact and ended up pointing out towards the wingtip. The starboard wing was badly damaged, with the outer fuel tank breaking away and resting under the wing. It was still connected to the inner tank and there were 12 gallons of fuel remaining inside when investigators removed it later. The fuselage was relatively undamaged (apart from the obvious damage to the underside resulting from a wheels-up landing) and the four men on board were able to walk away from the aircraft without any injuries.

As the accident was caused by the failure of the starboard engine, the investigators examined the fuel system carefully to check for fuel starvation. They traced the flow of fuel through the pipes and fuel cocks to the carburettors, which seemed normal. When they checked the non-return valve on the outer tank they found it to contain a yellow paint-like substance which had sealed the valve in the closed position. The component was sent to the Royal Aircraft Establishment at Farnborough where it was examined in its laboratories. They concluded that the substance was a hardened film which is formed when a slushing compound is used in a tank. This is a fairly common process which forms a fuel-resistant film on the inside of aluminium tanks and prevents corrosion; however, it should only be carried out after all the tank fittings have first been removed.

Examination of the paperwork for *Star Visitant* revealed that all four fuel tanks had received an application of a zinc chromate slushing compound at the last C of A in January 1949. Assuming the non-return valve had been stuck in the closed position since January it was concluded that in the twenty-two flights made since that date, no fuel other than a few gallons of leakage past the valve had flowed from the starboard outer tank to the engine.

There was an interesting postscript to this accident. The Accidents Investigation Branch had established the cause, but then set out to discover which engineer at BSAA's Langley maintenance base was responsible for using the slushing compound without removing the tank fittings. In doing so they sent a letter to one of the BSAA inspectors, whose initials were on the repair card, warning him that he would probably be blamed for the error and suggesting he may wish to avail himself of the services of a solicitor. After he replied three days later they sent him a second letter apologising that they had made a mistake as his initials were not on the side of the card marked 'Slushing'. Unfortunately they then wrote a letter blaming another engineer, who employed a solicitor to protest his innocence as he was not responsible for slushing the tank in question. This resulted in another letter of apology from the AIB for any pain caused to him or his wife and an offer to pay for any solicitor's bills incurred.

Occasionally, even a highly efficient organisation such as the AIB can get things wrong. The identity of the engineer actually responsible was never revealed.

* * *

At the end of the 1948–49 football season, London club Arsenal was invited by a wealthy Brazilian to tour Brazil. On 9 May the first half of the party took off on flight BA221 to Rio via Lisbon, Dakar and Natal to be joined two days later by the rest of the team. The Gunners, including celebrities such as Wally Barnes, Joe Mercer and goalkeeper George Swindin, were accompanied by their manager Tom Whittaker, and arrived in Rio to a rapturous reception by Brazilian football fans who called them *'major maquina futebolistica do mundo'* or 'the greatest football machine in the world'. Stargirl Sylvia Haynes recalled the trip and the photo she had taken with the team. Sadly she lent it to a journalist who never bothered to return it. The trip brought a little more good publicity, but it was all too late to save the airline.

* * *

Many accounts of the exploits of BSAA focused on the mistakes or errors of judgement which led in some cases to the loss of aircraft. There were examples of incidents which were not so widely publicised, where coolness under pressure and the flying skills of the crew led to a safe outcome, as did the one that occurred on 13 July 1949 over Brazil, on a flight from Rio de Janeiro to Montevideo; virtually the last thing to happen before the merger.

In command of York G-AHFG *Star Haze* was Captain E.D. 'Wyn' Fieldson, an experienced and skilful former RAF bomber pilot who had been awarded the DFC for courage and devotion to duty on operations, including on one occasion bringing home a crippled Handley Page Halifax after it had part of its tail removed by another Halifax pilot who took the term 'close formation' rather too literally.

The weather forecast available to Captain Fieldson had predicted a weak cold front at an indefinite position across the track of the aircraft and no cloud above 10,000ft. The aircraft took off from Rio at just after 13.00 and the flight was normal, in clear air, until 16.10 when the altitude was reduced to 8,200ft to remain below cloud. Soon after, they encountered moderate to heavy clear air turbulence which lasted for over half an hour by which time the air smoothed out once more, although it was noted that the sky seemed very bright. The remainder of the flight is best told in Captain Fieldson's own words taken from the report he produced at the time:

17.04   Enter unavoidable stratiform cloud, temperature 11°C.

17.05   Immense hammering of hailstones which carried away both windshields and holed curved front windows. I was flying manually at the time and strapped in. Ducking as low as possible over the control column, I immediately commenced a rate 2 turn onto a reciprocal course. Mr E.S. Brown who was navigating immediately came to my assistance and we both suffered minor scratches about the face, blood from which was whipped into our eyes by the wind and made I/F [instrument flying] difficult. Mr MacIlwaine came beside me and shielded my head from the hailstones and flying Perspex with the tech log, for which he suffered two large facial bruises himself. A point of note is that at no time was the turbulence more than light.

17.07   Able to see ground. 20° Flap, undercarriage down, speed 140 knots, descending VFR [Visual Flight Rules] having decided to make landing PPPA [Porto Alegre] flying contact below cloud. (Note: a 130 Kt gale, even at 11°C, feels almost unbearably cold.)

17.20   Flying 1,500ft, below cloud, homing on PPPA. Watching engines carefully for signs of coolant leaks.

17.30   Making large diversion to avoid storms. Starboard Inner coolant temp, with shutter open 120°.

17.35   Starboard Inner feathered as coolant temp 120°, oil temp 90° and oil press. fallen to 35 psi.

17.40   Port Inner and Starboard Outer coolant temps 115° each. Starboard Inner oil temp, although feathered, still rising and now 120°.

18.00   Flying over land at 1,000ft below cloud. Vis. 10 to 15 miles. Keeping eye open for emergency landing areas in case of necessity.

18.15   PPPA in sight.

18.25   Landed.

Letters of commendation for the actions of the crew were sent to BSAA from many quarters, including one from Major Hamilton-Gordon, the British Consul in Porto Alegre, and from Brigadier Fullerton, the Military Attaché, who had been a passenger in *Star Haze*. He described the behaviour of all the crew as exemplary in very difficult circumstances.

Photographs taken of the aircraft on the tarmac at Porto Alegre clearly show the extent of the damage. The nose of the York was badly dented and the windscreens had been smashed, as had the astrodome. Engine radiators were holed, aerials were bent and the whole aircraft was peppered with dents and scratches. There were even large holes punched right through the aluminium skin at the tail of the aircraft. This was a fine example of an incident where skill and professionalism prevailed over bad luck to bring about a safe outcome to a dangerous situation.

On 30 July, just two weeks after Captain Fieldson's heroic flight, the Royal Assent to the Airways Corporation Bill, allowing for the merger of BSAA and BOAC, was received and BSAA ceased to exist.

Epilogue

An Unpopular Merger

On the evening of 21 March 1949 around 400 men and women met in London's Caxton Hall to discuss how they could stop the government's plans to amalgamate them with BOAC, and to show how much BSAA meant to them. They spoke of their dismay at the prospect of the merger, their frustration at the grounding of their aircraft and their fears that the special spirit that was BSAA would be lost forever.

Someone asked why, if aircraft were available in BOAC to operate the South American routes, they could not just be loaned to BSAA until a solution to the grounding of the Tudors had been found. Another expressed disappointment that the management they had served so well had not even bothered to send a representative to the meeting, despite its pledges of support. An ex-BOAC employee said that if it were BOAC under threat, despite being a bigger company, it would not have managed to rally even half the number of protesters that BSAA had there that evening.

No one suggested it, but there must have been some who felt that they had been betrayed by the management and by the government and that pragmatism rather than principle had been the victor. There were definitely those who believed that their airline was being sacrificed for reasons more underhand than they could imagine.

They may all have been correct. Their fears were realised. The merger went ahead and the spirit that had been theirs vanished. Some of those who went on to work for BOAC were shunned by its staff for not belonging to the right union, the South American routes were not run profitably and eventually in 1965 BOAC, blaming the losses on its British VC10 aircraft, handed over the routes to British United Airways.

BUA also flew VC10s on its South American services and made them profitable, in much the same way that BSAA had with its Lancastrians, twenty years before.

* * *

As former BSAA pilot Frank Taylor said much later, when the pioneering little company had faded from the memories of all but those who worked for it: 'BSAA was a relatively small airline with a remarkable *esprit de corps*. There was a great communal feeling. Everyone gave of their best to make a success of the enterprise and because of this everyone was important in the organisation. They were wonderful days!'

APPENDIX I. Aircraft Performance Comparison

APPENDICES

	Avro 691 Lancastrian III	Avro 685 York I	Avro 688 Tudor 1	Avro 688 Tudor 4	Avro 688 Tudor 4B	Avro 689 Tudor 5
Dimensions						
Span (ft & inches)	102' 0"	102' 0"	120' 0"	120' 0"	120' 0"	120' 0"
Length (ft & inches)	76' 10"	78' 6"	79' 6"	85' 3"	85' 3"	105' 7"
Height (ft & inches)	19' 6"	16' 6"	20' 11"	20' 11"	20' 11"	24' 3"
Wing area (sq ft)	1,297	1,205	1,421	1,421	1,421	1,421
Weights						
Tare weight (lbs)	30,220	42,040	47,960	49,441	50,322	46,300
All-up weight (lbs)	65,000	68,000	71,000	80,000	82,000	80,000
Performance						
Maximum speed (mph)	315	298	260	282	282	295
Cruising speed (mph)	245	233	210	210	210	235
Initial climb (ft/min)	950	820	700	800	635	740
Ceiling (feet)	25,500	26,000	26,000	27,400	23,500	25,550
Range (miles)	4,150	2,700	3,630	4,000	3,500	2,330

Registration	Type	Date	Location	Total on board	Total fatalities	Crew	Passengers	Crew Killed	Crew Injured	Passengers Killed	Passengers Injured
G-AGWJ	Avro Lancastrian III	30-Aug-46	Bathurst, Gambia	17	0	5	12	0	2	0	4
G-AHEW	Avro York	7-Sep-46	Bathurst, Gambia	24	24	4	20	4	0	20	0
G-AHEZ	Avro York	13-Apr-47	Dakar, Senegal	15	6	6	9	0	2	6	3
G-AGWH	Avro Lancastrian III	2-Aug-47	Tupungato, Argentina	11	11	5	6	5	0	6	0
G-AGWK	Avro Lancastrian III	5-Sep-47	Kindley Field, Bermuda	20	0	5	15	0	1	0	0
G-AGUL	Avro Lancaster	23-Oct-47	Heathrow, England	4	0	4	0	0	0	N/A	N/A
G-AGWG	Avro Lancastrian III	13-Nov-47	Kindley Field, Bermuda	16	0	4	12	0	0	0	0
G-AHNP	Avro Tudor IV	30-Jan-48	Western Atlantic	31	31	6	25	6	0	25	0
G-AHEX	Avro York	5-Jan-49	Caravelas, Brazil	15	3	6	9	0	3	3	4
G-AGRE	Avro Tudor IVB	17-Jan-49	Western Atlantic	20	20	7	13	7	0	13	0
G-AIKM	Avro 19 Srs 2 Anson	21-Apr-49	Luton, England	4	0	2	2	0	0	0	0
				177	95	54	123	22	8	73	11

APPENDIX III. Accidents to BOAC and BEA Aircraft between 1 January 1946 and 31 December 1949

Registration	Type	Airline	Date	Location	Total on board	Total Killed
G-AHCS	Douglas DC-3	BEA	7-Aug-46	Oslo, Norway	16	3
G-AGBE	Douglas DC-3	BEA	18-Nov-46	Lons-le-Saunier	4	0
G-AHOK	Junkers Ju.52	BEA	26-Jan-47	Glasgow, UK	-	-
G-AHKR	De Havilland Dragon Rapide	BEA	15-Apr-47	Isle of Man	7	0
G-AGJF	De Havilland Dragon Rapide	BEA	6-Aug-47	Isle of Barra, UK	-	-
G-AHPK	Vickers Viking	BEA	6-Jan-48	Northolt, UK	18	1
G-AIVP	Vickers Viking	BEA	5-Apr-48	Berlin	14	14
G-AIVE	Vickers Viking	BEA	21-Apr-48	Largs, UK	20	0
G-AGIX	Douglas DC-3	BEA	30-Jul-48	Sywell, UK	18	0
G-AHXY	De Havilland Dragon Rapide	BEA	27-Dec-48	Glasgow, UK	-	-
G-AHXV	De Havilland Dragon Rapide	BEA	15-Jan-49	Isle of Man	-	-
G-AHCW	Douglas DC-3	BEA	19-Feb-49	Coventry, UK	10	10
G-AHCY	Douglas DC-3	BEA	19-Aug-49	Oldham, UK	32	24
G-AGIY	Douglas DC-3	BOAC	23-Jan-46	El Adem, Libya	-	-
G-AGET	Short Sunderland	BOAC	15-Feb-46	Calcutta, India	-	-
G-AGEM	Consolidated Liberator	BOAC	21-Feb-46	PEI, Canada	14	1
G-AGEV	Short Sunderland	BOAC	4-Mar-46	Poole, UK	-	-
G-AGHV	Short Sunderland	BOAC	10-Mar-46	Rod-el-Farag, Egypt	-	-
G-AGLX	Avro Lancastrian	BOAC	23-Mar-46	Nr. Cocos Is, Indian Ocean	10	10
G-AGHK	Douglas DC-3	BOAC	17-Apr-46	Oviedo, Spain	13	0
G-AGMC	Avro Lancastrian	BOAC	2-May-46	Sydney, Australia	-	-
G-AGMH	Avro Lancastrian	BOAC	17-May-46	Mauripur, India	-	-
PP325	Handley Page Halifax	BOAC	8-Jul-46	Aldermaston, UK	-	-
G-AGUC	De Havilland Dove	BOAC	14-Aug-46	West Howe, UK	-	-
G-AGHT	Douglas DC-3	BOAC	14-Aug-46	Luqa, Malta	5	1
G-AGLU	Avro Lancastrian	BOAC	15-Aug-46	Bournemouth-Hurn, UK	4	0
G-AGMF	Avro Lancastrian	BOAC	20-Aug-46	Broglie, France	8	8
G-AGKD	Douglas DC-3	BOAC	23-Dec-46	Luqa, Malta	-	-
G-AGJU	Douglas DC-3	BOAC	3-Jan-47	Whitchurch, UK	3	0
G-AGJX	Douglas DC-3	BOAC	11-Jan-47	Stowting, UK	16	8
G-AHYZ	Short Sunderland	BOAC	18-Jan-47	Belfast, UK	-	-
G-AHRA	De Havilland Dove	BOAC	13-Mar-47	Highcliffe, UK	3	3
G-AGNR	Avro York	BOAC	16-Jul-47	Basra, Iraq	18	6
G-AGHP	Douglas DC-3	BOAC	5-Aug-47	Croydon, UK	5	0
G-AHZB	Short Sunderland	BOAC	23-Aug-47	Bahrain	26	10
G-AGHW	Short Sunderland	BOAC	19-Nov-47	Isle of Wight, UK	4	1
G-AJHL	De Havilland Dove	BOAC	9-Feb-48	Ionian Sea	-	-
G-AGKN	Douglas DC-3	BOAC	14-Jul-48	Marseilles, France	6	6

G-AGMB	Avro Lancastrian	BOAC	27-Aug-48	Tengah, Singapore	14	0
G-AGEW	Short Sunderland	BOAC	5-Sep-48	Sourabaya, Indonesia	25	0
G-AHYC	Consolidated Liberator	BOAC	13-Nov-48	Prestwick, UK	-	-
G-AGJD	Avro York	BOAC	1-Feb-49	Castel Benito, Libya	15	0
G-AGJO	Short Sunderland	BOAC	21-Feb-49	Hythe, Kent, UK	-	-
G-AGMM	Avro Lancastrian	BOAC	7-Nov-49	Castel Benito, Libya	-	-
G-AHEJ	Lockheed Constellation	BOAC	21-Dec-49	Reykjavik, Iceland	20	0
				BEA (in 13 accidents)	139	52
				BOAC (in 32 accidents)	209	54
				TOTAL	348	106

APPENDIX IV. Proving Flight on 1 January 1946

Schedule for BSAA Lancastrian G-AGWG *Star Light* – 1 January 1946					
Airport		**Scheduled**	**Actual**	**Sector time**	**Date**
London (Heath Row)	Depart	12:00	12:05		01 January 1946
Lisbon (Portela)	Arrive	16:35	17:26	5:21	01 January 1946
Lisbon (Portela)	Depart	17:30	18:41		01 January 1946
Bathurst (Yundum)	Arrive	02:05	04:00	9:19	02 January 1946
Bathurst (Yundum)	Depart	03:05	05:06		02 January 1946
Natal (Parnamirim)	Arrive	11:30	13:11	8:04	02 January 1946
Natal (Parnamirim)	Depart	12:30	14:20		02 January 1946
Rio de Janeiro (Santos Dumont)	Arrive	18:30	20:22	6:02	02 January 1946
Rio de Janeiro (Santos Dumont)	Depart	09:00	09:26		03 January 1946
Montevideo (Carrasco)	Arrive	14:15	14:51	5:25	03 January 1946
Montevideo (Carrasco)	Depart	12:00	11:54		06 January 1946
Buenos Aires (Morón)	Arrive	12:50	12:55	1:01	06 January 1946
Buenos Aires (Morón)	Depart	11:45	11:44		09 January 1946
Rio de Janeiro (Santa Cruz)	Arrive	17:15	17:23	5:39	09 January 1946
Rio de Janeiro (Santa Cruz)	Depart	11:00	10:52		12 January 1946
Natal (Parnamirim)	Arrive	17:00	16:54	6:02	12 January 1946
Natal (Parnamirim)	Depart	19:00	19:30		12 January 1946
Bathurst (Yundum)	Arrive	04:00	04:15	8:45	13 January 1946
Bathurst (Yundum)	Depart	23:45	15:17		13 January 1946
Dakar (Mallard's Field)	Arrive	-	16:22	1:05	13 January 1946
Dakar (Mallard's Field)	Depart	-	00:17		14 January 1946
Lisbon (Portela)	Arrive	08:15	08:44	8:27	14 January 1946
Lisbon (Portela)	Depart	08:00	08:03		15 January 1946
London (Heath Row)	Arrive	12:45	13:16	5:13	15 January 1946

APPENDIX V.

Aircraft operated by British South American Airways

Percival Proctor 3
G-AGTH (H.291) (LZ715) and HM397, 06/10/46 **BSAA 'Star Pixie'**, to French Morocco as F-DAAO 08/51

Airspeed A.S.40 Oxford 1
G-AIVY 'Star Mentor'
C/N 891 (HM965), bought 14/10/46 from RAF by Airspeed, registered by Airspeed c/n 828, registered G-AIVY to **BSAA** 09/11/46, C of A No 8708 issued 08/03/48, aircraft named **'Star Mentor'**, transferred 30/07/49 and registered 05/09/49 to BOAC Training Flight Hurn, registered 01/10/53 Cyprus Airways Ltd, Nicosia, scrapped Nicosia 09/56.

Airspeed A.S.65 Consul
G-ALTZ 'Star Monitor'
C/N 3000 (Oxford) (HN844), C/N 5134 (Consul), bought 22/02/47 from RAF by Aer Rianta, Teoranta, delivered 30/06/47 and C of A No 9408 issued, registered EI-ADB to Aer Rianta 07/07/47, transferred 02/08/48 to Aer Lingus, Teoranta, bought by **BSAA** 15/06/49, registered as G-ALTZ **'Star Monitor'** to **BSAA** 21/06/49, transferred 30/07/49 to BOAC, delivered 10/49 to BOAC Hurn, bought 11/54 from BOAC by M.J. Conry t/a Aeromarine Salvage Co, registered 15/05/56 to Leon M. Berner & Co, Elmdon (Birmingham), 04/06/57 accident in Léopoldville, 13/11/57 abandoned unserviceable Léopoldville, Belgian Congo.

G-AIUX 'Star Master'
C/N 539 (Oxford) (LB527), C/N 5106 (Consul), bought 27/01/47 from RAF by Airspeed, originally registered with incorrect C/N 718 but corrected 06/03/47, converted to Consul and registered to Chartair Ltd, Thame 14/02/47, C of A No 9036 issued 15/04/47, registered to **BSAA** 20/11/48 named **'Star Master'**, used for evaluation of prototype Sperry Zero Reader by **BSAA** 1949, transferred 30/07/49 to BOAC, registered 05/09/49 to BOAC Training Flight Hurn, registered 05/54 to East

African Airways Corporation (Kenya) as VP-KMI, withdrawn from use 12/11/55 due to wood and glue failure in tropical conditions, reported as returned to service 1957.

Avro 19 Series 2 (Anson)
G-AIKM 'Star Visitant'
C/N 1364, bought 31/10/46 by Short, Rochester and Bedford, registered 27/06/47 to Short, re-registered 12/01/48 to Short Bros & Harland Ltd, registered 06/10/48 to **BSAA** named **'Star Visitant'**, crashed at Luton 21/04/49 and cancelled same day.

Vickers-Supermarine Type 309 Sea Otter 1
G-AJLT (C/N 181716) (JM982) 03/47 to **BSAA** (never converted for use), scrapped Langley 1949.

G-AJLU (C/N 129893) (JM985) 03/47 to **BSAA** (never converted for use), 10/10/47 ferried from Wroughton to Langley (Pilot - E.D. Fieldson), scrapped Langley 1949.

G-AKRX (C/N 1806/C/206) (JM968) 20/01/48 to **BSAA** (never converted for use), scrapped at Langley 1949.

G-AKWA (JM739) 02/07/48 to **BSAA** (never converted for use), second production Sea Otter. Used for catapult trials in 1943, scrapped Langley 1949.

Avro 683 Lancaster 1 (freighter conversion)
G-AGUJ 'Star Pilot' (PP689)
Registered 27/10/45, initially loaned to **BSAA** 19/12/45, fitted with Lancastrian-style nose cone by Avro Waddington, C of A No 7248 issued 12/03/46 to **BSAA** and aircraft named **'Star Pilot'**, first service flown 29/03/46 (London to Montevideo), bought by **BSAA** 03/47, transferred 30/07/49 to BOAC, registered 03/09/49 to BOAC, dismantled Langley 12/49, sold to R.J. Coley & Sons for scrap.

G-AGUK 'Star Gold' (PP688)
Registered 27/10/45, initially loaned to **BSAA** 11/12/45, fitted with Lancastrian-style nose cone by Avro Waddington, C of A No 7249 issued 30/01/46 to **BSAA**, aircraft named **'Star Gold'**, first service flown 05/02/46 (London to Buenos Aires), cancelled 20/01/47 and permanently withdrawn from use, bought by **BSAA** 31/03/47, dismantled Langley for spares during 03/47.

G-AGUL 'Star Watch' (PP690)
Registered 27/10/45, initially loaned to **BSAA** 29/12/45, fitted with Lancastrian-style nose cone by Avro Waddington, C of A No 7250 issued 01/04/46 to **BSAA** and aircraft named **'Star Watch'**, first service flown 12/04/46 (London to Montevideo), bought by **BSAA** 03/47, written off London airport 23/10/47 during night training exercise (ground-looped on landing).

G-AGUM 'Star Ward' (PP751)
Registered 27/10/45, initially loaned to **BSAA** 25/01/46, fitted with Lancastrian-style nose cone by Avro Waddington, C of A No 7251 issued 06/05/46 to **BSAA** and aircraft named **'Star Ward'**, first service flown 09/06/46 (London to Paris), bought by **BSAA** 03/47, to Airtech Ltd Thame 03/47 for the fitment of under-belly pannier, transferred 30/07/49 to BOAC, registered 03/09/49 to BOAC, dismantled Dunsfold 12/49, sold to R.J. Coley & Sons for scrap.

G-AGUN 'Star Belle' (PP744)
Registered 27/10/45, initially loaned to **BSAA** as **'Star Belle'** 07/02/46, C of A No 7252 applied for but never issued, returned to RAF (20 MU Aston Down) 17/05/46 after loan, registration cancelled 03/07/46, loaned to BOAC 02/07/46 for Development Flight Navaid Trials from 08/07/46, registered 17/07/46 to BOAC as G-AHVN, special category C of A 8103 issued 10/09/46, transferred 17/08/48 to Ministry of Supply but remained on BOAC charge and use, withdrawn by BOAC 22/10/48, returned to Ministry of Supply 23/02/49, bought 24/02/49 by Flight Refuelling Ltd, Tarrant Rushton, dismantled Tarrant Rushton 01/50.

G-AGUO 'Star Bright' (PP746)
Registered 27/10/45, initially loaned to **BSAA** as **'Star Bright'** 07/02/46, C of

A No 7253 applied for but never issued, registration cancelled 03/07/46, returned to RAF (20 MU Aston Down) as PP746 13/05/46, registration cancelled, bought by R.J. Coley & Sons for scrap 07/05/47.

Avro 685 York
G-AGJA 'Star Fortune'
C/N 1207 (MW103, WW541 and WW508), registered 08/01/44 and delivered 31/01/44 to BOAC as G-AGJA 'Mildenhall', C of A No 7057 issued 21/02/44 to BOAC, bought by **BSAA** 18/05/49, named **'Star Fortune'**, based Nassau, transferred 30/07/49 to BOAC, registered 03/09/49 to BOAC as 'Kingston', bought by Lancashire Aircraft Corporation Ltd 29/05/51 and used as WW541 and WW508 for trooping, bought by Skyways 28/02/55 and registered April 1955, scrapped Stansted 08/59.

G-AGJE 'Star Way'
C/N 1211 (MW129 and WW580), registered 11/09/44 and delivered 26/09/44 to BOAC as G-AGJE 'Middlesex', C of A No 7094 issued 26/09/44 to BOAC, bought by **BSAA** 06/05/49, named **'Star Way'**, based Nassau, transferred 30/07/49 to BOAC, registered 03/09/49 to BOAC as 'Panama', bought by Lancashire Aircraft Corporation Ltd 31/07/51 used as WW580 for trooping, bought by Skyways 28/02/55, registered 04/55, withdrawn from use scrapped Stansted 10/56.

G-AGNN 'Star Crest'
C/N 1216 (TS791 and WW465), registered 12/04/45, C of A No 7171 issued 10/10/45 to BOAC as 'Madras', leased 19/05/47 to South African Airways as ZS-BGU, returned to BOAC service 12/09/47, bought by **BSAA** 06/07/48 and named **'Star Crest'**, transferred 30/07/49 to BOAC, registered 03/09/49 to BOAC as 'Atlantic Trader', later reverting to 'Madras', used for trooping 08/51 serial WW465, returned to BOAC 1951, bought by Skyways for spares 04/04/57, scrapped Stansted 05/57.

G-AGNS 'Star Glory'
C/N 1220 (TS795 and WW466), registered 20/08/45, C of A No 7209 issued 20/10/45 to BOAC as 'Melville', leased 16/04/47 to South African Airways as ZS-BTT, returned to BOAC service 17/09/47,

bought by **BSAA** 30/05/49 and named 'Star Glory', used by **BSAA** as engine freighter and trainer, transferred 30/07/49 to BOAC, registered 03/09/49 to BOAC as 'Pacific Trader', used for trooping 08/51 serial WW466, damaged beyond repair in accident prior to take-off at Idris, Libya 22/4/56 when undercarriage was retracted on ground. Broken up on site.

G-AGNU 'Star Dawn'
C/N 1222 (TS797 and XD670), registered 20/08/45, C of A No 7211 issued 14/12/45 to BOAC as 'Montgomery', leased 10/01/46 to South African Airways as ZS-ATR 'Impala', returned to BOAC service 24/09/47, bought by **BSAA** 26/07/49 and named **'Star Dawn'**, transferred 30/07/49 back to BOAC, registered 03/09/49 to BOAC as 'Nassau', bought by Air Charter Ltd 29/08/52 and named 'New Endeavour', used for trooping 03/53 serial XD670, returned to Air Charter 08/55, bought by Trans Mediterranean Airways as OD-ACO 12/12/56, written off in emergency landing Azaiba, Muscat 24/05/61.

G-AGNX 'Lima'
C/N 1225 (TS800 and WW582), registered 20/08/45, C of A No 7214 issued 06/02/46 to BOAC as 'Moray', bought by **BSAA** 26/07/49 and named **'Lima'**, transferred 30/07/49 back to BOAC, registered 03/09/49 to BOAC, bought by Lancashire Aircraft Corporation 29/05/51, used for trooping 08/51 serial WW582, returned to Lancashire Aircraft Corporation 02/53, withdrawn from use and stored at Stansted 06/53, scrapped Stansted 02/55.

G-AGOC 'Star Path'
C/N 1230 (TS805), registered 20/08/45, C of A No 7219 issued 19/04/46 to BOAC as 'Malta', bought by **BSAA** 09/05/49 and named **'Star Path'**, transferred 30/07/49 to BOAC, registered 03/09/49 to BOAC, scrapped Hurn 11/49.

G-AHEW 'Star Leader'
C/N 1300, registered 20/03/46, C of A No 7594 issued 27/05/46 to **BSAA** as **'Star Leader'**, written off in accident after take-off at Bathurst, The Gambia 07/09/46.

G-AHEX 'Star Venture'
C/N 1301, registered 20/03/46, C of A No 7597 issued 20/06/46 to **BSAA** as 'Star Venture', written off in accident at Caravelas, Brazil 05/01/49.

G-AHEY 'Star Quest'
C/N 1302 (WW506), registered 20/03/46, C of A No 7596 issued 05/07/46 to **BSAA** as **'Star Quest'**, transferred 30/07/49 to BOAC, registered 03/09/49 to BOAC, bought by Lancashire Aircraft Corporation 08/04/52, used for trooping 04/52 serial WW506, bought by Skyways Ltd 28/02/55, leased 08/06/56 to Arab Airways as JY-ABZ, named 'Petra', returned to Skyways Ltd service 26/09/56, withdrawn from use and scrapped Stansted 08/62.

G-AHEZ 'Star Speed'
C/N 1303, registered 20/03/46, C of A No 7597 issued 24/07/46 to **BSAA** as **'Star Speed'**, written off in accident at Dakar 13/04/47.

G-AHFA 'Star Dale'
C/N 1304 (WW504), registered 20/03/46, C of A No 7598 issued 18/08/46 to **BSAA** as **'Star Dale'**, transferred 30/07/49 to BOAC, registered 03/09/49 to BOAC, bought by Lancashire Aircraft Corporation (Skyways) 11/12/51, used for trooping 04/52 serial WW504, returned to Lancashire Aircraft Corporation 02/53, lost in Atlantic (approx 46° 15' N, 46° 32' W) 02/02/53.

G-AHFB 'Star Stream'
C/N 1305 (WW499 and WW586), registered 20/03/46, C of A No 7599 issued 28/08/46 to **BSAA** as **'Star Stream'**, transferred 30/07/49 to BOAC, registered 03/09/49 to BOAC, bought by Lancashire Aircraft Corporation 27/09/51, used for trooping serials WW499 and WW586, bought by Airspan Travel Ltd 27/08/54, bought by Skyways Ltd 28/02/55, leased 05/06/57 to Arab Airways as JY-AAC, returned to Skyways Ltd service 02/08/57, withdrawn from use and scrapped Luton 04/63.

G-AHFC 'Star Dew'
C/N 1306 (WW507), registered 20/03/46, C of A No 7600 issued 12/09/46 to **BSAA** as **'Star Dew'**, transferred 30/07/49 to BOAC, registered 03/09/49 to BOAC, bought by Lancashire Aircraft Corporation 03/04/52, used for trooping serial WW507,

transferred 28/02/55 to Skyways Ltd, bought by Air Liban 13/10/55 as OD-ACJ, scheduled for lease to an unknown operator as HZ-CAA, but not taken up, bought by Persian Air Services (date unknown) as EP-ADD, withdrawn from use Beirut 10/59.

G-AHFD 'Star Mist'
C/N 1307 (WW500), registered 20/03/46, C of A No 7601 issued 21/09/46 to **BSAA** as **'Star Mist'**, transferred 30/07/49 to BOAC, registered 03/09/49 to BOAC, bought by Lancashire Aircraft Corporation 05/11/51, used for trooping with serial WW500, transferred 28/02/55 to Skyways Ltd, bought by BOAC associated companies 11/06/57, bought by Middle East Airlines 13/06/57 as OD-ADB, lost at sea 29/09/58 en route from Beirut to Rome.

G-AHFE 'Star Vista'
C/N 1308 (WW468 and WW578), registered 20/03/46, C of A No 7602 issued 30/09/46 to **BSAA** as **'Star Vista'**, transferred 30/07/49 to BOAC, registered 03/09/49 to BOAC, bought by Lancashire Aircraft Corporation 07/08/51, used for trooping serials WW468 and WW578, transferred 28/02/55 to Skyways Ltd, withdrawn from use and scrapped Stansted 02/60.

G-AHFF 'Star Gleam'
C/N 1309 (WW503), registered 20/03/46, C of A No 7603 issued 18/10/46 to **BSAA** as **'Star Gleam'**, transferred 30/07/49 to BOAC, registered 03/09/49 to BOAC, bought by Lancashire Aircraft Corporation 16/01/52, used for trooping serial WW503, transferred 28/02/55 to Skyways Ltd, withdrawn from use 09/59, scrapped Stansted 03/60.

G-AHFG 'Star Haze'
C/N 1310 (WW468), registered 20/03/46, C of A No 7604 issued 25/10/46 to **BSAA** as **'Star Haze'**, transferred 30/07/49 to BOAC, registered 03/09/49 to BOAC, bought by Lancashire Aircraft Corporation 14/09/51, used for trooping serial WW468, transferred 28/02/55 to Skyways Ltd, withdrawn from use 10/56, Scrapped Stansted 02/59.

G-AHFH 'Star Glitter'
C/N 1311 (WW502), registered 20/03/46, C of A No 7605 issued 31/10/46 to **BSAA**

as **'Star Glitter'**, transferred 30/07/49 to BOAC, registered 03/09/49 to BOAC, bought by Lancashire Aircraft Corporation 22/11/51, used for trooping serial WW502, transferred 28/02/55 to Skyways Ltd, bought by Middle East Airlines 03/06/57 as OD-ADA, bought by BOAC associated companies 11/06/57, written off in landing accident Azaiba II, Saudi Arabia, 11/09/62.

Avro 688 Tudor 1
G-AGRG 'Star Cressida'
C/N 1255, allocated serial TS870 but not taken up, registered 05/09/45, C of A No 8483 issued 10/01/47 to Ministry of Supply and Aircraft Production (MoSAP), transferred 16/06/48 to Ministry of Civil Aviation (MoCA), converted by Avro 03/48 to Tudor Freighter 1 (Tudor 1F), leased 14/07/48 to BOAC at Hurn, loaned 1949 to **BSAA** as **'Star Cressida'**, bought by Aviation Traders Ltd 02/09/53 and delivered to them 10/53, C of A renewed 02/02/54 by Air Charter as 'El Alamein', proving flight to Hamburg 14/02/54, converted by Aviation Traders Ltd 07/56 to Tudor 4 for Air Charter, converted by Aviation Traders Ltd 07/58 to Super Trader 4B for Air Charter, written off when attempting a crosswind take-off from Brindisi 27/01/59.

G-AGRH
C/N 1256, allocated serial TS871 but not taken up, registered 05/09/45, C of A No 8484 issued 10/12/46 to MoSAP, transferred 16/06/48 to MoCA, converted to Tudor Freighter 1 06/48 and leased to BOAC, loaned to **BSAA** 1949 and used as Tudor Freighter 1 on Berlin Airlift, was to have been **'Star Ceres'**, withdrawn from use stored 10/08/49 Woodford, Tarrant Rushton, then Ringway, sold 02/09/53 to Aviation Traders Ltd, converted to Tudor 4 and delivered 20/08/54, C of A renewed 25/10/55 for Air Charter, converted by Aviation Traders Ltd 03/58 to Super Trader 4B, returned to service in 1958 to Air Charter as 'Zephyr', written off en route from Ankara to Bahrain. Crashed on Mount Suphan Dag, Turkey 23/04/59 after deviating from track.

G-AGRJ
C/N 1258, allocated serial TS873 but not taken up, registered 05/09/45, C of A No

8486 issued 24/2/47 to MoSAP, transferred 16/05/48 to MoCA, leased 05/48 to BOAC, loaned 1949 to **BSAA** and converted to Tudor Freighter 1 and used on Berlin Airlift, was to have been **'Star Celia'**, withdrawn from use and stored 10/08/49 at Woodford, Tarrant Rushton, and Ringway, sold 02/09/53 to Aviation Traders Ltd, delivered 20/08/54 to Air Charter, withdrawn from use 08/56 and broken up Southend.

Avro 688 Tudor 4 and 4B
G-AGRE 'Star Ariel'
C/N 1253, allocated serial TS868 but not taken up, registered 05/09/45, C of A No 8475/A460 issued 25/09/46 to MoSAP, delivered 26/09/46 to BOAC for familiarisation trials, transferred 11/46 to MoCA, converted by Avro 03/48 to Tudor 4B, delivered 14/11/48 **BSAA 'Star Ariel'**, written off 17/01/49 lost over Western Atlantic en route from Bermuda to Jamaica.

G-AGRF
C/N 1254, allocated serial TS869 but not taken up, registered 05/09/45, C of A No 8482 issued 06/12/46 to MoSAP, delivered 21/01/47 to BOAC and named 'Elizabeth of England', type rejected 11/04/47 by BOAC, converted by Avro 03/48 to Tudor 4B, bought 12/12/48 by **BSAA**, transferred 03/09/49 to BOAC, cancelled 12/10/51 as transferred to MCA, delivered 02/09/53 by road to Southend for Aviation Traders Ltd, broken up 02/54 Southend for spares.

G-AHNI
C/N 1342, registered 20/5/46, MoSAP for BOAC but not taken up, for **BSAA 'Star Olivia'** but not taken up, transferred 21/10/49 and C of A No 8492 issued 24/02/50 to MoCA, withdrawn from use/ stored 02/50 at Ringway, bought 18/11/53 and converted 04/54 by Aviation Traders Ltd to Super Trader 4B, delivered 28/08/54 to Air Charter as 'Tradewind', withdrawn from use 08/60 and scrapped Stansted.

G-AHNJ 'Star Panther'
C/N 1343, registered 20/05/46, first flight 09/04/47 MoSAP, C of A No 8493 issued 18/07/47 to MoSAP, delivered 18/07/47 to **BSAA** initially as **'Star Lion'** then **'Star Panther'** shortly after, converted 1949 by BSAA to Super Freighter 4, transferred 30/09/49 to BOAC, withdrawn from use/ stored at Ringway, cancelled 12/10/51 as transferred to MoCA, bought 02/09/53 by Aviation Traders Ltd, broken up 1953 Ringway for spares.

G-AHNK 'Star Lion'
C/N 1344, registered 20/05/46, first flight 29/09/47, C of A No 8494 issued 30/09/47 to MoSAP, delivered 29/09/47 to **BSAA 'Star Lion'**, converted 1949 by **BSAA** to Freighter 4, transferred 30/09/49 to BOAC, withdrawn from use 03/50 and stored at Hurn, cancelled 12/10/51 as transferred to MoCA, withdrawn from use 01/53, bought 02/09/53 by Aviation Traders Ltd, delivered 02/54, dismantled and taken by road to Southend, fuselage used for cargo door mock-up for the Super Trader 4B, scrapped 1954 at Southend.

G-AHNN 'Star Leopard'
C/N 1347, registered 20/5/46, C of A No 8497 issued 23/3/48 (as Tudor IV) to MoSAP, delivered 23/3/48 to **BSAA 'Star Leopard'**, converted 1949 by **BSAA** to Freighter 4B, transferred 30/9/49 to BOAC, cancelled 12/10/51 as transferred to MoCA, withdrawn from use October 1951, stored at Ringway, broken up 1953 at Ringway, spares to Southend February 1954.

G-AHNP 'Star Tiger'
C/N 1349, registered 20/5/46, C of A No 8497 issued 5/11/47 (as Tudor IV) to MoSAP, delivered 5/11/47 to **BSAA 'Star Tiger'**, written off 30/1/48, lost over the Western Atlantic en route from Azores to Bermuda, cancelled 26/5/48.

Avro 689 Tudor 5
G-AKBZ 'Star Falcon'
C/N 1418, allocated serial number TS904 but not taken up, registered 16/8/47, converted 1947 by MoCA to Tudor 5, C of A No 10300 issued 3/11/48 to MoCA, delivered 4/11/48 to **BSAA 'Star Falcon'**, used as a fuel freighter on the Berlin Airlift, transferred 3/9/49 to BOAC, withdrawn from use 10/8/49 and stored at Woodford, bought 1/11/51 by Aviation Traders Ltd, bought November 1951 by Surrey Flying Services, withdrawn from use June 1956,

scrapped July 1959 at Stansted by Aviation Traders Ltd.

G-AKCA 'Star Hawk'

C/N 1419, allocated serial number TS905 but not taken up, registered 16/08/47, converted 1947 by MoCA to Tudor 5, C of A No 10301 issued 07/12/48 to MoCA, delivered 07/12/48 to **BSAA 'Star Hawk'**, used as a fuel freighter on the Berlin Airlift, transferred 03/09/49 to BOAC, withdrawn from use and stored 10/08/49 at Woodford, bought 21/09/51 by Aviation Traders Ltd (ATL), registered 05/10/51 to Surrey Flying Services (subsidiary of ATL), loaned 23/05/52 to Lome Airways (Canada) as CF-FCY, returned 1952 to Stansted and stored, withdrawn from use June 1956.

G-AKCB 'Star Kestrel'

C/N 1420, allocated serial number TS906 but not taken up, registered 16/08/47, converted by MoCA to Tudor 5, C of A No 10302 issued 31/12/48 to MoCA, delivered 31/12/48 to **BSAA 'Star Kestrel'**, used as a fuel freighter on the Berlin Airlift, transferred 03/09/49 to BOAC, withdrawn from use 10/08/49 and stored at Woodford, sold 05/04/50 to William Dempster Ltd, withdrawn from use June 1956, scrapped at Stansted July 1959 by ATL.

G-AKCC 'Star Swift'

C/N 1421, allocated serial number TS907 but not taken up, registered 16/08/47, converted by MoCA to Tudor 5, C of A No 10303 issued 26/01/49 to MoCA, delivered 26/01/49 to **BSAA 'Star Swift'**, used as a fuel freighter on the Berlin Airlift, transferred 03/09/49 to BOAC, withdrawn from use 10/08/49 and stored at Woodford, bought 05/04/50 by William Dempster Ltd in association with Pan African Air Charter and Mercury Airways of South Africa, damaged 17/04/51 in heavy landing at Livingstone, repaired in three months, damaged beyond repair at Bovingdon 26/10/51 when it over-shot the runway on a flight from Castel Benito, bought November 1951 by Surrey Flying Services.

G-AKCD 'Star Eagle'

C/N1422, allocated serial number TS908 but not taken up, registered 16/08/47, converted by MoCA to Tudor 5, C of A No 10304 issued 11/02/49 to MoCA, delivered 11/02/49 to **BSAA 'Star Eagle'**, used as a fuel freighter on the Berlin Airlift, transferred 03/09/49 to BOAC, bought 05/04/50 by William Dempster Ltd in association with Pan African Air Charter and Mercury Airways of South Africa, withdrawn from use by end of 1953 at Southend, bought 05/04/54 by Air Charter, scrapped at Stansted in June 1958 by ATL.

Avro 691 Lancastrian 2 (9 passengers)
G-AKMW 'Star Bright'

VL977, delivered 1946 to RAF 231 Sqn Full Sutton, bought and registered 28/11/47, C of A No 9902 issued 23/12/47, delivered 23/12/47 to **BSAA 'Star Bright'**, delivered December 1948 to Skyways 'Sky Empire', used in the Berlin Airlift, withdrawn from use May 1951 at Dunsfold.

G-AKTB 'Star Glory'

VM738, delivered March 1946 to RAF 231 Sqn, registered 17/02/48, bought 18/02/48 by **BSAA**, C of A No 10058 issued 28/04/48, delivered 28/04/48 **BSAA 'Star Glory'**, bought 14/01/49 and delivered April 1949 to Flight Refuelling Ltd, used on the Berlin Airlift, withdrawn from use April 1951, scrapped 26/09/51 at Tarrant Rushton.

G-AKTC

VL978, delivered 1946 to RAF 231 Sqn Full Sutton, registered 17/02/48 No C of A issued, delivered June 1948 to **BSAA 'Star Fortune'** but not taken up, broken up June 1948 for spares at Langley.

G-AKTG

VL967, delivered January 1946 to RAF 231 Sqn Full Sutton, registered 24/01/48 to **BSAA 'Star Crest'** but not taken up, C of A number 10216 prepared but not issued, bought 24/02/48 by **BSAA** for spares.

Avro 691 Lancastrian 3 (13 passengers)
G-AGWG 'Star Light'

C/N 1279, registered 28/11/45, first flight 29/11/45 MoSAP, C of A No 7281 issued 05/12/45, delivered 06/12/45 and registered 14/12/45 to **BSAA 'Star Light'**, written off 12/11/47 when crashed on landing in Bermuda.

G-AGWH 'Star Dust'
C/N 1280, registered 28/11/45, first flight 27/11/45 MoSAP, C of A No 7282 issued 09/01/46, delivered 12/01/46 and registered 16/01/46 to **BSAA 'Star Dust'**, written off 02/08/47 en route from Buenos Aires to Santiago when it crashed into Mount Tupungato.

G-AGWI 'Star Land'
C/N 1281, registered 28/11/45, first flight December 1945 MoSAP, C of A No 7283 issued 24/01/46, delivered 27/01/46 and registered 25/01/46 to **BSAA 'Star Land'**, registered 16/08/48 to MoCA, bought 16/01/49 and registered 18/01/49 by Flight Refuelling Ltd, used on the Berlin Airlift, scrapped 26/09/51 at Tarrant Rushton.

G-AGWJ 'Star Glow'
C/N 1282, registered 28/11/45, first flight January 1946 MoSAP, C of A No 7284 issued 28/01/46, delivered 21/02/46 and registered 28/01/46 to **BSAA 'Star Glow'**, first service 11/03/46 Heathrow to Buenos Aires, written off 30/08/46 when it crashed on take-off at Bathurst, The Gambia.

G-AGWK 'Star Trail'
C/N 1283, registered 28/11/45, first flight January 1946 MoSAP, C of A No 7285 issued 15/02/46, delivered 21/02/46 and registered 28/01/46 to **BSAA 'Star Trail'**, written off 05/09/47 when it crashed on approach at Bermuda.

G-AGWL 'Star Guide'
C/N 1284, registered 28/11/45, first flight 01/02/46 MoSAP, C of A No 7286 issued 13/02/46, registered 28/01/46 and delivered 15/02/46 to **BSAA 'Star Guide'**, registered 14/01/49 and bought 16/01/49 and delivered 18/01/49 by Flight Refuelling Ltd, used on the Berlin Airlift, scrapped 26/09/51 at Tarrant Rushton.

G-AHCD 'Star Valley'
C/N 1298, registered 20/02/46, first flight 07/12/46 MoSAP, C of A No 7497 issued 10/01/47, delivered 15/01/47 to **BSAA 'Star Valley'**, bought 15/04/47 by British European Airways Corporation (BEA), leased 16/04/47 to 06/06/47 to BOAC, leased 16/07/47 to 24/07/47 to BOAC, cancelled 17/12/47 as sold abroad, bought 17/12/47 by Alitalia 'Sirocco'.

Avro 691 Lancastrian 4
G-AKFF 'Star Flight'
TX284, registered 29/08/47, C of A No 9681 issued 10/09/47 Skyways Ltd as 'Sky Ruler', bought 24/02/48 by **BSAA 'Star Flight'**, bought 28/12/48 by Flight Refuelling Ltd, used in the Berlin Airlift, withdrawn from use April 1951, scrapped September 1951 at Tarrant Rushton.

G-AKFG 'Star Traveller'
TX286, registered 29/08/47, C of A No 9721 issued 29/09/47 Skyways Ltd as 'Sky Minister', bought 24/02/48 by **BSAA 'Star Traveller'**, bought 28/12/48 by Flight Refuelling Ltd, used in the Berlin Airlift, withdrawn from use April 1951, scrapped September 1951 at Tarrant Rushton.

Bibliography

Books

Ashworth, Chris, *Avro York in Royal Air Force Service 1942–1957*, Hall Park Publications Ltd, nd

Avro Tudor IV Pilot's Notes & Operating Instructions, A.V. Roe & Co. Ltd, nd

Baldry, Dennis, *Piston Airliners Since 1940*, Phoebus Publishing, 1980

Barker, Dudley, *Berlin Air Lift: An Account of the British Contribution*, HMSO, 1949

Barker, Ralph, *Great Mysteries of the Air*, Pan Books, 1968

Bennett, Air Vice-Marshal Donald, *Pathfinder*, Goodall, 1998

Benson, Erik, *Aviator of Fortune: Lowell Yerex and the Anglo-American Commercial Rivalry, 1931–1946*, Texas A&M University Press, 2006

Brackley, Frida H. (ed.), *Brackles, Memoirs of a Pioneer of Civil Aviation*, W.& J. Mackay & Co. Ltd, 1952

Bramson, Alan, *Master Airman – A Biography of Air Vice-Marshal Donald Bennett*, Airlife Publishing Ltd, 1985

Chandler, Robert, *Off the Beam – The Memoirs of an Aircraft Radio Operator*, David Rendel, 1969

Denham, Terry, *World Directory of Airliner Crashes*, Patrick Stephens Ltd, 1996

Harris, Marshal of the RAF Sir Arthur, *Bomber Offensive*, Greenhill Books, 1990

Hyde, H. Montgomery, *Strong for Service: The Life of Lord Nathan of Churt*, W.H. Allen & Co. Ltd, 1968

Jackson, A.J., *Avro Aircraft Since 1908*, Putnam & Co. Ltd, 1965

Jackson, A.S., *Both Feet in the Air: An Airline Pilot's Story*, Terence Dalton Ltd, 1977

— *Pathfinder Bennett – Airman Extraordinary*, Terence Dalton Ltd, 1991

— *Can Anyone See Bermuda? Memories of an Airline Pilot (1941–1976)*, Cirrus Associates (S.W.), 1997

Jackson, Robert, *Coroner: The Biography of Sir Bentley Purchase*, George G. Harrap & Co. Ltd, 1963

Ministry of Civil Aviation, *Official Accident Reports*, HMSO, various dates

Operator's Handbook for Avro Lancastrian Aircraft, A.V. Roe & Co. Ltd, nd

Orange, Vincent, *Coningham*, Methuen, 1990

Penrose, Harald, *Wings Across the World: An Illustrated History of British Airways*, Cassell Ltd, 1980

— *Architect of Wings*, Airlife Publishing Ltd, 1985

Pyle, Captain Mark S. (ed.), *Chronicle of Aviation*, Chronicle Communications Ltd, 1992

Taylor, H.A., *Airspeed Aircraft Since 1931*, Putnam & Co. Ltd, 1970

Thomas, Ivor, *The Socialist Tragedy*, Latimer House Ltd, 1949

Thomas, Sir Miles, *Out on a Wing*, Michael Joseph Ltd, 1964

Tusa, Ann and Tusa, John, *The Berlin Blockade*, Coronet Books, 1989

Woodley, Charles, *BOAC, An Illustrated History*, Tempus Publishing Ltd, 2004

Wragg, David, *Airlift, A History of Military Air Transport*, Airlife Publishing Ltd, 1986

Other Sources

British Airways Museum, www.bamuseum.com

The National Archives, Kew, document classes AVIA, BT, DR, FO, PREM and TS

The Aeroplane magazine – various dates

Flight magazine – various dates

Air France and KLM statistics from www.planecrashinfo.com

Biographical details of John McPhee from www.bermuda-triangle.org/html/john_mcphee.html

Index

A&AEE Boscombe Down 36
A.V. Roe 32, 33, 35, 37, 38–9, 78, 131, 134, 136, 144, 162, 166, 189, 191, 203
Aasfjord 15
Accident Investigation Branch (AIB) later Air Accident Investigation Branch (AAIB) 81, 119, 129, 163, 166, 220
Adams, Mr 66
Aer Lingus 12
Aérospatiale/BAC Concorde ix, 192, 202
Aerovias Brasil 5
Air France ix, x, 82, 192
Air Ministry 3, 4, 18, 19, 23–4, 35, 40, 73, 133
Air Registration Board (ARB) 79, 144, 160, 161, 163, 165–6, 167, 208, 212
Air Safety and Technical Committee 80
Air Transport Auxiliary (ATA) 49, 54
Air Transport Bill 46–7
Airflight 189
Airtech 34
Alabaster, Captain R.C. 48, 95, 98, 100, 103, 107, 108, 135
Albion Star 2
Alcock, John 177
Aldergrove airport 14
Aleppo, Syria 10
Alexandria, Egypt 11
Allcock, Captain Gilbert M. 75, 127
American Export Airlines 4
Andes x, 34, 66, 112, 113–14, 115–16, 117, 122, 124, 135, 214
Anglo Frigorifico 1
Annual reports 141, 214
Argentine Air Force 116
Argentine army 116
Aries, Captain Maurice 61, 202–3
Aries, Michael 202
Armstrong Whitworth Siskin 10
Arpthorp, Stargirl Cynthia 70
Arsenal football team 221
Atallah, Casis Said 113
Atlantic Ferry Organisation 13–14, 46, 51, 52
Attlee, Prime Minister Clement 39, 82, 168, 170, 178, 215
Aviation Corporation of America 218
Avro Anson 219–20
Avro Lancaster ix, 32, 33, 35, 79, 109, 113
Avro Lancastrian x, 32, 33–4, 39, 40, 48, 54, 60, 81, 94, 95, 112, 113, 115, 117, 127, 134, 210, 211, 224

Avro Lincoln 56
Avro Tudor ix, 24, 32, 33, 36, 37, 39, 54, 81, 94, 111, 112, 131–2, 134, 135–7, 160, 161, 162–4, 165, 171, 172, 176, 184, 185, 187, 188, 191, 203, 208, 210, 211, 212, 214
Avro York 24, 31, 36, 37–8, 39, 57, 68, 78–9, 81, 84, 87, 92, 113, 114, 127, 134, 181, 187, 192, 199, 201, 210, 214, 215–16, 221
Axten, Albert 58

Bad Nenndorf 185, 187
Bahamas Airways 141, 218
Bailey, Mr 189
Baines, Stargirl Rita 54, 55
Baker, Mrs 66
Balfour, Harold, MP 18–19
Bangors hostel 56
Barber, C.C. 5
Barnes, Wally 221
Barranquilla, Columbia 84, 203, 215
Barzilay, Stargirl Dora 127, 130
Bathurst, (now Banjul) 6, 24, 25, 26, 40, 44, 49, 50, 65, 74, 76, 77, 80, 82, 86, 87, 88–9, 143
Bay of Biscay 13, 75
BBC 174
Beach Hotel, Montevideo 49
Beane Field, Antigua 138
Beard, First Officer F. 84
Beaumont and Son solicitors 107
Beaverbrook, Lord 14
Beddoes, Richard 211
Belem, Brazil 214
Belfast 14
Bendall, Stargirl C.A.F. 'Crystal' 125
Bennett, Arnold Lucas 8
Bennett, Aubrey George 8–9
Bennett, Celia Juliana *née* Lucas 8
Bennett, Clyde Kinsey 8
Bennett, Air Vice-Marshal Donald C.T. x, 7, 8–19, 32, 37, 40, 41–2, 43, 44, 46, 48, 51, 53, 55, 56, 58, 59–60, 61, 63, 64, 66, 68, 70, 72, 75, 77, 80, 93–4, 96, 102, 109–10, 116, 118, 123–4, 134, 137, 139, 160, 161, 162, 164, 165, 166, 167–9, 170, 172, 174–6, 179, 180, 184, 187, 189–91
Bennett, George 8, 9
Bennett, Ly 10–11, 15, 16, 58, 68, 75, 135
Bennett, Noreen 15
Bennett, Torix 15
Berckemeyer, Señor 22

Berlin Airlift 137, 183–91, 214
Bermuda 34, 67, 69, 74, 109, 110, 125, 143, 150, 152, 154, 203, 204, 213
Bernadotte, Count 16
Bevin, Ernest, MP 74
Biggars, Captain 87–8
Black, S.W. 5, 23, 29, 30
Blackpool airport 14
Blair-Cunynghame, J.O. 158
Blue Star Shipping Line 1–2, 52, 71
BOAC pension scheme 65
Boeing 747, 209
Bogota, Columbia 66, 95, 108
Bomber Offensive 17
Booth Steamship Company 1, 3
Booth, John W. 3, 5, 23–6, 28, 30, 40, 41, 44–5, 46–7, 63, 73, 75, 88, 158, 165, 167, 168–9, 170, 171–2, 173, 176, 177, 180, 182, 188, 212, 217
Bortkievicz, Heleno 200–1
Botwood, Newfoundland 11
Bowhill, Air Chief Marshal Sir Frederick 14–15
Brackley, Air Vice-Marshal Herbert George 'Brackles' 170, 177–82
Brackley, David 181
Brackley, Frida 178, 179
Bramson, Alan 167–8
Branson, Richard 61
Branson, Ted 61
Bray, Stargirl Margaret 84
Brazilian Air Force 197, 201
Brazilian Air Ministry 199–200
Brennan, Radio Engineer John 69–70, 71
Brest 75
Brice, Captain David 51–2
Brindisi 11
Brisbane 9, 11
Bristol Hercules radial engine 36
British Admiralty 16
British Air Line Pilots Association (BALPA) 80
British Air Mission to Japan 177
British Airways (pre Second World War) 2, 6, 13
British Airways (post 1974) xi, 21, 61
British Aviation Insurance Company 174
British Embassy, Washington 99, 105
British European Airways (BEA) x, 20, 21, 81, 104, 124, 141–2, 164–5, 179, 215
British government 5, 12, 13
British International Air Lines (BIAL) 140
British Latin American Air Lines Ltd (BLAA) 5, 7, 8, 19, 20, 21, 22–3, 26, 28–9, 32, 39, 40, 43–4, 173
British Medical Association (BMA) 8
British Overseas Airways Act 74
British Overseas Airways Corporation (BOAC) x, 2, 4, 5, 6, 13, 14, 20, 21, 23, 26, 27, 33, 36, 39, 40–1, 42, 43, 44, 47, 50, 52, 61, 64, 73–4, 81, 104, 111, 133–4, 135, 136, 137, 141–2, 157, 164–5, 179, 184, 203–4, 210, 215, 217–18
British Overseas Airways Corporation Act 13, 44
British Overseas Airways Corporation Ltd Bill 2

British Pathé News 68
British South American Airways Corporation (BSAA) *passim*
British United Airways (BUA) 224
British West Indian Airways (BWIA) 4–5, 27, 140–1, 218
Brooks, Route Intelligence Officer Angus 61
Brown, Air Commodore Vernon 166–7, 213
Brown, H.A. 'Sam' 36
Brown, Pilot/Navigator E.S. 222
Brown, Arthur Whitten 177
Browne, Stargirl Maria Teresa del Soconne (Mary) 71
BSAA cricket team 58
BSAA Operations Standing Orders 80–1
BSAA pension scheme 65
BSAA staff meeting to discuss merger 224
Buenos Aires, Argentina 2, 20, 22, 23, 25, 26, 40, 42, 48, 49–50, 54, 62, 66, 112, 114, 117, 118, 135, 214
'Building 41' 64
Bunker, Radio Officer 126
BWIA Terminal Building Restaurant 66

Cabinet Committee on Socialisation of Industries 215
Cable and Wireless Radio Telegraphy Station, Bermuda 154
Cadman report 2, 3, 6–7
Cadman, Lord 2, 3
Campbell, Engineer Tom 48
Canadian Government Transatlantic Air Service 32–3
Cape Town, South Africa 12
Cape Verde Islands 24, 88
Caracas, Venezuela 66, 74, 95, 140
Caravelas, Brazil 194, 197, 199, 201
Cardew, Basil 162
Carlisle, Mr and Mrs 66
Carrasco airport, Montevideo 22, 49
Carrera Hotel, Santiago 74
Caxton Hall 179, 219, 224
Chadwick, Roy 35–6, 37, 131, 137
Chandler, Radio Officer Robert W. 48, 49, 52, 75, 110, 135
Chapman, Radio Operator S. P. 219
Chase, Captain 88
Checklin, Second Officer Donald S. 113
Cheetham, John 22, 28, 76
Chicago Convention 21, 22, 26
Chilean Air Force 116
Chilean army 116
Christofanini, Mr and Mrs J. 192
Churchill, Prime Minister Winston 13, 17, 37
City Hotel, Buenos Aires 49, 74
Civil Aviation Committee 42
Clayton, Stargirl Lynn 84, 144, 152
Clayton, Wing Commander 90, 92–3
Clifford, Sir Bede 5, 67
Clipper Maid of the Seas 209
Coates Cotton Company 71
Cobham, Sir Alan 12, 109, 110, 183

Colby, Captain David 49, 55, 143, 146
Coleman, Steward R.W. 204
Colgan, Flight Sergeant 16
Collier, Air Vice-Marshal Sir Conrad 123–4, 174
Collins, Mr 95–7, 101, 103
Condamine river 8
Coningham, Air Marshal Sir Arthur 145, 152
Consolidated B-24 Liberator 15, 204
Cook, Captain Reginald James 113, 114, 115, 119, 122
Cook, First Officer Norman Hilton 113
Copacabana Palace Hotel, Rio de Janeiro 181
Cormican, Paddy 60–1
Costa Pinheiro, Dr 90, 92–3
Costa Pinheiro, Fernando de Sousa 90
Court of Enquiry, *Star Tiger* 156, 166
Courtney Report 137
Courtney, Air Chief Marshal Sir Christopher L. 137
Cousillas, Miss J.V. 192, 199
Cox, May 53
Crabtree, H.S. 210
Cracknell, Captain D.A. 48, 68
Cribbett, George 25, 28, 41, 73
Critchley, Brigadier General A.C. 23–4, 26, 27, 30, 42
Croydon airport 50
Cumming, Captain John N.S. 77, 79

Daily Express 107, 162, 164, 165, 167, 169, 170, 171
Daily Graphic 166
Daily Telegraph 121, 175, 176
Dakar, Yoff 24, 26, 50, 82, 84–5, 88–9, 91, 109, 111, 112, 118, 135, 144, 202, 214, 221
Dakar Airport Authority 87
Dakar tower controller 86, 87, 88
Daniels heater 132, 143, 145, 152, 156, 210–11
Dare, Aubrey 56, 59, 191
Dauncey, First Officer F. 204
Davies, W.H. 5
Davis, Wing Commander 124
Dawes, Group Captain 15
Day, Second Officer Roy 184–5
de Arteaga, Señor 21
de Havilland Comet 124, 137
de Havilland Dominie 27
de Havilland Ghost engine 34
de Havilland Mosquito 26, 113, 123, 127
de Wilde, Roger C. 219
Debenham and Freebody 55
de-icing systems 115, 144
Denman, Mr 71
Dewey, L. 5
Dixon, Mrs and Miss 66
Dobson, Sir Roy 166
Dodero Argentine Finance Group 27
Dodero scheme 22, 27, 40
Dodero Shipping Line 20
Dodero, Señor Alberto 20, 27, 28
Dorval, Montreal 158
Douglas C-47 201

Douglas DC-3 (Dakota) 34, 81, 82, 162
Douglas DC-4, 210
Dunnett, Mr 73

Eade, Jack 187
Earnshaw, Captain Godfrey J. 84–5, 88, 201
Eden, Foreign Secretary Anthony 22–3
Edwards, D. 49
El Cristo Pass 114
El Diario 22
Elizabeth of England 134
Elizabeth, HRH Princess 134
Ellison, Navigator C. 84, 143–4, 151–2, 153
Elsan 38–9
Enser, Richard 57, 141
Entwistle, Group Captain 24–5
Eureka beacon 113, 186
Eureka/Rebecca radar equipment 111
Evans, Mr W. 99, 104
Evans, Stargirl Iris Moreen 113
Evill & Coleman solicitors 105

Falcão, Signor 49
Falconer, First Officer P. 215
FAMA, Argentinian airline 158
Farnborough 210–11
Fearon, Radio Officer G.C. 125
FIDO 18
Fieldson, Captain E.D. 'Wyn' 140, 202, 221–3
Flensburg 18
Fletcher, Air Commodore 188
Flight 122
flight forecast, *Star Tiger* 147
flight plan, *Star Ariel* 205; *Star Tiger* 149
Flight Refuelling Ltd 12, 109, 110, 183, 187
Flores, Azores 110
Flying Training School Sealand 9
Forbes, Mr 29
Forbes, Sergeant 16
Ford, Sussex 109
Foreign Office 20, 28, 29, 44, 93, 94, 95–6, 102
Forsyth, Bill 56
Freese-Pennefather, Mr 96
'Frood' 68
Fullerton, Brigadier 222

Gander, Newfoundland 14, 84, 150, 203
Gatow, Berlin 185, 186, 191
GEE 18
General Council of British Shipping 3
George VI, HM King 37
Georgetown, Guyana 214
Gibson, Dr Anne 192, 197
Glenny, Mr 86
Gloster Meteor 124
Gold, F.G. 55
Gooderham, Eric John 113
Goodwin, Flight Engineer J. 204
Gould, Radio Officer William Arthur 127
Grafton Street office 44, 50, 53, 141
Graham, Captain Albert Charles 127–30, 192, 193–6, 197, 202

Griffin, Captain Frank 77, 126, 146, 151, 152, 154
Groom, Wing Commander L.D. 96–7
grounding of Avro Tudor 214–15
Gummer, Eileen 50, 59, 68, 124
Gunnell, Eileen 59
Guthrie, Stargirl Mary 48, 49, 54

Hagerston, Stargirl 'Poppy' 70
Hagyard, Ken 190
Half Die flying boat base, Bathurst 180
Hall, Wing Commander 49, 90–1
Hamilton-Gordon, Major 222
Hancock, First Officer W. 125
Handley Page Halifax 15, 221
Handley Page Hermes 32, 121
Handley Page HP 42 biplane 11
Handley Page Transport Company 177
Handover, D. 170
Hardingham, R.E. 212
Harmer, Radio Officer Dennis B. 113, 119
Harmer, Steward Tom 71
Harris, Marshal of the Royal Air Force Sir Arthur 17–18
Harrison, First Officer W. 76
Hartley, Sir Harold 158
Harvey, Air Commodore, MP 160
Harvey, Wireless Operator Ian 12
Havana, Cuba 144, 154
Hawker Aircraft Company 57, 59
Hawker Hurricane 57
Hayden, Ted 59–60
Haynes, Stargirl Sylvia 221
Hayward, Keith 53–4
Heathrow airport ix, 7, 24, 48, 50, 57, 59, 62, 67, 72, 134–5, 144
Henry Snowman solicitor 104–5
Hepworth, Stargirl Celia 135
Herald 42
Herrington, Stargirl Miriam W. 77
Hilder Thomson & Dunn solicitors 97
Hildred, Sir William 23, 24–5, 27, 29, 30–1, 40, 44, 45, 62
Hillman's Airways 2
HMT Queen of Bermuda 58
Holmes, Miss 66
Hotel Hannover, Bad Nenndorf 185
Hough, Leonard 50, 125, 126
House of Commons 2, 160, 161, 214, 217
House of Lords 162, 176
Hoyer-Millar, Mr 92
Hoyl, Kurt 122
Huffner, Richard 130
Huntley-Flindt, Stargirl Evette 61
Hurn airport 17, 24, 44, 62, 118, 203–4
Hut 43, 61
Hyde, H. Montgomery 83
hypoxia 119, 210

Imperial Airways 2, 6, 11, 11, 12, 13, 50, 51, 52, 109, 177–8, 179
Imperial Chemical Industries (ICI) 178
Institute Geografico Militar 117

Inter-American Conference on Problems of War and Peace 21
International Civil Aviation Organisation (ICAO) 21

J. Lyons, caterers 68
Jackson, Captain Archie 71
Janitrol 132
Japanese Naval Air Service 177
Japanese surrender 31
Jenner, Stargirl Zoë 54
jetstream x, 122–3
Jewitt, Bill 61
Johnson, A. 78
Johnson, Mr 66
Johnstone, Keith 57, 141
Jones, Captain 87
Jones, Captain O.P. 44
Jones, pilot 70
Jornal de Noticias 93

KLM x
Kanimbla, Australia 8, 9
Keflavik, Iceland 84, 203, 219
Kelly, Sir David 42–3
Kelly-Rogers, Pilot Jack 12
Kenny, James W. 39, 50, 109, 219
Kerly, Stargirl Ruth Helen 54
Kerrigan, Captain P.P. 135
Khartoum, Sudan 26
Kindley Field, Bermuda 127, 128, 151, 155, 203, 206
King Street office 141
Kingston, Jamaica 69, 74, 126, 140, 203, 206, 213
Kinnaird, King's Messenger R. 192, 196, 199
Kinsey, R. Stuart 105
Knollys, Lord 40, 43, 213

Lagen, Azores 110
Lake Havel, Berlin 187–8
Lamplugh, Captain 174
Lamport and Holt Line 1
LAN Chile airline 116
Langley airfield xi, 57, 59–60, 65, 72, 75, 78, 140, 141, 185, 220
Langrehr, Mrs E.R. 192, 196, 199
Lawson, Wing Commander 49
Leao, Senhor Sousa 21
Leche, Ambassador John 4, 5, 67, 173
Les Mamelles semaphore station 85
Lima, Peru 25, 66, 84, 203, 215
Limpert, Martha 113
Lindgren, George 82, 158, 217, 218
Linton, First Officer James B. 137
Lipman, Flight Lieutenant D.D. 38
Lisbon, Portugal 6, 13, 25, 40, 44, 49, 50, 59, 65, 84, 90, 91, 93, 94, 112, 135, 145, 214, 221
Lloyd-Jones, Mr 66
Lockheed 14, 6, 16
Lockheed Constellation 87, 210
Lockheed Hudson 14, 15
Lockheed Lodestar 5, 140

Lockheed Vega monoplane 10
London Aeroplane Club 51
Londonderry, Lord 83
Los Cerrillos airport, Santiago 66, 113, 116, 119
Lowe, F.H. 6
Lucas, Mr 57
Lucas, T.P. 8
Lufthansa 13
Luton aerodrome 219

Macfarlane, Stargirl Jean 71
Macilwaine, Pilot Robin 61, 222
Macmillan, Lord 156, 158–9
MacRobertson Trophy Air Race 10
Madeira 209
Maia 11–12
Majestic Hotel, Dakar 82
map, Star Tiger 148
Marroquim, Signor and Signora 49
Marshall Type XV blower 132
Master Airman 167–8
Mayo, Major Robert 11
McGillivray, Radio Superintendent J.A. 'Mac' 48,
    49, 52, 70
McMillan, Captain Brian W. 76–7, 143–4, 145–
    6, 151, 152, 153, 154
McPhee, Captain John Clutha 204
Mendoza, Argentina 114, 116
Mercer, Joe 221
Mercury 11–12
merger of BSAA and BOAC 223
Mexico City 21, 84
MI5, 167, 168
Miami 5
Miani, T.B. 192, 199
Milner, Radio Officer/Navigator Arthur 192
Milson, Wing Commander Dennis 53, 63
Ministry of Aircraft Production (MAP) 13, 29,
    30, 35, 37
Ministry of Civil Aviation (MCA) 23–4, 26–7, 38,
    41, 62, 63, 64, 72, 73, 78, 80, 81, 88, 93,
    95–6, 104–5, 109, 111, 123, 129, 135, 156,
    163, 164, 168, 174, 175, 178, 184
Ministry of Petroleum Warfare 18
Ministry of Supply 37, 39, 109, 118, 135, 136, 212
Ministry of Transport and Civil Aviation 121–2
Mond, Alfred, 1st Baron Melchett 178
Mond, Sir Robert 178
Montevideo, Uruguay 22, 23, 25, 40, 44, 49, 56,
    66, 112, 118, 135, 221
Moody, G. 63, 64
Moore-Brabazon, John, MP, later Lord Brabazon
    of Tara 2, 212–13, 214
Morley, Engineer A. 186–7
Morón airport, Buenos Aires 113–14
Morris, Mr 189
Mortleman, Stargirl Jean A. 192, 193, 196, 197,
    198–9
Mosley, Oswald 56
Mosqueira, Mrs M.C. 192
Mount Tupungato 112, 117, 122–3
Mountney, Second Officer Kingsley 192, 193–6

Moxon, Stargirl Judith B. 204
Mulligan, Tony 146
Murray, Kenneth 140
Myrtle Bank Hotel, Kingston 74

Narkunda 9
Nassau, Bahamas 84, 126, 203, 208, 214
Natal, Brazil 25, 26, 40, 44, 49, 65, 66, 102,
    109, 118, 135, 200, 214, 221
Nathan, Lord 82, 142, 143, 156, 160, 161–2,
    163, 164, 165–6, 167, 168–70, 170–1, 174,
    175, 176, 178–9, 184
New York Air Sea Rescue 206
Nicholls, Stargirl Sheila 144, 152
Night and Day nightclub 74
Nisbet, Mr 66
Northolt airport 165
Norway 15–16

Oboe 18
Oceanic Air Traffic Control New York 206, 207
Off the Beam 110
Oporto, Portugal 90
Oppenheimer, Herbert 178, 179
O'Reilly, Sir Lennox 67
Orosz, Jagwida Irena and Stanislaw 95–108
Orrell, J.H. 'Jimmy' 132, 134
Ottaway, Reg 58
Out on a Wing x
Overo volcano, Chile 122
Owens, Stargirl Margaret M. 192, 193, 196–7,
    198, 199
Oxford University Cosmos Society 176

P&O Nedlloyd 2
Pacific Steam Navigation Company 1
Page, Pilot Humphrey 14
Pagh, Harald 113
Pakenham, Lord, later 7th Earl of Longford 179,
    188–9, 212, 214, 215
Palace Hotel, Lisbon 73
Palisadoes aerodrome, Kingston 207
Pan American Airways (PAA) 3, 4, 6, 22, 25, 26,
    27, 66, 76, 104, 183, 209, 218
Panagra 27, 66, 116
Panair 87
Parlaunt Park Farm 57
Parnamirim airport, Natal 192
Parry, Senior Engineer Bill 186
Pathfinder x, 8, 9, 18
Pathfinder Force 8, 17, 46
Patrick, Bernard 60
Payne, Air Commodore L.G.S. 175
Payne, Muriel 58
Percival Proctor 127
Perkins, Robert, MP 2
Phipps, Graham 57
Piarco International airport, Trinidad 5
Pierced Steel Planking (PSP) runway 76
Pointer, Air Commodore 168
Poole 13
Poole, Cecil, MP 215

Portal, Air Chief Marshal Sir Charles 19
Portela airfield, Lisbon 24
Porter, Bernard 50, 65, 212
Porto Alegre, Brazil 222
Port-of-Spain, Trinidad 66, 84, 140
Powell, Mr 208
Power, Stargirl Cecily 54
Powerscourt, Lady 212–14
Press Association 174
Price, Frank 56, 59, 191
Privy Council Office 215
Prowse, David 110
Purchase, Mr (later Sir) Bentley 105, 106, 107
Qantas 135, 136
Queens Park Hotel, Port-of-Spain 66

RAF Bomber Command x, 8, 15, 17, 32
RAF Coastal Command 51
RAF Transport Command x, 31
RAF Volunteer Reserve 57
Ralph, Wing Commander 157
Rees, Captain William Jeffrey 'Jeff' 154, 188
Rees, Engineer Gordon 48
Reid, Mr 121
Reith, Sir John 2
Rendell, Lord 162
Republica 93
Rettie, Radio Officer Gordon C. 204, 206
Riley, Stargirl B.J. 135
Rio de Janeiro, Brazil 22, 25, 40, 44, 49, 65, 112, 118, 135, 221
Rissen, Norman 52
Robertson, First Officer William C. 192, 194–6, 197, 198–9
Rodley, Captain E.E. 135
Rolls-Royce 34
Rolls Royce Avon engine 34
Rolls Royce Merlin engine 34, 36, 60, 133, 196, 203, 204, 208
Rolls Royce Nene engine 34, 137
Rome, Italy 13
Rose, John C. 50
Ross, Pilot Ian 14
Royal Aircraft Establishment (RAE) 220
Royal Mail Lines 5, 50
Royal Mail Shipping Company 75
Royal Mail Steam Packet Company 1, 50

Sal Island 24, 88
Salaman, Peggy 51
San Gabriel, Chile 122
San Juan, Argentina 114
Santa Maria, Azores 95, 102, 109, 110–11, 125, 145, 157
Santiago, Chile 25, 34, 40, 66, 68, 112, 114, 115, 116, 134, 135, 203, 214, 219
Santos Dumont airport, Rio de Janeiro 49, 75
Sao Paulo, Brazil 84
Sarsby, Group Captain Charles F. 55, 58
Scotchbrooke, Mr 66
Scotland Yard 107
Scott-Hall, S. 212

Scottish Airways 81
Serrador Hotel, Rio de Janeiro 74
Shannon 84
Shapley, Second Officer V.D.J. 204
Shawcross, the Right Honourable Sir Hartley 105
Shell oil company 26
Shepherd, Wing Commander W.J.R. 181
Short Brothers 12
Short S30 Empire flying boat 12
Short Sunderland flying boat 40
Sikorski, General 13
Silver, John 57
Simpson, King's Messenger Paul 112–13
Simpson, Mr 96–7
Sinclair, Sir Archibald 19
Siri, Señor 22
Skillman, Flight Lieutenant 49
Skoogh, Captain 16
Slater, Radio Officer Ernest D. 77
Smoker, Radio Officer P.A. 135
Smurthwaite, First Officer John 126
South African Airways 135, 136
South Atlantic 24, 25, 45, 54, 109
Spartan Airlines 2
Speke airport, Liverpool 219
Sperry A3 autopilot 211
Stanley, Oliver, MP 217
Star Ariel ix, 112, 133, 134, 166, 203–11, 212, 218
Star Bottom 52
Star Celia 184
Star Ceres 184
Star Dew 181
Star Dust x, 94, 112, 114, 115, 116, 117, 118, 119–23, 124, 211
Star Gleam 201
Star Glow 76, 80, 143
Star Guide 95, 146, 150–1, 153, 156, 157
Star Haven 75–6
Star Haze 221–3
Star Hoist 52
Star Land 66, 78
Star Leader 39, 77, 77–8, 80, 81, 82
Star Leopard 134
Star Light 48, 49, 50, 54, 58, 62, 126–31, 192
Star Lion 134–5, 137, 144, 156, 203
Star Mist 182
Star Panther 134, 137, 144, 206
Star Speed 84, 87–9, 90, 94, 144
Star Tiger ix, 55, 76, 112, 133, 134, 137, 139, 143–59, 160, 167, 171, 172, 176, 184, 208, 212, 218
Star Trail 66, 125
Star Venture 114, 192, 200–1, 202
Star Visitant 219–20
Star Vista 215
Star Ward 34
Star Watch 126
Starways House 141
STENDEC, explanations 119–21
Stephenson, Sir John 160, 161–2, 164, 165–6, 167, 168–9, 170, 171, 172–3, 174, 176–7

Stephenville, Newfoundland 84, 150, 203
Stevens, Squadron Leader 49
Stirling, Ambassador Charles 90, 92, 94
Stirling-Wylie, Colonel 49
Stocks, Major S. 119
Stonehouse, First Officer William G. 127
Store, Captain Gordon 12, 14, 51, 62, 87, 88, 109, 139, 212
Storey, Captain Jaime 117–18
Stott, Radio Officer D. G. 84, 86
stowaways 69–70
Straight, Whitney 210, 217, 218
Studart, Route Inspector M.R. 192, 193, 199
Sundell, Ake 16
Supermarine Southampton biplane flying boat 10
Supermarine Spitfire XI 117–18
Swindin, George 221
Swinton, Lord 21, 27–8, 39, 44, 141–2, 176

Taylor, Captain Frank 225
'Teasey Weasy', Mr 53
Terra Nova Hotel, Santa Maria 74
The Aeroplane 6, 81, 82, 131
The Air Mariner 11
'the bungalow' 67
The Complete Air Navigator 11
The Times 121, 122, 182
Thiès, Senegal 86, 87, 89–90
Thomas, Ivor, MP 41, 46, 215
Thomas, Sir Miles x
Thompson, Stargirl Joan 137, 139
Thorn, Avro Chief Test Pilot Sidney A. 'Bill' 132, 137
Tirpitz 15–16, 18
Toowoomba, Queensland 8
Trans Canada Airlines 32, 33, 214
Transportes Aeros Centro Americanos (TACA) 3, 4, 5
Trinidad 5, 214
Trinidad Guardian 141
Trippe, Juan 3, 218
Tuck, Radio Officer Bob 'Tucky' 144, 151, 153
TWA 183

United Airways 2
United Nations (UN) 21
United Nations Relief and Rehabilitation Administration (UNRRA) 67
United States Air Force (USAF) 151, 155, 206
Urquhart, Robert W. 95–108
Utting, Clement Wilbur 191
Uxbridge 62
Vereker, Ambassador Gordon 22–3
Vestey Group 1
Vestey, William 2
Vickers VC10 224
Vickers Viking 113, 140, 165

Vickers-Supermarine 309 Sea Otter 140–1
Victory Aircraft Ltd 32, 33
Vinyals, Stargirl Priscilla 55, 68–9, 71, 140, 154, 202

Wade, First Officer Michael G. 77
Ward, George, MP 217
Ware, Wing Commander 129
Warner, Second Officer M.J. 125
Warner, Wing Commander William W. 55
Warren, Wing Commander R. 201
Watson, J. 201
Webb, Radio Officer Howard 77–8
Webster, Radio Operator John 137
Westminster Airways 160
Wheatley, First Officer John 110
White Horse Tavern, Bermuda 70, 74, 155
White, Engineer Chalky 110
Whitfield, Edwin 184, 188
Whitney, Cornelius Vanderbilt 218
Whittaker, Tom 221
Whitworth, Fred 56–7
Wilby, Superintendent of Aircraft Development Raymond E. 135, 138–9
Wildman & Co. solicitors 105
Wildman, Lawrence J. 105–7
Williamson F.24, F.8 camera 117–18
Wilson, Group Captain 23
Wilson, Mr 66
Wilson, Squadron Leader D.J.B. 137
Winster, Reginald Thomas Herbert Fletcher, 1st Baron 39, 40, 43, 44–5, 46, 48, 63, 74, 82
Womersley, Captain Geoffrey 140
Wood, Sir Kingsley 2, 11–12
Woodford 32, 134, 137, 144
Woodhouse, Mr 208
Woods, Jimmy 10
Woods-Humphrey, George 2
Woolcott, Captain A.H. 125–6
world long-distance seaplane record 12
Worrall, First Officer Pete 126
Wright, Sir Andrew 180
Wright, Captain John 215–17
Wright, 'Wilbur' 56
Wroughton 140
Wunsdorf, West Germany 185, 186, 188, 189

Yarde, Group Captain B. 186
Yerex, Lowell 3–4, 5, 7, 67, 173, 174
Young, Lady 4
Young, Peter 113
Young, Sir Hubert 4
Yundum airport, Bathurst 24, 73, 77, 180

Zeiss Contessa Nettel plate camera 117
zinc chromate slushing compound 220